VIRGINIA'S GENERAL

In war men are nothing;
it is the man who is everything.
The general is the head,
the whole of an army.
—Napoléon Bonaparte

VIRGINIA'S GENERAL

Robert E. Lee and the Civil War

ALBERT MARRIN

ATHENEUM 1994 NEW YORK

Maxwell Macmillan Canada TORONTO   Maxwell Macmillan International NEW YORK OXFORD SINGAPORE SYDNEY

FOR A NEW GENERATION OF CIVIL WAR ENTHUSIASTS

Atheneum
Macmillan Publishing Company
866 Third Avenue
New York, NY 10022
Maxwell Macmillan Canada, Inc.
1200 Eglinton Avenue East
Suite 200
Don Mills, Ontario M3C 3N1
Macmillan Publishing Company is part of the Maxwell Communication Group of Companies.
First edition
Printed in the United States of America
10 9 8 7 6 5 4 3 2 1
Library of Congress Cataloging-in-Publication Data
Marrin, Albert.
Virginia's general : Robert E. Lee and the Civil War / by Albert Marrin.
p.   cm.
Includes bibliographical references (p.) and index.
ISBN 0-689-31838-3
1. Lee, Robert E. (Robert Edward), 1807–1870—Juvenile literature. 2. Generals—United States—Biography—Juvenile literature. 3. Generals—Confederate States of America—Biography—Juvenile literature. 4. United States. Army—Biography—Juvenile literature. 5. Confederate States of America. Army Biography—Juvenile literature. 6. United States—History—Civil War, 1861–1865—Campaigns—Juvenile literature. I. Title.
E467.1.L4M36 1994
973.7'3'092—dc20
[B]   94-13353
SUMMARY: A biography of Robert E. Lee, concentrating on the Civil War years.

PHOTO CREDITS

All photographs courtesy of the National Archives except as listed below. National Portrait Gallery, Smithsonian Institution: 8, 48, 57, 61, 90 (gift of Mrs. Chester E. King), 107, 196; Washington/Custis/Lee Collection, Washington and Lee University, Lexington, Virginia: 9; Schomburg Center for Research in Black Culture, New York Public Library: 23; Library of Congress: 40, 105, 112, 141, 166; Century War Book, 42; Gardner's Photographic Sketch Book of the Civil War: 185; Century Magazine: 187

CONTENTS

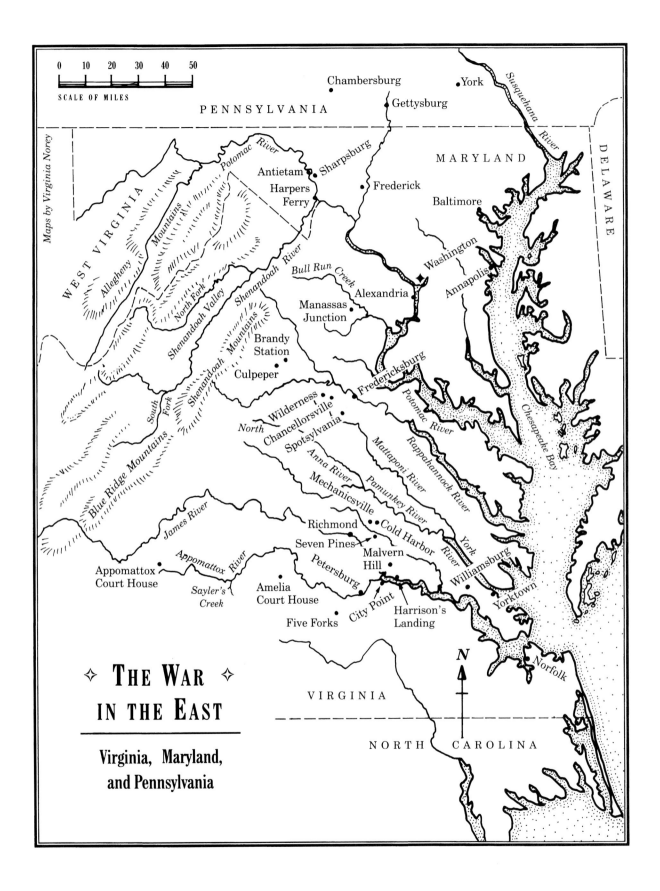

Maps by Virginia Norey

SCALE OF MILES
0 10 20 30 40 50

PENNSYLVANIA

Chambersburg

York

Susquehanna River

Gettysburg

MARYLAND

DELAWARE

Sharpsburg

Potomac River

Antietam

Frederick

Harpers Ferry

Baltimore

WEST VIRGINIA

Allegheny Mountains

North Fork

Shenandoah River

Washington

Annapolis

Shenandoah Valley

Bull Run Creek

Alexandria

Shenandoah Mountains

Manassas Junction

Brandy Station

Culpeper

Fredericksburg

Chesapeake Bay

South Fork

Blue Ridge Mountains

Wilderness

North

Chancellorsville

Spotsylvania

Potomac River

Anna River

Mattaponi River

Rappahannock River

Mechanicsville

Pamunkey River

James River

Richmond

Cold Harbor

York River

Seven Pines

Appomattox River

Malvern Hill

Williamsburg

Appomattox Court House

Petersburg

Yorktown

Sayler's Creek

Amelia Court House

City Point

Harrison's Landing

Five Forks

N

Norfolk

◆ THE WAR IN THE EAST ◆

VIRGINIA

Virginia, Maryland, and Pennsylvania

NORTH CAROLINA

PROLOGUE ✦ "MARSE ROBERT"

Thursday, April 18, 1861. A bright spring morning with high wispy clouds set off against a deep blue sky. Already the sweet scent of flowers filled the air.

At about nine o'clock, a lone horseman rode down from Arlington Heights on the Virginia side of the Potomac River, directly opposite Washington, D.C. He wore the uniform of a colonel in the United States Army and sat tall in the saddle, the reins held loosely between his fingers. He rode easily, effortlessly, as one who had been around horses all his life and knew their ways.

He was an impressive figure at fifty-four years old, said by both men and women to be the handsomest fellow alive. Solidly built, and a picture of health, he had been sick only once in his adult life, and then not seriously. He stood five feet eleven in his socks and weighed just under 170 pounds. His hair was black with flecks of gray, his face close shaven except for a thick mustache of the blackest black. He had brown eyes, a long, straight nose, and a ruddy complexion. His lips were pressed tightly together and his jaws set, his face showing no expression whatsoever.

He began to cross the Long Bridge, a mile-long span over the Potomac. Off to the right, the United States Capitol dominated the landscape, its unfinished dome topped by a crane and surrounded

The unfinished United States Capitol as Robert E. Lee would have seen it when he crossed the Long Bridge in April 1861

with scaffolding. It would be another two years before the twenty-foot bronze statue of Freedom would be hoisted into the place it occupies today. To the left was the marble stump of the Washington Monument, only a third of the way on its five-hundred-foot climb upward. All was quiet, save for the water lapping against the bridge's stone pilings and the clippity-clop of his horse's hooves against the wooden planks. Occasionally, the man hunched his shoulders and shuddered in his overcoat, as a cold breeze whipped across the river.

He ignored the scenery. He had made this journey hundreds of times and knew the nation's capital like his wife's estate, Arlington. Besides, a lot had happened recently; it preyed on his mind, giving him sleepless nights.

Events had moved quickly—*too* quickly—since Abraham Lincoln's election as president five months earlier. Hating the man and fearing he would abolish their "peculiar institution"—slavery—seven Southern states had already seceded from the Union to form their own country, the Confederate States of America. It was a time for painful choices, especially for people such as the colonel.

The army was breaking up as officers obeyed their consciences and took sides. But how sad, how dreadful, it was to choose! Someday soon, men who had been friends all their adult lives might be killing one another in the line of duty.

The explosion came on April 12. At dawn, Confederate guns fired on Fort Sumter in the harbor of Charleston, South Carolina. President Lincoln declared a state of rebellion and called for seventy-five thousand volunteers to put it down. The Civil War had begun.

Leaving the Long Bridge, the colonel rode up Fourteenth Street to Pennsylvania Avenue, the city's main thoroughfare. Despite the imposing government buildings, Washington still resembled a frontier town—a very *dirty* frontier town. "The town," an English visitor wrote, "looks like a large straggling village reared in a drained swamp." Its unpaved streets were a horror. Rain turned them into streams of slippery mud. In dry weather, the slightest breeze blew clouds of dust into people's eyes, made them sneeze, and caused the dust to crunch between their teeth. Cattle, pigs, and sheep roamed freely, leaving their droppings to blend with the dust and mud. The Old City Canal ran the length of Pennsylvania Avenue from Capitol Hill to the rear of the White House. Actually an open sewer, the canal stank of floating garbage and dead animals. Living in the White House required a strong stomach as well as a keen mind.

Washington was already a city at war. Troops, rushed in by train, camped on the lawns of government buildings. Barracks had sprung up on the Mall, one of the oldest federal parks and today lined with some of the world's finest art and science museums. Checkpoints stood at intersections and along key avenues. At one of these, guards snapped to attention and saluted the colonel. They were saluting both the man and the uniform, since Robert E. Lee had been a respected figure in the army for thirty-two years. It seemed that everyone either knew him or knew of him.

Colonel Lee dismounted in front of 1651 Pennsylvania Avenue, a pale yellow building across from the White House. Known as Blair House today, it is a guesthouse for visiting foreign heads of state. Back then, it was the home of Francis Preston Blair, Sr., a close political ally of the president.

After showing his guest to a chair, "Old Man Blair" came straight to the point. President Lincoln wanted him to ask Lee a question: Would he take battlefield command of the United States Army?

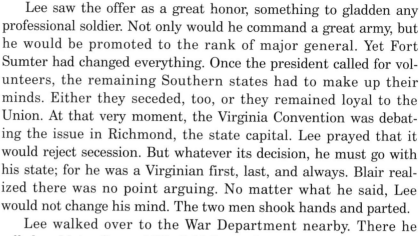

Lee saw the offer as a great honor, something to gladden any professional soldier. Not only would he command a great army, but he would be promoted to the rank of major general. Yet Fort Sumter had changed everything. Once the president called for volunteers, the remaining Southern states had to make up their minds. Either they seceded, too, or they remained loyal to the Union. At that very moment, the Virginia Convention was debating the issue in Richmond, the state capital. Lee prayed that it would reject secession. But whatever its decision, he must go with his state; for he was a Virginian first, last, and always. Blair realized there was no point arguing. No matter what he said, Lee would not change his mind. The two men shook hands and parted.

Lee walked over to the War Department nearby. There he called on Major General Winfield Scott, the army's general-in-chief and his friend for fifteen years. Although they had no way of knowing it, this was to be their last meeting. When Lee told of Blair's proposal and his refusal, Scott shook his head and looked "pained." "Lee," he said, "you have made the greatest mistake of your life; but I feared it would be so."[1]

General Winfield Scott, one of America's greatest soldiers and Robert E. Lee's friend, in a photo dating from the early days of the Civil War. Scott's greatest regret was that Lee had decided to resign from the United States Army to serve the Confederacy.

Lee headed back to the Long Bridge. Newsboys were shouting that the Virginia Convention had voted to secede. Virginia was the South's richest and most powerful state. With it in the Confederacy, the Civil War was bound to last longer and be more terrible than anything Americans had ever known before.

The Civil War is the central event in our country's history. It is the American *Iliad*, because, like the poet Homer's tale of ancient Greece, it is filled with action, danger, and characters larger than life. And, like the *Iliad*, it has never lost its fascination. More than fifty thousand books on the war have been published since the guns fell silent more than a century and a quarter ago. Still the printing presses turn out a hundred new titles, more or less, each year.

The Revolution, 1775–1783, gave us our independence. The Civil War, 1861–1865, gave us our character as a nation. In doing so, it answered two vital question. First, it decided whether the United States should remain one nation or become two. Second, it showed that this nation could not endure half slave and half free. But at what a price! The dead numbered 620,000, of whom 360,000 were Union and 260,000 Confederate soldiers. Never before had Americans experienced such a frightful bloodletting; nor have they since. The men who died almost equaled the 680,000 Americans who died in all their country's other wars combined. The Union alone had 275,000 men *wounded*, compared to the total of 231,000 who *served* in the armies of the American Revolution.

Robert E. Lee played a key part in the Civil War; indeed, it is impossible to imagine that struggle without him. So much of what happened, happened because of what he did or failed to do. Had he accepted President Lincoln's offer, it is likely that the war would not have lasted as long, saving countless lives. But, instead, Lee became the champion of the South, its very fighting soul. For three years he led the Army of Northern Virginia, one of the greatest fighting forces in history.

Lee's men called him "Marster Robert"—"Marse Robert" for short. The term "marse" originated with the slaves as a slurring of master. On earth, the master was at once their owner and overseer. In heaven, he was the Lord God, Master of all Masters.

The Confederate soldier borrowed the term from the slave. In a way, his life was not all that different from the slave's. True, he was a free man, and the slave was not. Yet each had to obey the authorities without question or protest. And those authorities could be good or bad, kind or cruel, depending on the individual. A decent master was addressed as "Marse So-and-So"; God was simply "Old Marster." In speaking of Lee, Confederate soldiers might easily confuse the two. Once a private asked his friend, who had spoken of "Old Marster," whether he meant "the one up at headquarters or the One up yonder." Lee was for him and many others, Godlike, the living embodiment of wisdom and strength.[2]

Robert E. Lee was both a decent man and a fearsome warrior. War by its very nature is cruel, and civil wars particularly so. Marse Robert, however, rose above war's cruelty. He demanded that his men remember they were civilized human beings, respecting the rights of civilians, prisoners, and the wounded. Despite occasional lapses, they followed his principles and example to the end. They did so out of love for the man. They knew he loved them in return and would not waste their lives. They also feared his wrath, knowing he would not hesitate to hang lawbreakers. But the love came first.

Lee was a soldier's soldier. Although calm and deliberate, never raising his voice, he was extremely aggressive. Few generals have ever done so much with so little. He fought against tremendous odds. Yet in campaign after campaign, he defeated the cream of the Union army, humiliating its generals and bringing Abraham Lincoln to the edge of suicide. True, he was defeated in the end. The wonder is that he held out so long.

Lee influenced the way Americans make war. General John J. Pershing, commander of American forces in Europe during World War I, revered him. In World War II, General George Patton, grandson of a Confederate colonel, learned from Lee's use of mobility and bold thrusts to achieve victory. But instead of using infantry and cavalry, Patton's thrusts were spearheaded by tanks and dive-bombers. General Douglas MacArthur, who commanded in the Pacific against the Japanese, was the son of Arthur MacArthur, one of the Union's "boy generals." Douglas learned to admire Lee at the same time as he learned to talk. At bedtime, his mother would say: "You must grow up to be a great man like your father, or like Robert E. Lee."[3]

Today Lee, the former Rebel, is considered one of America's greatest heroes. Our task is to understand him as both a person and a soldier, setting him in his own time.

I ✦ AN OFFICER AND A GENTLEMAN

Robert E. Lee is the best soldier in Christendom.

—General Winfield Scott

Robert E. Lee was born January 19, 1807, at Stratford Hall, the "big house" of his family's plantation on the Potomac River in Westmoreland County, Virginia. Located in the eastern part of the state, this region belongs to the Tidewater, a network of creeks and rivers emptying into Chesapeake Bay. The Tidewater was glorious country, a land of fertile soil and vast plantations worked by black slaves. Although plantations further south grew cotton, those of the Tidewater had specialized in tobacco since colonial times. Plantation owners lived like royalty, waited upon hand and foot by "servants," a polite term for household slaves. It had always been so, and, as far as they knew, would be so forever.

It was something to be one of the Tidewater Lees. The Lee family, said John Adams, second president of the United States, had "more men of merit in it than any other family."[1] Adams was not exaggerating. Generations of Lees had served first the kings of England, then the American republic, with distinction. Two signers of the Declaration of Independence had been born in the same room, indeed, in the same bed, in which Robert later came into the world. Kinsmen had been diplomats, soldiers, naval officers, judges, town mayors, members of the Continental Congress, and United States congressmen. The Lee women were noted for their intelligence, grace, and beauty.

Robert E. Lee's father, Henry ("Light-Horse Harry") Lee, was a general during the Revolutionary War and later governor of Virginia. From a painting attributed to James Herring in the National Portrait Gallery, Washington, D.C.

Robert was the fourth child of parents who were as different as day and night. His father was Henry Lee, a restless, reckless man who enjoyed getting in harm's way. As a cavalry officer during the Revolution, he was nicknamed "Light-Horse Harry," because his men were "lightly" armed and he led them on daring raids behind British lines. George Washington, who gave him command of a unit called Lee's Legion, admired his gallantry. Sometimes, however, he went too far. During a crackdown on deserters, Harry had a man hanged, the body decapitated, and the head paraded around camp on the point of a spear.

After the war, Harry was elected to Congress, and also served three one-year terms as governor of Virginia. It was he who described Washington in the famous phrase: "First in war, first in peace, first in the hearts of his countrymen."

Robert's mother was Anne Hill Carter, daughter of Charles Carter, probably the richest man in Virginia. A kind, gentle person, she fell in love with the handsome Harry the moment she set eyes on him. He was a thirty-seven-year-old widower and she was twenty when they married in 1793 and moved into Stratford Hall, one of America's most elegant homes. It had brick walls four feet thick, a huge ballroom, and seventeen other rooms, each painted a different color. There was a blue room, and a green room, and a red room, each with a fireplace big enough for a tall man to stand in. A massive outdoor staircase led directly to the ballroom. Portraits of Lee ancestors hung from the walls in gilt frames, clad in their finery.

The honeymoon did not last long. Anne soon learned that her groom was a ne'er-do-well. He had a roving eye, and his affairs with other women broke her heart. He poured money into every get-rich-quick scheme that came his way, investing in canal companies that never dug a ditch and in western lands that no one wanted to buy. His own fortune, and then his wife's, ran through his fingers like so many grains of sand. In desperation, he borrowed money for other, riskier ventures to recoup his losses. But when these failed, too, he sold Stratford's furnishings to raise cash; he even sold the outdoor staircase. The massive oak doors were chained to keep out bill collectors.

By 1807, Anne was about as miserable as a person could be. Early in January, her father died. Her husband was too "busy" to comfort her; she seldom saw him, since he was always roaming the countryside, trying to borrow money or find investors for his crazy schemes. Already the mother of three, two boys and a girl, Anne was expecting once again. The last thing she wanted, she admitted, was another child. Nevertheless, she gave birth to a "little black-eyed brown Boy, very healthy, good-tempered, lively and sweet," whom she named Robert Edward after her two brothers.[2] In time, that unwanted child would become her darling.

Had Anne's father not left her some money, the family would have gone hungry. As it was, things went from bad to worse. When Robert was two, his father's creditors had him arrested and sent to debtor's jail. This was legalized kidnapping, a way of forcing a debtor's loved ones to pay up or see him rot behind bars. The jail was at Spotsylvania Court House, where Robert would fight one of the bloodiest battles of the Civil War.

Somehow Light-Horse Harry raised the money and was released after about a year. Yet he could not return to Stratford. The estate did not belong to him, but to his first wife's family, and it was inherited by their son from this earlier marriage. According to her will, Light-Horse Harry could live on the estate until the boy, Henry, Jr., turned eighteen. Since he had just come of age, the family was forced to leave.

In the summer of 1810, the Lees moved into a rented house in Alexandria, eighty miles up the Potomac and six miles from the nation's capital. Moving, however, did not improve life. During a visit to Baltimore, Maryland, in July 1812, Harry was beaten in a riot. Thugs knocked him unconscious and rolled him into the gut-

Ann Hill Carter Lee was the wife of "Light-Horse Harry" Lee and the mother of Robert E. Lee. This painting, the work of an unknown artist, dates from about the year 1795. Notice that she is wearing a picture of George Washington, a family friend, hanging on a chain around her neck.

ter. Seeing him lying helpless, a drunk dripped hot candle wax into his eyes and tried to cut off his nose. The knife slipped, slashing him across the face. He was no longer handsome.

Harry returned home after several months, broken in body and spirit. His family went in constant fear, lest the smallest "error" trigger a temper tantrum. He would sit for hours babbling to himself, or charge around the house, cursing the world for the "wrongs" it had done him. Hoping to regain his health, he sailed for the West Indies in 1813. After five years of wandering from island to island, he died while trying to return home. A family friend wrote the best epitaph: "Light-Horse Harry a fool was born, a fool he lived, and a fool he died!"[3] Anne said nothing, at least for the record, and, for all we know, shed no tears. Almost from the day he left, he was dead to his family; indeed, his wife took to calling herself the Widow Lee while he still lived.

Alexandria was a good place to live. It had schools for the older children and was home to many of Anne's relatives; in fact, it seemed that every other person they met was either her aunt, uncle, or cousin. The children, though "poor kin," always found a warm welcome in their homes.

Anne had no qualms about letting Robert go out alone. Wherever he went, there were kindly adults to keep an eye on him. Veterans of Lee's Legion lived in town, and they adopted their old commander's son as a mascot. Did these men know how to spin a yarn! The boy would sit open-mouthed, listening to stories about "Swamp Fox" Francis Marion, the gallant Frenchman Lafayette, and other heroes of the Revolution. But this was Alexandria, and talk eventually turned to its greatest citizen.

Alexandria had been George Washington's favorite town, and his spirit could still be felt everywhere. Here, in Market Square, he had drilled his Virginia Rangers during the French and Indian War. There, at the City Tavern, he and his wife, Martha, had celebrated his last birthday in 1799. The Lees worshiped in Christ Church, where pew number five still held Washington's personal Bible. Small wonder that the son of a ne'er-do-well should have idolized the Father of His Country. Washington's virtues—honesty, loyalty, duty, thrift, courage, fair play, hard work—became his watchwords.

Anne took a keen interest in her son's education. In the early years, she helped him with the basics of reading and writing. When he turned nine, she sent him to a Carter family school. The Carters were such a large family that they had their own separate schools for boys and girls. Robert attended school at Eastern View

Plantation, the home of Anne's sister, Elizabeth Randolph. After learning all he could there, at thirteen he was enrolled in the Alexandria Academy. There he studied Latin, Greek, and mathematics, a subject that gave him as much pleasure as other boys found in games. Not that he didn't enjoy sports. He was an excellent rider, swimmer, and ice-skater; he could run two miles without stopping for breath.

Usually, however, he had little time for athletics. His mother's health had become so poor that she was often too weak to get out of bed. Her older sons, Carter and Smith, were studying law or serving in the navy. Daughter Anne was herself sickly, and Mildred, born after the move to Alexandria, was still playing with dolls. So Robert took charge; or, as they said in the Old South, "carried the keys." He became the housekeeper, cared for the horses, and did the marketing, going out with a basket over his arm each day after school. He was a good manager, keeping track of every penny in the budget.

By the time Robert was fifteen, he had also become his mother's nurse. He mixed her medicines and saw that she took them on time. Robert himself was a medicine for the ailing woman. If she was well enough to go out, he took her on coach rides. "He would entertain and amuse his mother," an aunt recalled, "assuring her, with the gravity of an older man, that unless she was cheerful the drive would not benefit her. When she complained of cold or drafts, he would pull out from his pocket a great jack-knife and newspaper and make her laugh with his efforts to improvise curtains and shut out the intrusive wind which whistled through the crevices of the old family coach."[4]

Much as Anne depended upon her son, she knew she could not keep him home forever. On his seventeenth birthday, they discussed the future. She wanted to send him to college, but could not afford the expense. Still, there was a college that offered a free education: the United States Military Academy at West Point, New York. An army career seemed ideal for a son of Light-Horse Harry Lee and an admirer of George Washington.

The academy's admission requirements were modest by today's standards. An applicant needed to be between fourteen and twenty years of age, a minimum of four feet nine inches tall, and able to read, write, and do elementary arithmetic. Robert easily met these requirements. The problem was that the academy admitted only a few dozen cadets each year, and competition was fierce. His relatives, however, knew the "right" people. One introduced him to

Andrew Jackson, the hero of the War of 1812 and a future president. "Old Hickory" was so pleased with the boy that he got him an appointment. A letter of recommendation signed by five senators and three congressmen was also helpful.

So Robert E. Lee packed his bags and headed north in June 1825. As the carriage pulled out of the driveway, his mother was heard to say, "How can I live without Robert? He is both son and daughter to me."[5]

The United States Military Academy is set on a bluff overlooking the Hudson River. But the natural beauty of its setting was in sharp contrast to the drabness of the school itself. In Robert's day, it consisted of some gray stone buildings clustered around a parade ground. There was a mess hall, a chapel, a library, classroom buildings, and barracks for the four hundred students, or "cadets." The rooms were too tiny for beds; cadets were issued thin mattresses and slept on the floor.

Everything about West Point was calculated to build discipline and character; that is, to make an officer and a gentleman. The training began on day one and continued without letup for the next four years. That training could be hard to take, if you didn't see the purpose behind it. A new cadet, for example, had to get used to upperclassmen calling him "Plebe" (slang for commoner) or "Animal" or "Thing." Being called names, the argument went, taught self-control, vital for one responsible for other people's lives. Losing your temper brought extra duty and demerits, black marks against your name. You might also get demerits for breaking any of the academy's scores of rules and regulations. A cadet soon learned that he could not have a wife, own a horse, use tobacco, gamble, or play a musical instrument. Enough demerits and you were out of the academy.

The school day began with reveille at 4:30 A.M. After roll call and cleaning their quarters for inspection, cadets studied mathematics until breakfast at seven o'clock. This meal, leftovers from the night before, was usually meat, bread, butter, and coffee.

Classes started after breakfast and lasted until four o'clock in the afternoon. Instructors expected students to be prepared; there was no such thing as missing an assignment and catching up later, or borrowing a classmate's notes. Every cadet had to recite every day in every subject. Mathematics was the most important; West Pointers graduated with degrees in engineering, and engineering is based on mathematics. French was second in importance, since the best military books were written in that language. In addition, cadets studied drawing, physics, chemistry, history, geography, and military science. The rest of the day was taken up by inspections, weapons drill, guard duty, and study periods; at ten o'clock the bugler sounded lights-out.

Lee became the star of the academy. He made friends easily, owing to his consideration for others and his sense of humor. He always found time to help fellow cadets with mathematics. During off-duty hours, he told funny stories that made his listeners laugh, while he laughed "until the tears ran down his face"; only later did he become the serious, unsmiling man known to history.[6] Joseph E. Johnston, his classmate and best friend, recalled that "he was full of sympathy and kindness, genial and fond of gay conversation, and even of fun, while his . . . attention to all duties, personal and official . . . gave him a superiority that everyone acknowledged in his heart. He was the only one of all the men I have known who could laugh at the faults and follies of his friends in such a manner as to make them ashamed without touching their affection for him, and to confirm their respect and sense of his superiority."[7] In short, Robert E. Lee was a born leader.

He vowed to be a perfect cadet, and almost succeeded. Because of his mathematical ability, he was named an assistant professor with a salary of ten dollars a month, thus becoming both teacher and student. In his senior year, he became adjutant to the corps of cadets, West Point's highest honor; the adjutant assisted the commander in issuing orders and keeping records. He graduated second in the class of 1829, narrowly missing the top place; that went to a fellow who soon quit the army to become a lawyer. Lee graduated without a single demerit, an academy record that has never been equaled.

The new second lieutenant went home on leave before reporting to the Army Corps of Engineers. He arrived just in time to nurse his mother through her last illness. Anne had missed him terribly and could not bear to be without him. She watched his every move, and if he left the sickroom, she kept her eyes on the door until he returned. Widow Lee died on June 26, 1829. Robert, who had been closer to her than had any of her other children, said he owed her everything.

He used the rest of his leave to settle his mother's affairs and pay social calls. One place drew him like a magnet. It was Arlington House, a white-columned mansion overlooking the Potomac. There lived George Washington Parke Custis, George

Mary Custis about the time of her marriage to Robert E. Lee. Mary and her husband were always proud of their relationship to George Washington.

Washington's adopted son and the grandson of Martha Washington. Rich in land and slaves, Mr. Custis had turned Arlington into a shrine to the first president. Its rooms contained furniture from Mount Vernon, Washington's estate, and the late president's clothing, field tent, watches, and books, as well as boxes of his personal letters; there was even the bed in which he had died. Mr. Custis liked nothing better than to talk about his adoptive father, and Robert liked nothing better than to hear about the great man from one who had been so close to him.

As a child, Robert had often visited the Custises with his mother. While the adults socialized, he played with their daughter, Mary Anne, a year younger than himself. He had not seen her since going off to West Point. Now he found her different—fascinatingly different. She had grown from a gangly teenager into a slim beauty of twenty-one. They took long walks, losing track of time in one another's company. What passed between them is unknown. What we do know is that they fell in love and he asked her to be his wife. They married on June 30, 1831, after his first tour of duty. Robert had joined the Washington family, becoming, a relative said, "the representative of the family of the founder of American liberty."[8] It was the closest thing America had to royalty.

Mary Anne bore seven children in fourteen years. Her first, born in 1832, was named George Washington Custis Lee. Then came Mary, William Henry Fitzhugh, Annie, Agnes, Robert E. Lee, Jr., and Mildred. She was a good mother, but it was Father who made the deepest impression upon their children.

Lee had a way with children, all children. Throughout his life, he was attracted to them and they to him. His own children always knew they were loved—*powerfully* loved. That love was shown in

countless ways. Whenever he came home or left, he called them to
him, "kissing us—caressing us in his sweet way."[9] He gave them
pet names, which he used even when they became adults. Baby
Custis was "Dear Mr. Boo"; when he got older, his father called him
"Mr. Custis." His second son became "Rooney," and Robert, Jr.,
was "Rob." Agnes was "Daughter," and Mildred "Precious Life";
their mother was called "The Mims." Despite a busy schedule, he
found the time to take them rowing, to swim with them in the
Potomac, and to teach them to ride horses. On Sunday mornings,
he'd invite them into bed to listen to stories. All he asked in return
was that they tickle his hands and feet. If they stopped, he
declared, "No tickling, no story."[10]

Lee's engineering duties took him away from home for months
at a time. During these absences, he wrote long letters telling the
children about his adventures and how much he missed them. "My
precious Annie," he wrote his second daughter,

> *I take advantage of your gracious permission to write to you,
> and there is no telling how far my feelings might carry me
> were I not limited by [time]. . . . But my limited time does
> not diminish my affection for you, Annie, nor prevent my
> thinking of you and wishing for you. I long to see you
> through the dilatory nights. At dawn when I rise, and all
> day, my thoughts revert to you in expressions that you can-
> not hear nor I repeat. I hope you will always appear to me as
> you are now painted on my heart.[11]*

But Lee was not merely a nice man who said nice things to children. He was also a stern disciplinarian who had strong opinions
and expected to be obeyed. His sons, he believed, must be kept to a
high standard, lest they become like Light-Horse Harry. He
demanded reports on their progress in everything from mathematics to swimming. He made regular room inspections, as in an army
barracks, to make sure everything was neat and clean. The children were constantly lectured on their reading habits. Reading
novels was bad, since novels painted imaginary pictures of the
world. History books and "works of truth" were good, since they
depicted reality. The word "can't" was banned from the children's
vocabulary. "I Cannot admit their assertion that 'they can't,'" he
wrote Mary. "They *Can* if they *try* & I say in addition they *Must*."[12]
No wonder Rob found it impossible to disobey his father; none of
the children could.

Lee was happy as a husband and father. Still, as a professional soldier, he must have found life dull. Civil engineering, the building of harbors and docks, was a routine part of his job. Although vital to the growing nation, and to his own reputation, it offered no real challenge. It was child's play compared to combat engineering, building roads and bridges to open the way for advancing armies. But in his chosen field, he had no experience at all. After seventeen years in the army, he was a thirty-nine-year-old captain who had never heard a shot fired in anger. Apart from Indian troubles in the West, none of them serious, the nation had been at peace since the close of the War of 1812 with Great Britain.

Then came the Mexican War.

The war grew out of a boundary dispute between the United States and its southern neighbor. Texas had belonged to Mexico until 1836, when its American settlers broke away and formed the Lone Star Republic. After nine years of independence, it joined the Union as the twenty-eighth state. The Mexicans, however, refused to recognize the Rio Grande as the border. Tempers flared as both sides staged across-the-border raids to rustle cattle and kill ranchers. On May 13, 1846, Congress declared war after Mexican troops overran an American outpost near the present-day city of Brownsville.

Americans disagreed on the justice of their first war on foreign soil. In New England, people chose jail rather than pay taxes to buy weapons. Congressman Abraham Lincoln of Illinois condemned it as a war of conquest, ruining his career in the House of Representatives. A young lieutenant named Ulysses S. Grant thought the war "the most unjust ever waged by a stronger against a weaker nation."[13] But he stayed in the army because, he said, a soldier must serve his country whether it be right or wrong. So did Robert E. Lee. He confessed to being "ashamed" at the United States for having "bullied" its smaller neighbor. Nevertheless, as a professional soldier, he could not choose his wars. He would obey orders and leave political decisions to politicians.[14]

Lee's engineering skills won him a place on the staff of Major General Winfield Scott. Known as "Old Fuss and Feathers" because of his devotion to army regulations, Scott was the ablest commander of the day. His mission demanded every ounce of ability he possessed, and then some. He was to land an army on Mexico's eastern coast, march inland across the mountains, and take Mexico City, the capital.

The invasion fleet sailed from the mouth of the Rio Grande on March 3, 1847. Lee and "Joe" Johnston shared a cabin aboard the flagship *Massachusetts*. It was a fine cabin, large and comfortable, except that nothing in it stood still for more than a few seconds at a time. High seas tossed the ship about like a cork. Lee had a strong stomach; Johnston did not. "My poor Joe," he wrote his sons, "is so sick all the time that I can do nothing with him. . . . The ship rolls so that I can scarcely write."[15]

The American force, ten thousand strong, landed near the city of Vera Cruz after a two-day voyage. It found the Mexicans waiting behind breastworks, log barriers covered with mounds of earth. Rather than risk a direct assault, Scott decided to lay siege to the town. Everything now depended on the engineers.

Robert E. Lee in 1838, from a painting by William E. West. The dashing young lieutenant was said to be the handsomest man in the United States.

Lee put his men to work digging trenches and placing the guns. The Mexicans replied by shelling the work parties. Their gunners, however, were poorly trained, and most of their shots went wild. The worst menace, Lee found, was trigger-happy Americans. One night, he and a fellow officer were walking along a trail cut through some thick brush. Rounding a bend, they were challenged by a guard.

"Who goes there?" he cried.

"Friends!" Lee replied.

"Officers!" shouted his companion.[16]

The guard fired, sending a bullet between Lee's left arm and his body, but without leaving a scratch. It was a close call, the first of many. History is full of fascinating ifs. If that bullet had been off by a quarter of an inch, the Civil War would surely have been fought differently.

When all was ready, the Americans cut loose with heavy guns that threw thirty-two-pound and sixty-eight-pound shells a mile. In two days of shelling, the Mexican breastworks were blown to bits and Vera Cruz surrendered. Captain Lee had mixed feelings about the result. He had always seen war as an exercise or a game.

Now, for the first time, he fired guns at live targets. It was a strange feeling, at once thrilling and horrifying. The shells, he wrote Mary, were "so beautiful in their flight," trailing fiery streamers as they sped across the sky. But their effect was definitely not beautiful. "It was awful! My heart bled for the inhabitants. The soldiers I do not care so much for, but it was terrible to think of the women & children."[17] It would always be so. Lee marveled at the pageantry of war, but hated what it did to human beings.

The Americans pushed inland. At Cerro Gordo, they found the Mexicans waiting at the top of a steep mountain pass. It was an astonishing sight. The enemy position, soldiers said, was so strong that the defenders did not need cannon and muskets; all they had to do was throw rocks at the "gringos" below. The only hope of avoiding a slaughter was to attack from behind.

General Scott called Captain Lee to his tent. His question was short and sharp: Could he find a way around? Lee said he would try his best.

Setting out with a scout known as Juan Diablo—John the Devil—he did discover a trail that ran behind the enemy positions. All was well until they stopped to refresh themselves at a stream before returning to camp. Kneeling to drink, they heard the voices of men speaking Spanish. Mexican soldiers were coming to the spring!

Juan Diablo hid in some rocks, while Lee dropped behind a log screened by thick brush. The Mexicans drank from the spring, then loafed about and sat with their legs dangling over the log, inches from Lee's head. He hugged the ground, envying the earthworms. A lizard walked in front of his nose. Ants crawled into his shirt. He lay still, not daring to move a muscle, let alone scratch. At last, the sun set and the soldiers left and the Americans escaped. Next day, Lee showed his engineers where to cut their road.

The Battle of Cerro Gordo began on April 17, 1847. One troop column held the Mexicans' attention while another struck from behind. By nightfall of the second day, the enemy was in full retreat, having lost over a thousand killed and wounded.

Although proud of his role in the victory, Lee saw no reason for joy. "You have no idea what a horrible sight a field of battle is," he wrote Mr. Boo. He had found a Mexican drummer boy with a shattered arm pinned beneath a dying soldier. A little girl was trying to help the boy, possibly her brother, but she could not move the full-grown man. Lee ordered them both taken to a field hospital. The girl stared at the stranger, a giant compared to most of her countrymen. She seemed so small, so delicate. "Her large black eyes were streaming with tears," he wrote, "her hands crossed over her breast. . . . Her plaintive tone of 'Mille gracias, Señor' [a thousand thanks, sir] . . . still lingers in my ear."[18]

After leaving the mountains, the Americans headed for Mexico City. It was the rainy season, and the capital was surrounded by soggy fields and lakes that had overflowed their banks. The most direct approach lay across the Pedregal, a huge lava bed resembling petrified ocean waves. The ground was strewn with chunks of lava that could easily slice through a man's boots. It was the same problem Scott had faced at Cerro Gordo. To avoid a head-on assault, he had to slip behind the enemy positions; that is, cross the Pedregal.

Scott believed that if anyone could succeed, it was Robert E. Lee. He was right. Not only did Lee's engineers build a road, Lee crossed the Pedregal three times. The first time was with a scouting party to mark the trail; the other times he went alone to report to Scott and receive further orders. He crossed at night, in a thunderstorm, with only lightning flashes to show the way. Scott was amazed. Lee's trips, he said, were "the greatest feat of physical and moral courage performed by an individual" during the entire campaign.[19]

Lee's daring enabled the Americans to reach the outskirts of Mexico City with only light casualties. One obstacle still barred their way: a massive fortress atop Chapultepec, the "Hill of Grasshoppers." It was Lee who guided the first assault troops to the fort on September 13, 1847. But he did not take part in the fighting; his job was to report its progress to Scott and keep him in touch with the field commanders. Lee went about his task, ignoring the bullets whizzing past his head. One grazed him, drawing blood but otherwise doing no harm. It was to be his only battle wound.

The assault troops set up ladders and bellied over the fortress walls. Present that day were men who would win fame fighting one another in the Civil War. A husky lieutenant named James Longstreet was hit as his men neared the wall. He was carrying a flag, which he passed to George Pickett, a recent graduate of West Point. Joe Johnston was there, too, along with Thomas J. Jackson, P. G. T. Beauregard, A. P. Hill, D. H. Hill, John B. Magruder, and Richard S. Ewell. All were destined to serve alongside Lee as generals in the Confederate army. Their comrades, men like John Pope, Joseph Hooker, George Gordon Meade, Ambrose E. Burnside, and George B. McClellan, would be Union generals. Ulysses S. Grant, the man who finally defeated Lee, hauled a light cannon into a church steeple to shell the defenders at one of the city gates.

Mexico City surrendered the next day. General Scott was thrilled with his men's performance; so much so that he said he could hug them all. He was especially proud of Lee, promoting him to the rank of colonel. The promotion was "by brevet," a reward for courage that carried the title but not the pay of a higher rank. Nevertheless, it was a milestone in Lee's career. Until then, he had been just another good officer. The brevet showed that he was a man to watch. Scott thought so. "I tell you," he wrote a friend, "that if I were on my death bed tomorrow, and the President of the United States would tell me that a great battle was to be fought for the liberty or slavery of the country, and asked my judgment as to the ability of a commander, I would say with my dying breath, 'Let it be Robert E. Lee!'"[20]

After the excitement of Mexico, Lee's life became pretty tame. He returned to Arlington and a hero's welcome. "Here I am again, my dear Smith," he wrote his brother, "perfectly surrounded by Mary and her precious children, who seem to devote themselves to staring at the furrows in my face and the white hairs in my head."[21] The younger children could not stop touching him, kissing him, and questioning him about his adventures. Whenever they could, he and Mary would sit on the porch and look across the Potomac at the rising Capitol.

His work was not demanding. There were the usual engineering projects, notably the building of Fort Carroll in Baltimore harbor. In 1852, thanks to General Scott, he was named superintendent of the United States Military Academy. It was a choice post, normally reserved for older men.

"The Point" had changed little since his student days. Yes, there was more of everything: more cadets, more professors, more rules. But the spirit was the same, and that is what gives a school its character. Among the Plebes were the superintendent's son, Custis, and his nephew, Fitzhugh. Like his father before him, Custis was a near-perfect cadet; Fitzhugh, a high-spirited young-ster, managed to pass by the skin of his teeth.

Lee was an able superintendent, not an outstanding one. He tightened discipline and introduced some needed reforms. His great-est successes, however, were on a personal level. Nothing pleased him more than a cadet who did well, and the best ones were invited to sup-per at his house. A special favorite was James Ewell Brown Stuart, known to everyone by his first three initials, "J. E. B." or "Jeb."

Nothing pained him more than having to expel a cadet, "the most grievous office I am called on to perform."[22] When it became necessary, he tried to persuade the cadet to resign before final examinations, to spare him the shame of expulsion.

Early in 1855, Lee received a genuine promotion. In the years since his return from Mexico, Indian wars had flared across the Southwest. Congress replied by authorizing two new cavalry regiments to protect the frontier. Lee became a lieutenant colonel, second in command of the Second Cavalry based in Texas. This meant leaving West Point and the Corps of Engineers, but it was a move he relished. The army was small, and a promotion to lieutenant colonel of engineers might never come. Besides, after twenty-five years in the service, he felt it time to have a fighting command.

Lee was soon disappointed. Texas in winter was "blue northers," tornadolike winds that blew from the north, burying the countryside in snow. Texas in summer was "fiery hot," with winds "like the blast from a hot-air furnace."[23] His life became an endless round of escorting wagon trains, chasing Mexican *banditos*, and keeping tabs on the warlike Comanche. He had to ride hundreds of miles to attend courts-martial, trials for soldiers charged with breaking army rules. He found the trials boring, but read every document and heard every word of testimony. His reputation for fairness spread among the troops. Once he faced a cavalryman accused of some offense. "You shall have justice," he said softly, trying to put him at ease. "That is what I am afraid of, sir," answered the trooper.[24]

Missing his own family, the colonel befriended those of his men. He told their children stories, played games with them, and gave

Colonel Robert E. Lee, Second Cavalry, in the 1850s. During this time he was stationed in Texas, chasing Mexican outlaws and keeping tabs on the Comanche Indians.

them little gifts. To ease his boredom, he took long rides and adopted stray animals. Lee's choice of pets was odd. He started with a rattlesnake, only it refused to eat the frogs he caught, and died. Next came a wildcat cub, which he freed when it got too big to handle. His third choice was a gorgeous tabby cat. It was so appealing that no one could resist giving it food. That was too bad. "I foretold its end," Lee wrote jokingly. "Coffee & cream for breakfast. Pound cake for lunch. Turtle & oysters for dinner. Buttered toast for tea, & Mexican rats, taken raw, for Supper! Cat nature could not stand such luxury. He grew enormously & ended in a spasm. His beauty could not save him."[25]

In October 1857 an urgent telegram arrived. Lee's father-in-law had died and he must return home.

He arrived to find Mary old at forty-nine. During his absence, she had been crippled by arthritis, so that even the slightest movement caused agonizing pain. The estate was also in poor condition. Mr. Custis had been more interested in good living than good business. If Arlington was to be saved, Lee would have to take charge to pay off the debts and make needed repairs. He applied for a few months' leave, only to find that he needed more time. It would be nearly two years before he saw Texas again.

Arlington's slaves were another problem. Mr. Custis had left orders to emancipate (free) all his slaves—196 black men, women, and children—within five years of his death. Lee was planning to do that when unsigned letters appeared in two New York City newspapers. The writers accused him of stripping a slave woman and then whipping her on the bare back. The charge was false. There is no record of Lee's ever whipping an animal, let alone a person. Even during the Civil War, his worst act of personal "violence" was to shake his fist at the enemy. He did not reply to the charge, recognizing it as part of the deepening conflict over slavery.

Black slavery had existed in the New World ever since Spain introduced it into her colonies in the 1520s. During the next three centuries, twelve million Africans were shipped across the Atlantic, of whom at least two million died en route. The majority of slaves worked in the sugar industry of Brazil and the West Indies, where they died in droves of disease, overwork, and brutal treatment. The first blacks came to North America in 1619, brought by a Dutch warship to Jamestown, Virginia. From then on, slavery grew as the English colonies prospered. By 1860, there were four million slaves in the United States, living almost entirely in the South.

All slaves were equal in that they were unfree; they were chattel, property to be bought and sold at auction like so many head of cattle or bushels of wheat. Slaves had no legal rights in the United States. Slave marriages were not recognized by the law, nor could slaves be taught to read and write. In fact, they were not regarded as entirely human; the Constitution declared each slave was to be counted, for census purposes, as three-fifths of a person.

Slaves were divided into three classes. House servants dressed well, had fine manners, and got along nicely with their owners. These slaves were often regarded as members of the family; indeed, a white child might be closer to its black "mammy," or nursemaid, than to its real parents. Mechanics—carpenters, blacksmiths, stonemasons, wagon builders—were skilled craftsmen who might earn enough from work after hours to buy their freedom. By 1860, there were 250,000 free blacks in the South, of whom approximately 4,000 owned slaves of their own; some free blacks in Louisiana and South Carolina had as many as seventy or eighty slaves.[26] Most slaves, however, were field hands, farm laborers who grew tobacco, sugar, rice, and cotton. These lived under the harshest conditions

Slave sale in Charleston, South Carolina, based on a sketch by the English artist Eyre Crowe.

and could be punished for anything, or nothing, depending on the master's whim. Nevertheless, they were usually better fed than the poorest Southern whites, whom even they despised as "poor white trash."

Slavery was justified by racism, the belief that certain peoples are naturally inferior to others. It was said that slavery was good for blacks, because it rescued them from "African barbarism," enabling them to learn useful trades and save their souls by becoming Christians. According to Jefferson Davis, a senator from Mississippi and a former secretary of war, Africans had been "reared in heathen darkness and, sold by heathen masters, [and] were transferred to shores enlightened by the rays of Christianity. There, put to servitude, they were trained in the gentle arts of peace and order and civilization. They increased from a few unprofitable savages to millions of efficient Christian laborers. Their servile instincts rendered them contented with their lot. . . . Never was there happier dependence of labor and capital on each other."[27]

Black people did not share this rosy view. Although no one ever took a poll of slaves, there is evidence that the vast majority resented being exploited. They knew that, if their owners took care of them, it was for the same reason a farmer cares for his oxen: to make them work better. This comes through in a plantation song:

> *We raise de wheat,*
> *Dey gib us de corn;*
> *We bake de bread.*
> *Dey gib us de crust;*
> *We sift de meal,*
> *Dey gib us de husk;*
> *We peel de meat,*
> *Dey gib us de skin;*
> *And dat's de way*
> *Dey take us in;*
> *We skim de pot,*
> *Dey gib us de liquor,*
> *And say dat's good enough for nigger.*[28]

Slaves resisted in various ways. They were careless, "losing" or "accidentally" breaking tools. They slowed down on the job, pretending illness or ignorance. Thousands fled to Canada and the Northern cities, where slavery did not exist. Or they turned on their masters and killed them. There had been a massive rebellion in Santo Domingo in 1803, where slaves overthrew French rule and founded the republic of Haiti. In the United States, slaves ravaged the countryside around Charleston, South Carolina, in 1822. Nine years later, the followers of Nat Turner, a black preacher who had taught himself to read and write, killed sixty white Virginians. The rebels were hunted down without mercy.

Blacks also had white allies. In both the Old World and the New, whites were coming to believe that slavery was evil. It was outlawed in England in 1772 and abolished in the British West Indies in 1834; Mexico ended slavery in 1829.

Americans had always been of two minds about their "peculiar institution." On the one hand, it was legal and profitable; indeed, by 1860, Southern slave-grown cotton accounted for three-quarters of the world's supply. On the other hand, it made a mockery of the Declaration of Independence's claim that "all men are created equal."

By the 1840s Americans were turning against slavery in growing numbers. Opponents came from all sections of the country and every walk of life. Southerners, particularly small farmers, resented the aristocratic planters, who controlled state politics. The planters' wives had another grievance. Black women were often sexually abused by their white owners. As a result, numerous blacks—estimates range as high as one in four—had a white father or ancestor. Mary Chesnut, the wife of a U. S. senator from South Carolina, hated slavery for this very reason. "God forgive us," she wrote in her diary, "but ours is a *monstrous* system [of] wrong and iniquity. . . . Like the patriarchs of old our men live all in one house with their wives and their concubines, and the mulattos one sees in every family exactly resemble the white children. . . ."[29] The master's offspring, black and white, slave and free, were brothers and sisters. But if cash was short, masters might sell their own flesh and blood. A healthy field hand could bring $1,500 at auction.

The loudest opposition came from Northern abolitionists, those who wanted slavery abolished immediately. Slavery, they insisted, was a moral question pure and simple. If blacks were God's children, as they surely were, then enslaving them was a sin. If the Constitution legalized slavery, then it must be ignored in favor of a "higher law." William Lloyd Garrison, a leading abolitionist, publicly burned a copy of the Constitution, declaring, "So perish all compromises with tyranny." He demanded that the North secede from the Union, taking as his slogans "All Hail Disunion" and "No Union with Slaveholders." Garrison was a radical, part of a small

William Lloyd Garrison, a leading abolitionist and editor of The Liberator, *was willing to risk anything, including the breakup of the United States, to bring about the end of slavery.*

group willing to break up the United States to achieve their ends. Although a minority in the abolitionist movement, the radicals had influence far beyond their numbers, drowning out the voices of more moderate abolitionists.

Robert E. Lee had despised slavery since boyhood. He recalled how, while running errands for his mother, he passed the Alexandria city jail, its chimney studded with rusty spikes that had once held the heads of rebellious slaves. He knew that the Founding Fathers—John Adams, Thomas Jefferson, Benjamin Franklin, James Madison—had opposed

slavery. Richard Henry Lee, his uncle and a signer of the Declaration of Independence, had denounced slavery as "iniquitous and disgraceful."[30] George Washington, his hero, had inherited slaves from his father but vowed never to buy another and supported a ban on importing slaves into the young nation. The ban took effect in 1808.

Lee had once owned six slaves, a wedding gift from Mr. Custis, but he freed them straightaway. He described slavery as an evil under any and all circumstances. It is interesting to note that Lee and Abraham Lincoln, soon to be on opposite sides in the Civil War, agreed on this matter. It was Lincoln, after all, who said: "If slavery is not wrong, nothing is wrong."[31] Yet Lee also believed, along with Jefferson Davis, that blacks were better off as slaves in America than as free people in Africa. Slavery, he told Mary, was a "painful discipline" for blacks, albeit "necessary for their instruction as a race."[32]

He was not being hypocritical. Lee had few dealings

with slaves, except as house servants. He lived among "enlightened" people who treated slaves well, compared to those in the Deep South; he once nursed an old slave, a devoted family servant, during his last illness. Lee showed how one could be a good person, hate slavery, and still think blacks belonged to an inferior race.

Racism was not restricted to any geographic area or social class. It was a basic part of the American outlook in the nineteenth century, and beyond. Like so many of his countrymen, North and South, Lee saw blacks as inferiors. Unlike whites, he claimed, blacks were unfit for steady work on their own. Nor could they govern themselves; he opposed giving free blacks the right to vote. Here, too, he and Lincoln agreed. During a debate on September 18, 1859, "Honest Abe" spoke out against racial equality: "I am not nor ever have been in favor of bringing about in any way the social and political equality of the white and black races. . . . I am not nor ever have been in favor of making voters or jurors of negroes, nor of qualifying them to hold office. . . ."[33]

Lee and Lincoln agreed on yet another point. Both disliked abolitionists. Lee saw them as blustering bigots who did more harm than good. Slavery, he argued, would end only when a majority of whites realized it was wrong. And that required time—time to think, time for polite discussion, time to get used to the idea of change. Abolitionists, however, inflamed people's emotions. Their harsh words, Lee feared, were destroying the goodwill that bound the nation together. Lincoln said much the same. On July 6, 1852, he denounced "those who would shiver into fragments the Union of these states; tear to tatters its now venerated Constitution; and even burn the last copy of the Bible, rather than slavery should continue a single hour [longer.]"[34]

John Brown was such a person. Born in 1800, Brown was a lean man with ferocious gray eyes; he claimed his stare made cats run out of the room. Yet he could be as gentle and playful as a kitten. He loved children, and would hold them on his lap for hours, joking with them and tickling them. Sad music made him cry. An inept businessman, he had spent most of his life in shady deals, including horse stealing.

Brown's passion was abolitionism. He was, said his brother Jeremiah, "insane upon the subject of slavery."[35] Somehow he convinced himself that God had chosen him to free the slaves not by argument, but by force. While living in Kansas, he led a band of his followers to Pottawatomie Creek, where on May 25, 1856, they dragged five proslavery men from bed and hacked them to pieces with swords. What others thought a beastly crime, he thought an act of divine vengeance.

On the night of October 16, 1859, Brown invaded Virginia with an "army" of seventeen men. Moving swiftly, they seized the federal arsenal at Harpers Ferry at the junction of the Potomac and Shenandoah rivers. Brown planned to carry rifles from the arsenal into the mountains and rally runaway slaves. Then, with him at their head, a mighty army would move southward, killing whites, burning plantations, and destroying slavery. The whole accursed system would vanish in the twinkling of an eye, Brown thought.

He was wrong. The first casualty was a free black, shot by Brown's men as he fled. The local militia—hundreds of armed whites—turned out, trapping the raiders in the arsenal's fire-engine house, a brick building with thick wooden doors. It was a standoff. Brown was holed up in the arsenal with plenty of ammunition and thirteen hostages, innocent men taken as "insurance" in case of trouble. The militiamen were content to pop away from the distance. Rushing the building would endanger themselves and the hostages. This was a job for professionals.

Next morning, Colonel Lee was in a store in Alexandria when a soldier came up to him. It was Jeb Stuart, his West Point favorite, now a lieutenant in the First Cavalry. Stuart had an urgent order from the War Department. Lee was to go to Harpers Ferry with a company of marines. His mission: retake the arsenal at once and get John Brown, dead or alive. Lee left without changing out of his civilian clothes.

The marines were in position by sunrise, October 18. One of Brown's men peered through a window and saw a "civilian" standing in the open, looking through a spyglass. He was taking aim when Brown pushed his gun aside; there was no need to shoot a harmless stranger. The Lee luck held.

John Brown about the year 1855. Brown planned to capture Harpers Ferry, Virginia, as a first step in a slave rebellion that he believed would end slavery in one mighty, bloody action.

Moments later, Jeb Stuart came up to the door with a white flag and a message. Colonel Lee demanded his immediate surrender in return for "the mercy of the government." Brown said he was not interested in mercy. He wanted safe passage out of town, or he would fight to the death.

Stuart stepped back and waved his hat in a prearranged signal. Lee sent in the marines. The leathernecks broke through the door with a heavy ladder and went after the defenders with bayonets; they had been ordered not to shoot for fear of hitting the hostages. John Brown's crusade to free the slaves ended three minutes later. Seventeen men lay dead, including ten raiders, among them two of Brown's sons. Not one slave joined the rebellion.

Brown and six accomplices were sentenced to death for murder, inciting a slave rebellion, and treason against the state of Virginia. Brown's execution was set for December 2, 1859. As they walked him to the gallows, Brown handed a note to a guard. It said: "I John Brown am now quite *certain* that the crimes of this *guilty* land will never be purged *away*; but with Blood."

The bleeding would soon begin. And more blood would be shed than even John Brown could have imagined.

II ✦ THE STORM BREAKS

John Brown's body lies

a-mould'ring in the grave,

His soul is marching on.

Glory! Glory Hallelujah!

His soul is marching on.

—"John Brown's Body"

Colonel Lee returned to duty in February 1860. He was no longer with the Second Cavalry, but commander of the department of Texas, an area covering most of the Southwest. Yet his work was no different than when he had been with the regiment, except there was more of it. He was up to his ears in paperwork, inspection tours, and courts-martial. This time, however, life on the Texas plains was anything but dull.

Even in faraway Texas, he could hear the rumblings from back home. John Brown's body lay mould'ring in the grave, but his ghost could not be laid to rest. After his capture, letters were found implicating six leading abolitionists—the Secret Six—in his scheme. Worse, the court's sentence caused an outpouring of sympathy in the North. But that sympathy was not always for the condemned man. Some abolitionists believed he was worth more to them dead than alive. They *wanted* him hanged, and feared he might be spared at the last moment. That would harm the cause, said the Reverend Henry Ward Beecher, begging his congregation not to pray for a pardon. "Let no man pray that Brown be spared," he said from the pulpit. "Let Virginia make him a martyr."[1]

It did.

Abolitionists used their martyr for all he was worth. The minute Brown died, bells tolled and flags were lowered to half-mast in the North. Cannons fired salutes and people attended "Martyr Services" dressed in black. Henry David Thoreau, a famous author, called Brown "an angel of light." Poet Ralph Waldo Emerson declared that Brown would "make the gallows as glorious as the Cross." Enthusiasts spoke of "Saint John the Just," and even compared him to Jesus Christ.[2] It was as if Northerners had forgotten Brown's record in Kansas, or his intentions in Virginia.

Southerners were outraged. These statements, they assumed, reflected the feelings of the entire North. Of course they did not; Abraham Lincoln, for one, believed Brown was a criminal. On the day of the execution, he said he got what he deserved, although he, Lincoln, agreed that slavery was wrong. "That cannot excuse violence, bloodshed and treason."[3]

But it is not easy to listen to reason when you are terrified. A tidal wave of fear, anger, and hatred rolled across the South, unifying it as never before. Harpers Ferry confirmed Southerners' worst fears. Abolitionists were plotting slave rebellions! Abolitionists wanted "to Brown" them, to incite "howling savages" to murder women and children! Even Southerners opposed to slavery asked how they could remain in the Union under these circumstances. Perhaps, they wondered, it would be best to secede and set up a nation of their own. Radicals, called "fire-eaters," began to take charge.

Brown's execution came as the country was preparing for the presidential election of 1860. The Democrats, supporters of slavery, opposed the Republicans led by Abraham Lincoln. Emotions ran high, particularly in the South, where Lincoln's party was denounced as "black Republicans," traitors to the white race. No one was hated more than Lincoln himself. The man from Illinois was said to have "Negro blood" in his veins and to be a taller, smarter version of John Brown.

Lincoln despised slavery, but accepted it as legal under the Constitution and state laws. Thus, wherever slavery existed, it could not be disturbed by the central government, he said. Lincoln also believed that Congress could bar slavery from the territories before they became states. Here was the weak point in the whole slave system. Cotton exhausted the soil. If slavery could not expand, it must die out along with the cotton plantations. Its death would take longer than abolitionists wished, but the end result would be the same.

Lincoln's election was the last straw for the South. On December 20, South Carolina seceded from the Union, followed by Mississippi,

Florida, Alabama, Georgia, Louisiana, and Texas. They formed a separate country, the Confederate States of America, with Montgomery, Alabama, as its capital and Jefferson Davis as president.

Confederates stood for "states' rights," the idea that a state, not the central government, must decide on vital issues. By 1860, the idea of a unified nation had not yet become fixed in people's minds. It was said that "the United States *are*," not that "the United States *is*." The plural *are* indicated separate countries that had voluntarily bound themselves together but still reserved the right to go their own way. For the individual, national citizenship came through state citizenship. If you were an American, it was because your state was part of the Union. Your state came first— always. It, not the United States, was your true home and had first claim to your loyalty. Secession, therefore, seemed natural. Radical abolitionists also approved of secession, albeit for different reasons.

The Confederacy meant to defend itself. An army was formed, federal arsenals seized, and agents sent abroad to buy weapons. Not that these weapons would be used. At first, Confederate leaders felt there would be no war; a show of force would be enough to guarantee Southern independence. Robert Barnwell Rhett, a prominent South Carolina politician, was so sure of this that he swore to eat the bodies of all those killed in the fighting. A common saying was: "A lady's thimble will hold all the blood that will be shed."[4]

Even if war came, it could not last long. "Yankees," slang for Northerners, were pictured as greedy shopkeepers who would cheat their mothers for a penny. In the words of a poem:

> *Yankee Doodle is a knave,*
> *And everybody knows it,*
> *And swindling is his natural trade,*
> *For by his tricks he shows it.*
> *He'll go to church and sing and pray,*
> *Be full of grace on Sunday,*
> *With wooden hams and paper shoes,*
> *He'll cheat you on a Monday.*[5]

It was funny just to imagine such people on a "field of honor," a battlefield. A Yankee might dress in a smart uniform, but deep down he was a coward. Why, at the first shot he would "skedaddle" as fast as his legs could carry him. Compare such a low creature to a "Rebel," slang for a Southerner! Rebels were said to be naturally brave, having learned to ride and shoot as children. Victory was certain, because "one Rebel can lick ten Yankees."

In January 1861, Lee gave his view of the crisis. "As an American citizen, I take great pride in my country," he wrote Custis. "But I can anticipate no greater calamity for the country than a dissolution of the Union. . . . Secession is nothing but revolution. . . . Still, a Union that can only be maintained by swords and bayonets, and in which strife and civil war are to take the place of brotherly love and kindness, has no charm for me. . . . If the Union is dissolved, and the Government disrupted, I shall return to my native State and share the miseries of my people, and save in defense will draw my sword on none."[6]

No one who spoke with Lee then or after doubted his sincerity. Despite his education and worldly experience, he was a simple man with simple beliefs. He considered himself an American. He hated secession, as he hated slavery. Above all though, he was a Virginian. He called Virginia his "mother State"; Light-Horse Harry had said "Virginia is my country." Robert hoped Virginia would not secede. But if she did, he must go with her. If he had to fight, it would be only in her defense, even against the armies of the United States. Even against his friends. Even against relatives like Samuel P. Lee, a cousin who was siding with the Union.

Early in February, General Scott ordered him back to Washington. Hoping to keep Lee loyal to the Union, the wily old fox wanted him to make a decision while Virginia was still debating the secession issue. Scott himself was a Virginian who supported the Union.

Virginia opposed secession. On April 4, its state convention voted against secession by an overwhelming majority. At the same time, it upheld secession as a sacred right. The Declaration of Independence says that governments get their powers from the consent of the governed. Well, the Confederacy no longer wished to be governed by the United States. Virginia, therefore, could not stand by if her Southern sisters were attacked.

On April 12 Confederate guns fired on Fort Sumter. Two days later, the fort surrendered after a gallant defense in which no lives were lost on either side. On April 15 President Lincoln called for volunteers to put down the rebellion. Virginia would have to furnish her share of troops for a cause she rejected.

Apart from Lee's surrender at Appomattox Court House four years later, the week after Fort Sumter must have been the worst in his life. On April 16 the Virginia Convention met to discuss its

Fort Sumter here has fallen to Confederate troops in the opening battle of the war between the Union and the Confederacy.

next step. On April 17 Lee was again called to Washington. On April 18 he rejected Lincoln's offer to head the Union forces. With Virginia's secession all but certain, he was in an impossible position. Serving in the Union army would mean going against everything he held dear. He would be fighting his beloved state, his neighbors, and his own kin. The very idea brought tears to his eyes. On April 19 Virginia officially seceded, quickly followed by Arkansas, North Carolina, and Tennessee. The Confederacy had grown to eleven states.

That night, Mary sat alone in her wheelchair at Arlington House. All was quiet, except for the sound of her husband's footsteps in the room above. He was pacing the floor, back and forth, to and fro, into the small hours. Once she thought she heard him drop to his knees in prayer; a devout Christian, he often sought God's counsel.

"Well, Mary, the question is settled," he said when he came to breakfast in the morning. In his hand he held a letter of resignation. On April 20 he resigned his commission in the United States Army after thirty-two years of faithful service.

The tragedy of Robert E. Lee is that, in choosing Virginia over the United States, one side of him had triumphed over the other. By fighting for his "mother" state, he would also be fighting for slavery and secession, which he despised. Victory would not only win Confederate independence, but fasten the chains more tightly on millions of fellow human beings. It was an agonizing choice to make, but he saw no honorable way out. To have chosen otherwise would have violated his deepest convictions. He could not have done that and remained true to himself.

Mary understood. "My husband has wept tears of blood over this terrible war," she wrote a friend, "but as a man of honor and a Virginian, he must follow the destiny of his state."[7]

Lee's services were urgently needed. On April 23 he was offered, and accepted, command of Virginia's armed forces with the rank of major general. His job was to organize the state's defenses. Time was precious, and he had no patience with the silly optimism of people who knew nothing about war. One day a man brought his five-year-old son to Lee's office. The boy was the apple of his father's eye, and he wanted him to show off.

"What is General Lee going to do to General Scott?" the father asked.

"He is going to whip him out of his breeches," replied the youngster, who had been well coached. The father laughed, imagining the three-hundred-pound general standing in his drawers.

Placing his hand on the boy's shoulder, Lee looked the father squarely in the eye. It was a hard stare, the kind that made grown men cringe. "My dear little boy," he said to the child, "you should not use such expressions. War is a serious matter, and General Scott is a great and good soldier. None of us can tell what the result of the contest will be."[8] It was a message to all Southerners. Unless they thought realistically and pulled together, the Confederacy was doomed.

Lee knew the Yankees would be no pushover. The Union had tremendous resources for war. Its population numbered 23,000,000, compared to the 5,220,000 whites who lived in the Confederacy. It had 85 percent of the nation's factories, 67 percent of its farm acreage, and 66 percent of its railroad mileage. It manufactured all goods in greater quantity than the South, with a special advantage in weapons production. Southern railroads—where they existed—had no common gauge the distance between rails, making it necessary to transfer goods from the cars of one line to another. Time, Lee predicted, would also show that Southerners had no monopoly on courage. This was going to be a war for survival that might last ten years.

Lee's warnings aroused distrust. Accusations flew thick and fast. He was a "defeatist," some said. No, he was a Yankee spy, others insisted. "At heart Robert E. Lee is against us," the ignorant muttered. There was even talk of charging him with treason.[9] But President Davis trusted him, and *that* made all the difference. Lee and "Jeff" Davis had been cadets together at West Point. Davis, the carefree youth Lee had known then, had grown cold and conceited, someone who looked down on others. Lee's success would be due in part to his ability to get along with his chief.

After Virginia joined the Confederacy on May 23, Richmond became the new nation's capital. A few days later, her armed forces were transferred to the Confederate States Army. Lee's job was unchanged: Get ready for the coming struggle.

That was a tall order. Everything was scarce during that spring of 1861. Weapons of all kinds were needed. Maps were obtained from bookstores or torn from atlases. There was a shortage of chloroform, used to knock out patients during surgery. Even when supplies were available, there was no general staff to plan campaigns or pass orders to field units.

Only manpower was abundant. After Fort Sumter, Southerners mobbed recruiting stations. War was thrilling to those who had never known it. To farmers who spent their days behind a plow, and townsmen who worked at dull jobs, war was an adventure, a once-in-a-lifetime chance to escape the grind of civilian life. War was glory and romance and, if you fell, a painless death with a bullet through the heart. Few imagined what real bullets striking real flesh could do. Newspaper drawings showed men returning to admiring families with "fashionable" wounds, like an arm in a sling or a bandaged forehead. No one expected the war to last until Christmas, and everyone wanted to enjoy the "fun" while it lasted. "So impatient did I become for starting," wrote an Arkansas volunteer, "that it felt like ten thousand pins were pricking me in every part of the body."[10] Even eight-year-olds ran away, only to be told that the army was for "grown menfolk."

Johnny Reb—the Confederate soldier—also had more serious

reasons for enlisting. Slaveowners, surely, fought to protect their "sacred right" to have human property. The majority, however, cared little about slavery or the legalities of secession and states' rights. Two-thirds of white Southerners owned no slaves at all; many Virginia mountain people never saw a black person until they came down to the lowlands. They did, however, care for "hearth and home." It was for these, rather than any abstract ideal, that Lee's sons joined the army. Custis rose to the rank of major general of infantry. Rooney, a giant of a man described as "too big to be a man and not big enough to be a horse," became a major general of cavalry. Rob rose from a private to a captain of artillery. They owed their ranks to merit, not to their father's influence.

You didn't have to be a genius to understand Union strategy. To crush the rebellion, the Union army had to invade, conquer, and occupy the Rebel states. That meant turning the South into an immense battlefield. It meant uprooting civilians from their homes and destroying property created by generations of hardworking people, white and black. The typical Southerner, therefore, was fighting a defensive war. He had neither the desire, nor the ability, to conquer the North.

A soldier named Alexander Hunter spoke for countless Johnny Rebs. After his capture, a Yankee officer asked, "What are you Rebels fighting for, anyway?" Hunter was astonished at the fellow's ignorance. "The question struck me then and there as supremely ludicrous. Here were we Virginians standing on our own soil, fighting for our native hearth against an invading army, defending what every man holds dear—his home and fireside. As well ask a game-cock why he crows and bares his spurs on his own dunghill."[11]

Southern women, even those who disliked slavery, agreed. Every man who enlisted made them feel that much safer. A man's willingness to serve became the test of his suitability as a husband and father. To encourage enlistments, women went about singing "I Am Bound to Be a Soldier's Wife or Die an Old Maid." Men who didn't get the message were treated with contempt. They were called "craven cowards" unfit to speak to "decent girls," let alone marry them. Those who still held back might receive a skirt and a petticoat with a note: "Wear these or volunteer."

Women disguised themselves as men and went to war. Over four hundred women have been identified as having fought in the Confederate ranks. One of these gave her Yankee captives a surprise. A Northern newspaper reported that prison camp guards discovered a Johnny Reb who was actually a Janie Reb. "One day last week one of the rebel officers . . . gave birth to a 'bouncing boy.' This is the first instance of the father giving birth to a child, that we have heard of."[12] Until then, she had performed all of her soldierly duties.

Volunteer units took names calculated to inspire courage in themselves and fear in the enemy. Among these were the Southern Avengers, Dixie Heroes, Cherokee Lincoln Killers, Yankee Terrors, Hornet's Nest Riflemen, Lexington Wild Cats, and Louisiana Tigers. Each unit, when complete, received a battle flag sewn by the local ladies, and its members were sworn into the Confederate service.

What a send-off they received! With flags waving and bands playing, each unit marched to the local railroad station. Men and boys lined the route, cheering. Ladies showed their gratitude with kisses. An Alabama volunteer recalled: "Every young fellow who went to war got a kiss from his 'best girl,' and as it was the first that many of us had ever enjoyed, it is not surprising that a last farewell was repeated over and over again before we actually took our departure."[13]

Amid waving handkerchiefs and tooting whistles, the train chugged out of the depot. Women cried. Men watched dry-eyed, as it was not considered "manly" to cry in public. "I hid away from the other soldiers and took a big cry," recalled a Mississippian. "It seemed to help, and after it, I felt better about leaving home."[14] But since this was usually Johnny Reb's first train ride, he settled down to enjoy the experience. The train barreled along at a fantastic twenty-five miles an hour!

During the spring of 1861 troop trains stopped at Richmond every day. Richmond was not only the Confederacy's capital, but its largest manufacturing center and the key to its eastern defenses. The city lay at the hub of a giant wheel whose rim stretched in an arc from the Blue Ridge Mountains in the west to the mouth of the James River in the east. Only a hundred miles from Washington, it shielded the states farther south from a land attack. It had to be held.

Richmond's population of thirty-eight thousand doubled, and doubled again, within a few weeks. The city never seemed to sleep. Lines of army wagons rumbled through its streets at all hours. Squadrons of cavalry galloped to their posts. Vacant lots blossomed with white tents. The Central Fair Grounds on its outskirts became a training camp.

The camp, visitors noted, held blacks as well as whites. Blacks were vital to the Confederate war effort. Free blacks bought government bonds. Slaves worked as army cooks, teamsters, hospital attendants, ambulance drivers, and stretcher bearers. Black construction crews dug trenches, built forts, laid railroad tracks, and repaired roads and bridges. Black craftsmen worked in machine shops and factories. Each black worker freed a white for military service. Although Southerners feared a slave uprising, it never came. Why, is a question historians have yet to answer.

Owners usually sent household slaves along with their sons who enlisted. Known as body servants, they looked after the recruit's clothing, cleaned his quarters, and cared for his horse. Master and servant had often been raised together as children. Now that the master was a soldier, the servant might feel responsible for his safety. Such was Kent, owned by a soldier named Harry. Before he left, Kent's mother told her son "he need not come home if he let anything hu't Mas' Harry . . . an' I tells Affy, de gal he's courtin', it's no use for she to fret, fur 'less Kent brings Mas' Harry back, dere won't be no weddin' fur him."[15] Kent did his duty. Some body servants did more; they took guns and fired at the enemy. One black killed four Yankees; another won praise as a sharpshooter.[16] All of which shows that slavery was, in human terms, a very complicated system.

Lee molded his recruits into a fighting force. He began simply, gathering smaller units into ever-larger formations as they went up the "chain of command." The company, 100 men under a captain and his lieutenant, was the basic building block. Ten companies, 1,000 men led by a colonel, formed a regiment. Four regiments, 4,000 men commanded by a brigadier general, made up a brigade. Named for its commander, the brigade was a mini-army with all "combat arms"—infantry, artillery, cavalry—plus signal units, medical teams, and supply details. A division consisted of three brigades, 12,000 men under a brigadier or major general. Three divisions, 36,000 men under a major general, became a corps. The largest formation was an army consisting of two or three corps, 72,000 to 108,000 men. A Confederate army was named for its area of operations and commanded by a lieutenant general. The Union adopted a similar organization, only its armies were named for rivers and led by major generals.

The purpose of camp was to turn civilians into soldiers. This meant teaching essential skills, toughening bodies, and instilling discipline in the shortest possible time. Lee found discipline to be his greatest problem. The majority of soldiers were independent

A photo of Confederate infantrymen taken early in the war. They carry the "stars and bars," the Confederacy's official flag. Because it looked so much like Old Glory, and might easily be mistaken for it in combat, it was replaced by the famous battle flag consisting of a red cross with thirteen stars.

small farmers, people used to being their own bosses. But an army is a team, each member depending on others to do their duty correctly and on time. Thus, Johnny Reb was bound to see discipline as a violation of his rights; indeed, as a form of slavery. "I love my country as well as any one but I don't believe in the plan of making myself a slave," a Georgian wrote his folks. "A private soldier is nothing more than a slave and is often treated worse. I have . . . gone through more hardships than anyone of ours or Grandma's negroes; their life is a luxury to what mine is sometimes."[17]

Johnny Reb's ordeal began before sunup. Reveille sounded at 4:30 A.M., rain or shine. Rubbing the sleep from his eyes, he groped for his uniform. It is only partially true that the Civil War was between "the Blue and the Gray." Billy Yank—the Union soldier— did wear blue, hence the nicknames "bluecoat" and "bluebelly."

The official Confederate uniform was gray, but gray dye was always scarce. More often than not, soldiers wore butternut, a dusty brown color made from butternut bark or walnut shells, hence the nickname "butternuts." Hats were of every shape and description. But whatever its appearance, Johnny Reb held on to his hat for dear life. A hat was a regular part of a man's costume. Appearing bareheaded was the same as going out naked.

Soldiers always complained about their food. Official Confederate rations were meat, corn bread, coffee, and, in summer, vegetables such as corn and onions. Rations, however, were better on paper than in reality. Meat was fatty bacon or tough beef preserved in salt. Nicknamed "salt horse," it was said that iron horseshoes could be found in the barrels. "The beef is so poor it is Sticky and Blue," a Rebel observed; "if a quarter was thrown against the wall it would stick." A comrade agreed, noting that "buzzards would not eat it at any season of the year."[18] Corn bread was so hard and moldy that a Virginian said it would "have thrown our mammies into spasms."[19] So would some of the dishes Johnny Reb invented on his own. A favorite was "sloosh," as in "slush." Several men chipped in, each donating a chunk of beef or bacon. These were fried in boiling grease thickened with cornmeal to form a paste. Sloosh was not very digestible, but it was tasty and easy to prepare.

Companies and regiments assembled for drill after breakfast. Then, hour after hour, they slogged across fields, up and down hillsides, and through streams. Drill hardened muscles and built team spirit. Each man carried at least forty pounds of equipment and personal items. He marched with a nine-pound musket slung over his shoulder. A bayonet, bowie knife, canteen, and cartridge box hung from his belt. On his back he carried a knapsack. Private Carlton McCarthy, Richmond Artillery, made an inventory of his knapsack. It contained "a full stock of underwear, soap, towels, comb, brush, looking-glass, tooth-brush, paper and envelopes, pens, ink, pencils, [shoe] blacking, photographs, smoking and chewing tobacco, pipes, twine string, and cotton strips for wounds . . . needles and thread, buttons, knife, fork, and spoon. . . . On the outside of the knapsack, solidly folded, were two great blankets and a rubber [ground cloth]."[20] (Note the cotton strips: there were no such things as first aid kits or bandages wrapped in sterile packages.) It was no fun to carry this load when the sun beat down and the straps dug into your shoulders. Rain soaked the knapsack, making it heavier.

A Confederate gunner posing near his weapon. Civil War artillery were "muzzle loaders"; that is, the shell and gunpowder charge were rammed down the front of the barrel and ignited by a piece of burning rope or a flint setting off a small gunpowder charge placed in the touchhole at the rear.

As the troops marched, sergeants bellowed "right turn," "left turn," "half turn," "quarter turn," "about face." These motions were essential for getting around on a battlefield. The ability, for example, of thousands of men to turn together could make the difference between halting a flank attack (that is, one on an unprotected side) and disaster. Nevertheless, soldiers considered drill "an affliction to be endured while it lasted."[21] Men became bored. If, as often happened, a rabbit appeared, they broke ranks and chased it until it escaped or they had extra meat for the cooking pot.

The chief weapon was the musket. Until the 1850s, the infantryman was a glorified spear carrier. Battles were not won by gunfire but by bayonet charges. The musket was a smoothbore; that is, the inside of its barrel, or bore, was smooth. This meant that the bullet, a one-ounce lead ball, wobbled when it left the barrel. It was deadly at up to a hundred yards; but anyone hit beyond that range was most unlucky, since no one should have been able to hit him with an aimed musket shot that far away. The idea was not to shoot the enemy down, but to advance shoulder to shoulder and let him get off a volley of shots. Many would fall, but that did not matter if there were large numbers of attackers. While the enemy reloaded, the survivors sprang forward with bayonets.

By 1860, the smoothbore had given way to the rifle musket. It was still called a musket, because it kept some of the musket's features. It fired a single shot, was loaded through the muzzle, and was about five feet long. But unlike the musket, it had rifling, spiral grooves cut on the inside of the barrel to spin the bullet in flight, giving it greater range and speed. The bullet, an inch of soft lead shaped like the end of a crayon, could travel a thousand yards in a few seconds. The rifle musket made the soldier a true gunman. Although he still carried an eighteen-inch bayonet, it no longer decided the battle. Bayonets caused about 1 percent of all wounds in the Civil War. They were, however, useful as can openers and candleholders.

The rifle musket was loaded "by nines"; that is, a soldier had to go through nine separate steps before firing. He began by taking a cartridge from his cartridge box; the cartridge was a paper tube, closed at each end, containing gunpowder and a bullet. He then tore open the cartridge with his teeth, poured the gunpowder down the muzzle, inserted the bullet, jammed powder and bullet down with a ramrod, removed the ramrod, half cocked the hammer, inserted a firing cap at the rear of the barrel, and brought back the hammer all the way to fire. The long barrel meant that a musket could only be loaded from a kneeling or standing position, exposing the shooter to enemy fire.

A skilled soldier could fire every thirty seconds. Early in the war, however, most Rebels were unskilled. It is one thing to shoot a squirrel at leisure, another to shoot a man who is firing back. Besides, rifles were still scarce in the South; in fact, officers sometimes had to advise their men to throw stones at the Yankees until

A Union training camp near Washington, D.C., in 1861. This camp, and hundreds of others like it, existed to toughen civilians physically and teach them basic soldiering skills.

they could take weapons off the dead. Ammunition was too precious to waste on target practice. Rebels in training would point their weapons at targets, shout "Bang!," and drop to the ground in laughter. Even when ammunition became plentiful, firing on both sides continued to be inaccurate. Confederate veterans said it took a man's weight in lead to down a single enemy. Union experts claimed that it took 240 pounds of gunpowder and 900 pounds of lead to kill each Confederate. Civil War casualties were high not due to marksmanship, but because many men were firing many bullets in the same direction.

Johnny Reb and Billy Yank used their spare time in much the same way. The typical soldier was not well educated, but he could read and write. Newspapers and the Bible were his favorite reading materials. He wrote letters and received them by the millions. These letters tell us much about the experiences of ordinary people and how they viewed the Civil War. Married men missed their wives, as this Rebel poem indicates:

The rose is red
The violet is blue
Shogar is sweet
And so are you.

The sea is deep
And in your arms
I long to sleep
A heap Nancy.[22]

Owners might send their slaves some words at the end of a letter. A common postscript was "tell the Negroes howdy," or "give my respects to the colored members of the family," probably a reference to house servants.[23]

Spare time also involved less wholesome activities. An army camp, a Rebel wrote his wife, was a place where you could "smell hell." General Lee agreed. Despite his best efforts, he was "pained" by the way men let go of themselves in their spare time.[24]

An army camp was a cross between a saloon and a gambling den. Soldiers, it seemed, would drink anything alcoholic. If they could not get proper "drinkin' likker," they settled for the "distilled damnation" brewed by local farmers. The names they gave this stuff indicate its potency: "Tanglefoot," "Rifle Knock-Knee," "Bust Skull," "Rot Gut," and "Rock Me to Sleep, Mother."

Johnny Reb's gambling tastes ranged from cards and dice to raffles and horse races. In fact, he would bet on anything that could move under its own power, including lice. One fellow boasted of having the fastest louse in creation. He would challenge a competitor to place his louse on a metal dish, the winner being the one who climbed off first. His louse never lost. It was later found that his louse's plate was heated before each race.

In matters of discipline, Lee expected officers to be fair, not gentle. Soldiers who broke the rules paid heavily. Lee had deserters shot. Thieves might get more of a stolen object than they ever imagined. Take the six Rebels caught with a stolen rowboat: Four had to carry it around camp all day, while the others sat inside, "paddling" in thin air. Being absent without leave or insulting an officer meant "bucking and gagging." The culprit was made to sit grasping his knees with his hands, his chin touching his knees. A stick was then tied between his arms and under his knees, while a bayonet was placed in his mouth and kept there by a string tied behind his ears. Two hours of this treatment normally cured even the worst offenders.

In two months Lee organized, trained, and equipped sixty regiments of infantry totaling nearly fifty thousand men. Most of these he sent to the railway center of Manassas Junction thirty miles southwest of Washington. But Lee himself did not go with them. President Davis decided he was more valuable at his desk in the capital than at the front. Joe Johnston and P. G. T. Beauregard commanded the troops defending Richmond.

"On to Richmond!" had become the Union war cry. On July 16, 1861, Brigadier General Irvin McDowell led a splendid army across the Long Bridge west of Washington. Five days later, he was defeated at the Battle of Manassas, or Bull Run, the first major fight of the war. (Southerners named battles after towns, Northerners after the nearest geographical feature.) Still, it had been a close call for the Confederates. Pressed hard, the Rebs were about to give way when an officer saw a brigade under Thomas J. Jackson holding its ground on a hillside. To rally his troops, the officer shouted: "There stands Jackson like a stone wall!" The name stuck. Next to Marse Robert, "Stonewall" Jackson would be the South's greatest hero.

Lee was delighted at the news from Manassas and sent both commanders his congratulations. "I almost wept for joy," he wrote Johnston, "at the glorious victory achieved by our brave troops."

But he was being a good sport. Not that he was jealous of brother officers, only disappointed for himself. In words written only for Mary's eyes, he confessed to being "mortified" at not having taken part "in the struggle for my home and neighborhood."[25]

President Davis released him from desk duty soon after Manassas. He was needed elsewhere. Virginia's western counties were about to give the state a taste of its own secession medicine. These counties were home to mountaineers who cared nothing for slavery and despised Tidewater aristocrats; "traitors," they called them. So, when war began, they welcomed Union forces with open arms. These forces were led by Major General George B. McClellan, a rising star in the Union army. McClellan's invasion was serious; for if he gained a foothold, he might push eastward into the Shenandoah Valley. Lying between the Allegheny and Blue Ridge mountains, this wide, fertile valley was known as "the bread-basket of the Confederacy."

Lee was not given total control of Confederate forces in this vital area. They were already commanded by three generals, which was exactly three too many. Incompetent to begin with, the generals hated one another more than the enemy and refused to cooperate. Whenever they met, they fell to bickering and name-calling. Davis wanted Lee to make peace among them and help them work out an attack plan.

Lee tried his best, but it was like talking to a barn door. Occasionally, he lost his temper. There was no shouting, for he never raised his voice to anyone. But his neck reddened and his words stabbed like daggers. A lieutenant, guilty of a minor error, had a dressing-down he would remember for the rest of his life. He stood before the general, trembling at every word. "This," said Lee, "is in keeping with everything else I find here—no order, no organization, nobody knows where anything is, and no one understands his duty!"[26]

It rained for twenty days straight. Streams became raging rivers. The mud was so deep that dead mules lay in the road with only their ears showing. Although it was summer, it was so cold that Lee wore his winter coat, and even slept with his aide, Colonel Walter H. Taylor, for warmth.

Sickness spread through the camps. Soldiers became their own worst enemy. "They bring it on themselves by not doing what they are told," Lee wrote Mary. "They are worse than children, for the latter can be forced."[27]

The average Johnny Reb was a country boy who brought country habits into crowded army camps. Used to the outdoors, he relieved himself wherever he pleased, rather than using the latrines, particularly at night. He seldom washed himself, let alone his clothing. Lines of marching soldiers could be seen with a musket in one hand and the other inside their shirts, scratching. Lice and fleas multiplied, bringing a host of diseases. For every Confederate killed in action, three others died of disease; the Union army lost two men to disease for every one lost in battle. Just being in the army was life-threatening.

Lee's worst problem was the generals, who would not stop their feuding. In September, he retreated, leaving a small force to guard the passes of the Shenandoah until winter halted operations in the mountains. But by leaving western Virginia, Lee abandoned it to the enemy. Late in October, it seceded and became West Virginia, the thirty-fifth state to enter the Union.

General Joseph E. Johnston commanded Confederate forces defending Richmond until wounded at the Battle of Seven Pines. His successor was his dear friend, Robert E. Lee.

A discouraged General Lee returned to Richmond. All he had to show for three months in the mountains was a beard, which he wore the rest of his life. Lee himself was blamed, unfairly, for the setback. Newspapers dubbed him "Evacuating Lee." People said he was soft, "too tender of blood," and even called him "Granny Lee" behind his back.

Jefferson Davis ignored such nonsense. Two weeks after Lee's return, he sent him on another mission. Union warships were prowling off the southeastern coast of the Confederacy, and shore defenses needed strengthening. Once again Lee became an engineer. His first assignment after graduating West Point had been at Savannah, Georgia. Now at Savannah, he blocked the mouths of coastal rivers to keep Yankee gunboats away from inland railroad bridges. At Charleston, he repaired the harbor forts and reinforced them with heavy guns.

During his stay in Charleston, Lee saw a big gray horse named Greenbriar. A high-strung animal, Greenbriar made even good riders uneasy. Not Lee. He bought him for two hundred dollars in gold and renamed him Traveller, "because he was such a good traveller."[28] Traveller was to become Lee's favorite mount, a veteran of more battles than most Confederate soldiers.

No one saw any battles in Lee's future when he returned to Richmond. Early in 1862, he became President Davis's military assistant. Like a twentieth-century chief of staff, he was to advise on strategy and, "under the President," direct Confederate military operations. *Under the President*: Lee did not like that idea at all. He was still a desk general, one with responsibility but no authority to act in the field.

But things were about to change. Soon he would have enough action to last a lifetime.

Lee astride his favorite horse, Traveller, a veteran of many battles.

III ✦ SAVIOR OF RICHMOND

I was too weak to defend,

so I attacked.

—Robert E. Lee, *1862*

Lee's setback in western Virginia was mild compared to the Union disaster at Manassas. The Yankees had suffered 3,500 casualties—killed, wounded, captured—before fleeing in dazed confusion. Although their losses were small compared to later Civil War battles, Manassas was the worst bloodbath in American history up to that date. "It's damned bad," Lincoln told a friend from Illinois. It was the only time he ever heard the president swear.[1]

The job of rebuilding went to George B. McClellan, who seemed the ideal replacement for the ailing Winfield Scott. Born in 1826, he had graduated West Point with honors and earned a name for himself as an engineer in the Mexican War. He was five feet nine inches tall and had the body of a weight lifter; he could bend a quarter with his thumb and forefinger and flip a 250-pound man over his head. McClellan believed he was God's gift to the nation, smarter, braver, and better than anyone else. He scorned politicians, particularly Lincoln, calling him the "original gorilla" and "a well meaning baboon."[2]

McClellan *was* a brilliant organizer. Things began to improve the moment he took charge. The army was reorganized and named the Army of the Potomac. Its troops were drilled until they could go through their paces in their sleep. Grand reviews were held to the music of massed bands, as McClellan galloped along the ranks

General George B. McClellan created the Army of the Potomac. A timid, blundering commander who despised President Lincoln, he was still a brilliant organizer.

on a gleaming black stallion. "I am to watch over you as a parent over his children," he promised, "and you know that your General loves you from the depths of his heart."[3] They did know, and loved him for it. He was their "Little Mac," their "Young Napoleon"; like the French emperor, he liked to stand with one arm folded behind his back and the other thrust into the front of his coat.

Joe Johnston stood between Richmond and Washington with fifty thousand men. It was a strong force, well dug in and eager for another crack at the enemy. Little Mac refused to take the bait. Rather than attack head-on, he planned to bypass the Rebel defenses entirely. He would sail down the Potomac to Fortress Monroe at the tip of the peninsula formed by the York and James rivers; the fortress lay seventy miles southeast of Richmond and had remained in Union hands when Virginia seceded. This is historic country, the place where America began. In 1607 English colonists sailed into the mouth of a river they called the James in honor of their king, and built Jamestown, the first permanent English settlement in the New World, on its bank. Across the Peninsula, at Yorktown on the York River, Lord Cornwallis surrendered to General Washington in 1781, ending the Revolutionary War.

McClellan had three forces totaling 175,000 men. One was at the northern end of the Shenandoah Valley; another at Fredericksburg, fifty miles north of Richmond; and the third, the Army of the Potomac, at Washington. Once ashore on the Peninsula, he planned to push ahead with the 107,000-man Army of the Potomac. Resistance was expected to be light, since only 13,000 Rebels were on the Peninsula. Meantime, his other forces would sweep southward. The Confederates would be caught in the jaws of an immense nutcracker. McClellan expected to end the war within two weeks. Better yet, he would do so with light casualties; he hated to lose men, and the sight of blood made him sick to his stomach.

The expedition's success depended on control of the sea. If a

Confederate gunboat slipped among the unarmed transports, it would be like a wolf in a flock of sheep. And the enemy seemed to have just the vessel for the job. The *Merrimac,* her sloping sides covered by iron plates four inches thick, was the world's first "ironclad" warship. When the Union learned of her existence, it hurriedly built its own ironclad, the *Monitor.*

On March 8, 1862, the *Merrimac* sank two wooden warships off Fortress Monroe; the Yankees hit her again and again, but the heaviest cannonballs bounced off harmlessly. That night, as Confederates celebrated their victory, the *Monitor* arrived. She was long and low, with only a single round turret on deck; sailors called her "a tin can on a shingle." But what a tin can! That turret could rotate, bringing its guns to bear from any direction. Next morning, the ironclads slugged it out for two hours. Although the battle ended in a draw, the *Merrimac* never put to sea again. Little Mac set sail for the Peninsula without delay.

The Peninsula was an eye-opener for Billy Yank. Moving inland from Fortress Monroe, he had his first glimpse of slavery. Along the way were farms whose owners had fled, leaving behind their slaves. One regiment met a mulatto woman with a handsome baby in her arms. "He is the child of a white man," she said. "He is

The Monitor *and the* Merrimac *slug it out on March 9, 1862. History's first encounter of ironclad vessels, this battle changed naval warfare forever.*

worth four hundred dollars. I began at fifteen, and I am nineteen now. I have four already."[4] Elsewhere, slaves gathered along roadsides to shake soldiers' hands and cheer them on. Billy Yank had enlisted to save the Union, not to abolish slavery, but such experiences began to work a strange chemistry. Without realizing it, the Union soldier was coming to see himself as a liberator.

He also had his first taste of "Southern hospitality." It was not pleasant. Wherever he turned, he was reminded of who he was: an invader. White women went out of their way to be rude. In small towns, they stepped into the gutters to avoid sharing a sidewalk with "dirty Yankee mudsills." Once, when two pretty girls passed a group of soldiers, the older burst out: "Oh! Oh! What have you done? Your skirt touched a Yankee!"[5]

Soldiers stopping at houses for a drink of water met women who said they were surprised that so many Northerners had "come down to invade our soil." A dignified lady, told that McClellan would soon be in Richmond, disagreed. "No!" she snapped. "You-all will drink hot blood before you-all get thar!"[6] Women served as spies for the Rebel army, and even took potshots at passing troops. Some Yankees admired their high spirits. A soldier remarked that if Southern girls loved as strongly as they hated, "it would be well worth trying to get one of them."[7]

McClellan's advance stalled at Yorktown. It needn't have, since he outnumbered the defenders by at least eight to one. Unfortunately, there was nothing Napoleonic about Mac except his nickname. Although he could inspire his troops, he was cautious to the point of timidity, if not plain cowardice. This Young Napoleon lacked fighting spirit, the single most important quality in a general. He certainly talked a good fight, but at the last moment he would hesitate, finding excuses for inaction. He once refused to advance because his horses had sore mouths!

Major General John B. Magruder, the local Confederate commander, gave him reason to hesitate. Outnumbered and outgunned, Magruder had to buy time for Lee to bring troops from farther south and for Johnston to come down from the north. An amateur actor, "Prince John" was a brilliant showman. He marched a few regiments through a clearing in full view of the Yankees, had them come around a small forest out of sight, and then marched them across the clearing again—and again, and again. It worked! McClellan decided that *he* was outnumbered and must await reinforcements. Meanwhile, Johnston arrived with forty thousand men. "No one but McClellan would have hesitated to attack," he wrote Lee.[8] Both had known him in Mexico and were not surprised that he would fall for such a trick.

The armies dug in for a siege. It was like digging back into America's past. Johnston's men restored the trenches that had been used by Lord Cornwallis's troops eighty-one years earlier. McClellan's men burrowed into General Washington's old siege line. A few inches below the surface, they found relics of the Revolution: rusty bayonets, crushed canteens, tin plates, the remains of clay smoking pipes.

After four weeks of digging, McClellan's guns were in position. But the cannonade, set for dawn on May 4, never took place. Sunrise revealed empty trenches across the way. Johnston had escaped in the nick of time. All he left behind were logs on wheels painted black to resemble cannons, scores of straw-man gunners, and "torpedoes," buried shells set to explode on contact. This was something new in warfare, as several Yankees discovered when they sat in the wrong place. One poor fellow was blown to bits when he picked up a pocketknife left as a booby trap.

Johnston slowly fell back until he reached Richmond's outer ring of defenses. This began five miles from the city and swept in an arc from the east to northeast, across the Chickahominy River. McClellan was overjoyed. Soon his northern forces would arrive to close the trap, he thought. Victory was certain. And if all went well, as it must, in two years he would replace the original gorilla in the White House.

Then Robert E. Lee spoiled his daydream.

Lee had been watching McClellan's advance with growing anxiety. Richmond was in a panic. The Yankees were coming! The roar of their cannons rattled windows in the center of town. Day and night, he heard the scuffle of feet and the clatter of wagons as thousands fled with their belongings; others buried valuables in gardens or sewed them into the linings of women's dresses. Railroad trains were crowded with refugees; people gladly paid anything for a ticket to anywhere, so long as it was far away. On May 14 Jefferson Davis met with his cabinet to discuss the situation. He was for accepting the inevitable. The purpose of the meeting, he announced, was to decide on the next move after the city's fall.

Lee was outraged. Richmond was Virginia's capital as well as the Confederacy's. And Virginia meant everything to him. "Richmond *must* not be given up; it *shall* not be given up!" he said. "Richmond *must* be defended!" He spoke in a booming voice, tears welling up in his eyes. No one present had ever heard him use that tone, or seen him so emotional. The cabinet could easily have brushed the protest aside, but the force of Lee's conviction won them over. They agreed to defend the capital.

Already a plan was forming in Lee's mind. He put himself in Lincoln's place. One thing was certain: the president of the United States must defend its capital city. Washington itself had little military value; its real importance was symbolic. Losing Washington would sway public opinion both at home and abroad. At home, people would lose faith in the Union cause, demanding peace at any price. Abroad, European governments, monarchies resentful of the American republic, would recognize Confederate independence and intervene on its behalf. Lee could save Richmond by threatening, or seeming to threaten, Washington. He would defend by attacking.

Members of the Confederate high command. From left to right: Stonewall Jackson, Joseph E. Johnston, and Robert E. Lee.

A glance at the map told him where the blow should fall: in the Shenandoah Valley. The Valley, as it is called, runs from southwest to northeast, a real advantage to the Confederacy. A Northern army moving up the Valley would actually be going away from Richmond, while a Southern army moving down the Valley would be heading toward Maryland, Pennsylvania, and Washington. A Union defeat in the Valley would open the road to Washington. To protect his capital, Lincoln must pull back the army around Fredericksburg, depriving McClellan of reinforcements.

Stonewall Jackson commanded a small Confederate force in the Valley. As the president's adviser, Lee could recommend how this force should be used. But he had to do so quietly, tactfully. Joe Johnston, not he, was in charge of Richmond's defenses. Although Johnston was a dear friend, he resented inter-ference, and Lee did not want to hurt his feelings. So, without con-sulting Johnston, he ordered several scattered units to join Jackson. Then he wrote Stonewall, "suggesting" he use them as he thought best. Did he!

Stonewall's seventeen-thousand-man force began a game of hide-and-seek with forty thousand enemy troops. The Yankees could easily have crushed them, had they been able to pin them down. Stonewall never gave them the chance. In a whirlwind cam-paign, he struck one unit and disappeared, only to strike another unit miles away. The secret was in his soldiers' legs. He marched them long distances so rapidly that they began calling themselves "Jackson's Foot Cavalry." He set a strenuous pace, and hundreds fell by the wayside, panting and exhausted. But those who kept going were the strongest of the strong. To quicken the pace, he made them carry only the necessities. A captured Rebel said it best. "You uns is like pack mules—we uns is like race horses," he noted, staring at the Yankees' full packs. "All Old Jackson gave us was a musket, a hundred rounds, and a gum blanket, and he druv us like hell."[9] It was a compliment, back then, to be called "old." A brave soldier of twenty might still be called "the old man."

In May 1862 Stonewall won five battles, took hundreds of pris-oners, and sent to Richmond wagons loaded with captured mus-kets, ammunition, and supplies. He advanced toward Harpers Ferry, hurling the enemy backward. Retreating Yankees called it "the big skedaddle," a desperate run for their lives. Once they decided to run, nothing could stop them. A Union general tried to rally his troops after a battle. "Men, don't you love your country?" he cried. A private paused long enough to blurt out: "Yes—and I'm trying to get back to it as fast as I can."[10]

President Lincoln took the bait. With Washington in danger, he recalled the force from Fredericksburg just as it was moving to join McClellan. Little Mac was unprepared for this sudden change of plan. Expecting reinforcements, he had sent large forces across the Chickahominy, opening a gap in the northern part of his line. Worse, on the night of May 30, a rainstorm flooded the river, cut-ting his army in two.

Joe Johnston saw his chance. Next day, he attacked south of the river at a place called Seven Pines, or Fair Oaks. President Davis and General Lee had ridden out to watch the battle. What they saw was a savage brawl in which units lost their way and wounded men drowned in muddy pools of water tinged with blood.

At the height of the battle, which ended in a draw, Johnston was carried past them on a stretcher with broken ribs and a punctured lung. Although the injuries were not life-threatening, the wounds would keep him out of the war for months to come.

Johnston was taken to Richmond, where a friend called his wounding a national calamity. "No, sir!" he replied. "The shot that struck me down was the best ever fired for the Southern Confederacy, for . . . now a man . . . will succeed me and be able to accomplish what I never could." The *Philadelphia Press,* a Union newspaper, later described the bullet that struck Johnston as "the saddest shot fired during the war," because it changed Southern tactics and gave it "skillful generalship."[11]

Both had a point. Johnston was right in believing the Confederacy must turn to Lee, whom he had admired since their days at West Point; President Davis ordered Lee to take over that very night. But Johnston was wrong to believe this was best for the Confederacy, much less the Southern people. As the *Press* noted, until then the Confederate military had lacked a driving spirit, a strong leader who knew exactly what he wanted and how to get it. Lee was the man they needed, but not even he could do the impossible. He fought magnificently, as we shall see, but could never deliver the knockout blow or match the North's growing power. The war, thanks largely to him, dragged on with growing ferocity and destructiveness. The North paid heavily in lives and money, but ended the war richer than when it started. The South, bled of its manpower and resources, lay in ruins. It paid dearly for the genius of Robert E. Lee.

Lee called his command the Army of Northern Virginia. That name is important, revealing as it does how he viewed his task. The army was to operate in northern Virginia, where he expected to do most of his fighting. For the next three years, this would be the most fought-over area in America.

But digging came before fighting. Within days of taking charge, Lee ordered the trenches around Richmond deepened and extended. It was not a popular order. Johnny Reb grumbled that he had done enough digging on the peninsula. He had joined to fight, he said, not to dig; besides, digging in the South was considered slave work. Soon he was calling his general the "King of Spades" and again "Granny Lee." Newspapers again wrote about "Evacuating Lee," who had given up western Virginia without a fight. Lee kept on digging. "There is," he wrote, "nothing so military as labor, and nothing so important to an army as to save the lives of its soldiers."[12] Apart from saving lives, there was another reason for digging trenches, which Lee was not ready to discuss just yet. Meantime, he made his plans and built his team.

That team was among the most outstanding in the history of warfare. Next to Lee himself, the team's star was Stonewall Jackson. Born in western Virginia in 1824, he stood six feet one inch tall, had large hands and feet, and walked with an awkward stride. He had a big nose, reddish brown hair, and piercing blue eyes with a gleam that earned him the nickname "Old Blue-light." A West Point graduate, he left the army after the Mexican War to become professor of artillery at the Virginia Military Institute in Lexington. An uninspiring teacher, he could make the most interesting subjects dull. Students made fun of him behind his back. "Tom Fool," they said, was "crazy as damnation."[13]

Stonewall *was* strange. Forever worrying about his health, he believed that one of his legs was bigger than the other and that one of his arms was too heavy. To keep in shape, he would raise his right arm straight up, hold it there for several minutes, then suddenly drop it to his side, draining the "surplus blood" from the "heavy arm." He never ate pepper because, he insisted, it "weakened" his left leg. He constantly sucked lemons as an aid to digestion. In battle, officers who came to him often got their orders between lemon sucks.

A devout Christian, Stonewall never touched whiskey, tobacco, or a deck of cards. Like Lee, he disapproved of secession, preferring that the South fight for its rights inside the Union rather than as a separate country. Although he hoped for an end to slavery, he believed it to be supported by the Bible. Slaves thought him a decent man who started a Sunday school for their children. In Lexington he took off his hat to black people on the street, explaining: "I could be no less polite than a colored man who raised his hat to me."[14] Once a slave named Albert begged Stonewall to buy him away from a harsh master. He did, allowing Albert to work as a hotel waiter and to give him so much a week until he repaid the debt and could be freed.

Before battle, Stonewall would go off by himself to have

Stonewall Jackson, Lee's "right arm," as he appeared in 1862, a year before his death. His loss was a major blow to the Confederacy, one from which it never recovered.

lengthy, and loud, conversations with God. His soldiers took these conversations seriously, as we learn from this poem:

Silence! Ground arms! Kneel all! Caps off!
Old Blue-light's going to pray;
Strangle the fool that dares to scoff!
Attention! It's his way![15]

Old Blue-light rode into battle with his arms raised, his eyes lifted toward heaven, and his lips moving in silent prayer. Danger, he admitted, filled him with "delicious excitement." A believer in "hard war," he wanted to fight with every means available. He called for hurling "thunderbolts of war" against Yankee cities. He wanted to invade the North to destroy its factories, blow up its coal mines, tear up its railroads, burn its crops, and take its leading citizens hostage. Nor were bluebellies to be taken prisoner. During the Valley campaign, a Confederate officer tried to spare the life of a brave Union officer. Stonewall objected. "No," he snorted. "Shoot them all. I do not wish them to be brave."[16]

Stonewall was just as hard on his own men. Soldiers were expected to go to their deaths without flinching or asking questions. But that could be too much even for loyal officers. One day a general rode up with a question. "Did you order me to advance over that field, sir?" he asked. "Yes," came the reply. "Impossible, sir! My men will be annihilated! Nothing can live there! They will be annihilated!" Stonewall answered coolly: "General . . . I always endeavor to take care of my wounded and to bury my dead. You have my order—obey it!"[17] No wonder his name was a terror to all concerned. Confederate soldiers joked that, if the Yankees were all in hell, they would be down there after them, with Stonewall leading the chase. His very name sent chills up the spines of Union troops.

James Longstreet, aged forty-one, was different. "Pete," or "Old Pete," as everyone called him, hailed from South Carolina. A hulking bear of a man, he stood six feet two inches tall, weighed over two hundred pounds, and had a chest-length beard. Never one to pass up a good time, he ate heartily, drank deeply, and played a wicked game of poker. He laughed a lot and, if the spirit moved him, would leap on a table to sing opera arias at the top of his voice. Then three of his four children died of scarlet fever in the same week. After that he was a serious, often silent and brooding, man.

Pete's courage and luck became legends in the Army of Northern Virginia. Always in the thick of the fight, he seemed to defy death. His men said he had a charmed life, and that his luck was contagious; those standing near him were supposedly immune to bullets. No general ever cared so much about the welfare of his troops. As he used to say, "If we only save the finger of a man, that's enough."[18] Lee called him "my old war horse."

At age twenty-nine, Jeb Stuart was the team's youngest member. Of medium height, he had blue eyes, a bushy brown beard, and a huge mustache, its ends curled upward. A dandy if there ever was one, "Beauty" Stuart wore a splendid uniform, high boots, a yellow silk sash, and a brown hat with a sweeping ostrich plume. The army, to him, was a fellowship of cheerful youths dedicated to laughing, singing, and having a good time. He meant it. Wherever Stuart went, he brought gaiety in the form of his own minstrel troupe: banjo player Sam Sweeny, plus a fiddler and a guitarist. He never outgrew the notion that war is an exciting sport.

General James Longstreet. Nicknamed "Old Pete," Longstreet was one of Lee's most trusted field commanders.

But when it came to fighting, Jeb Stuart was all business. A born horseman, his job as chief of Lee's cavalry force made him one of the most important men in the army. Before the airplane, the cavalry served as an army's eyes. Its duty was to scout ahead, observing the enemy's strength and movements while screening those of its own army. Armed with sword, pistol and carbine, a lightweight rifle, cavalry seldom charged infantry, which were usually more numerous and heavily armed. When cavalry fought, it was usually in raids on enemy supply lines or in small patrol actions. Stuart was a master at this kind of cut-and-slash warfare. And he led by example, from the front. As a trooper put it: "Jeb never says 'go, boys,' but always 'come, boys.'"[19] Stuart felt that death on the battlefield was the ideal end for a professional soldier. All he asked of fate was to be killed leading a cavalry charge. He would get his wish.

✧   ✧   ✧

Lee revealed his plan during the first week in June. From now on, he told the team, he would take the initiative, fighting at points selected by himself and not by the enemy. He would still be on the defensive, since conquering the North was out of the question. But his defense would be aggressive, dynamic, bold. Above all, bold! No longer would the Confederates wait to be attacked. They would hit first, hit hard, and keep on hitting to keep the Yankees off balance. And, at the right time, they would destroy the Army of the Potomac.

Those trenches outside Richmond were essential to his plan. Their purpose was not merely to defend the city, but to do so with as small a force as possible. About twenty-five thousand Rebels would be left in the trenches opposite seventy-five thousand Yankees. As before, Prince John Magruder would try to mislead the enemy about his true strength. Meanwhile, Lee would slip away with a strike force of fifty-five thousand. They would march northward, cross the Chickahominy, whose waters had subsided, and attack McClellan's right wing, a corps of thirty thousand. A victory would put them across McClellan's overland supply line, forcing him to retreat. It was a gamble, Lee admitted. If McClellan attacked while he was away, Richmond could fall in an hour, allowing him to pass through the city and hit the Rebels from behind. But doing the unexpected was his only hope of evening the odds.

Jeb Stuart set the plan into motion. On June 12 he took 1,200 men to scout enemy positions and find a weak point. Stuart left Richmond in a gay mood. Among his commanders were his general's son, Rooney, and his nephew, Fitzhugh. Sam Sweeny strummed his favorite tune, "If You Want a Good Time Jine the Caval-ree!" As the squadrons set out, flags waving and sunlight glistening on steel, troopers sang:

> *Come tighten your girth and slacken your rein;*
> *Come buckle your blanket and holster again;*
> *Try the click of your trigger and balance your blade*
> *For he must ride sure that goes Ri . . . ding a Raid!*[20]

Stuart found what he wanted in a day. But once Jeb got started, there was no stopping him. Instead of reporting to Lee at once, he decided to ride completely around the Army of the Potomac. That ride is still a legend in the South.

Luck was with him every step of the way. Startled Yankees were captured and mounted on stolen horses. Yankee supply

columns were overtaken and looted. In one place, Stuart found a thirty-acre field covered with wagons. All were burned. Yankee cavalry gave chase, but Stuart always kept a few hours ahead of them. Still, the fast pace took its toll. Entire squadrons fell asleep in the saddle. Stuart himself would throw one knee over the pommel of his saddle, drop his chin to his chest, and sleep soundly, rocking from side to side as his horse picked its way over rough roads. He returned to headquarters on June 15, having lost only one man. Richmond was elated, as citizens told one another how McClellan "had got his rear well-spanked."[21]

Lee acted on Stuart's information. On June 25, before dawn, he left Richmond with the strike force. By early afternoon, his forward elements were skirmishing with enemy patrols. These were the first shots of Lee's first campaign. Since it lasted a week, it is known as the Battle of the Seven Days.

The Confederates crossed the Chickahominy and camped near Mechanicsville, a village near the river. For Johnny Reb, as for Billy Yank, the night before battle was much the same. After supper, troops filed past the ammunition wagons to receive the stan-

Jeb Stuart and his men as portrayed in an English magazine, the Illustrated London News *of October 4, 1869. Surely, the artist never saw a Confederate battle flag. The one in this picture has twenty-three stars, while the real flag had only thirteen.*

dard sixty cartridges per man. Then they settled down for the night. It was almost impossible to sleep; there was too much going on, too many cavalrymen clattering by, too many guns being hauled into position, too many orders being shouted. Most men didn't even try to sleep. They wrote letters home, checked rifles for the hundredth time, or simply stared into the darkness, thinking private thoughts.

On June 26, at 3:30 A.M., drummers beat the "long roll," or call to arms. After a hasty breakfast, the troops formed ranks and officers made a final inspection. This was followed by some words of encouragement and advice: Hold your fire until the enemy is in range, aim low to allow for the musket's upward "kick," and always—*always*—follow your flag. The regimental flag was not just an ornament for parades. It was the regiment's identity; indeed, its very soul. On it were stitched the names of past battles, and every patched hole held special meaning. Where the flag was, there was the regiment. If it advanced, so must all true men, even over the bodies of friends. If it retreated, one might honorably do the same. Besides its own flag, each regiment had a Confederate battle flag showing a diagonal blue cross with thirteen white stars on a red field. Losing either flag was like losing a brother, and reason to cry. Men fought to the death to save their colors. Captured colors were dragged across the ground as an insult.

The morning fog lifted, revealing ambulances parked nearby. These were a sure sign that somewhere the surgeons were laying out their tools: knives, saws, tourniquets, forceps, probes, needles, and thread. The waiting men became nervous, began to perspire, felt a tightness in the stomach, and breathed heavily. No matter how much water they drank, their mouths stayed dry. Their minds raced. What if the worst happened? What if they were killed, or wounded, or captured? Would their families learn their fate? Perhaps not, for Civil War soldiers wore no identification tags. A man needed friends at such a time. Friends promised to search for each other should they go missing, and send home their belongings should they be killed. One could not help thinking of the folks back home, and how they would take the sad news. "This was my first battle," a Rebel wrote his wife afterward. "I thought . . . a heap . . . of you and those dear little ones [and it] hurt me worse than anything else."[22]

Lee was nervous that morning. Something had gone wrong. Stonewall Jackson was supposed to attack the enemy's rear while Lee struck head-on, but Jackson was still miles away. Jackson and

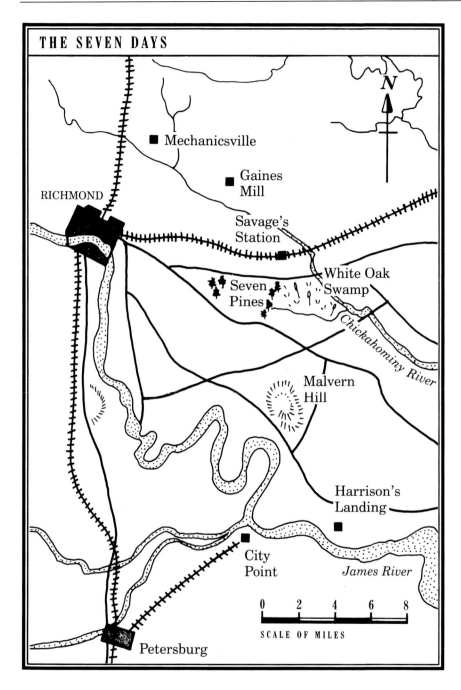

THE SEVEN DAYS

Mechanicsville

Gaines
Mill

RICHMOND

Savage's
Station

White Oak
Swamp

Seven
Pines

Chickahominy River

Malvern
Hill

Harrison's
Landing

City
Point

James River

0   2   4   6   8

SCALE OF MILES

Petersburg

his "foot cavalry" were exhausted from their Valley campaign and
would not arrive until the following day. The Battle of
Mechanicsville had to go on without them.

A first battle is a never-to-be-forgotten experience. It is truly a
"baptism of fire," a kind of rebirth. Rebels recalled how its sights

and sounds suddenly turned them into different men. Before, they had only been soldiers in training. After, they were veterans.

The noise and action drove away fear, at least for a while. So did their war cry, the famous "Rebel yell," a spine-tingling screech given on the run: *Yip-yip-yip-e-e-e-ee-e-e! Yah-ah-ah-yah-e-e-e-e-e-e-e!* It had an opposite effect on the enemy. A Yankee might hear it in battle after battle, and still not be used to it. Years later, a veteran of the Sixth Wisconsin regiment recalled: "There is nothing like it this side of the infernal region, and the peculiar corkscrew sensation that it sends down your backbone . . . can never be told. You have to feel it, and if you say you did not feel it, and heard the yell, you have *never* been there."[23]

Lee's timing was off, and Stonewall was sorely missed. After a six-hour fight, he had to admit defeat. Nearly fifteen hundred Rebels had been killed or wounded, compared to three hundred and sixty Yankees. Yet luck, in the form of the Young Napoleon, came to the rescue. Another general might have used the victory to push on to Richmond, as his staff urged. But McClellan saw Mechanicsville as a narrow escape rather than a clear-cut victory. As on the peninsula, he believed himself outnumbered, only now the Confederates had two hundred thousand men to his one hun-

A Union crew prepares to fire its gun. Note the man on the right with his arm extended; he is about to pull a rope which will trigger a gunpowder charge in the barrel, sending a piece of solid shot or an exploding shell on its way.

dred thousand! So he fell back to a stronger position at Gaines's Mill. It was a retreat from victory. Next day, June 27, Lee won his first battle.

During a lull in the fighting, an eighteen-year-old artilleryman lay curled up under a caisson. He was sleeping soundly when a friend nudged him awake, saying he had a guest. Groggy with fatigue, his uniform covered with dust, he rose to meet his guest. Before him was an officer in an elegant gray uniform on a big gray horse. It took a moment for him to realize what was happening, but then "I saw my father's loving eyes and smile." General Robert E. Lee had come to see how Private Robert E. Lee, Jr., was getting along.[24]

Meantime, McClellan completely lost his nerve. Fearing his "outnumbered" forces would be surrounded, he ordered all Union troops back across the Chickahominy. Then, on the afternoon of June 28, Lee and his staff saw an immense cloud rising to the south. It was dust raised by thousands of marching men and wagon trains that stretched for miles. The Army of the Potomac was in retreat from Richmond!

The retreat was so hasty that valuable supplies could not be taken along. McClellan ordered them destroyed. Tent cities were burned. Barrels of flour, sugar, coffee, and meat were heaped into mounds and put to the torch. Three brand-new locomotives were blown up. A hundred-car ammunition train was set ablaze and sent speeding toward a ruined bridge over the Chickahominy. On it went, faster and faster, flames shooting from the cars. Reaching the bridge, it hurtled across the gap, hung in space for an instant, and exploded like the crack of doom. Even a field hospital with twenty-five hundred sick and wounded was abandoned to the Confederates.

The retreat was a bonanza for Lee's men. Hard as the Yankees tried, they failed to destroy everything. Tons of supplies remained behind, neatly stacked and ready for use. Rebels who had gone for days on salt meat and moldy corn bread had a feast. They sat beside the Chickahominy, eating canned beef, white bread, and cake washed down with lemonade. Equally welcome was the chance to replace obsolete weapons with the latest models from Northern factories. A soldier-poet wrote:

> *Want a weapon?*
> *Why, capture one!*
> *Every Doodle has got a gun,*

Belt and bayonet, bright and new;
Kill a Doodle, and capture two![25]

Lee decided to press forward, hoping to destroy the invader before he recrossed the James. But it was not to be. The Union rear guard fought him to a standstill at Savage's Station and White Oak Swamp. Finally, on July 1, Lee caught up with McClellan at Malvern Hill, a strong defensive position along the James. Two hundred Union cannons lined the crest, wheel to wheel, supported by thousands of infantry. The slope was bare of trees, making any attacker a perfect target.

Lee brought up his own guns, but these were too few for the job. Whenever a Confederate gun fired, fifty Union guns replied, destroying it at once. Losing patience, he sent in his infantry without covering fire. It was one of the worst blunders of his career.

The Yankee gunners took their time, selecting their ammunition carefully. For targets up to a mile away, they used round shot, six- or twelve-pound iron balls known as "solid shot," or exploding shells that showered a wide area with red-hot fragments. When attackers came to within 250 yards, the gunners switched to shrapnel and canister. Shrapnel was a thin-walled shell filled with a dozen iron balls the size of golf balls; canister was a sheet-metal tube containing two hundred lead slugs. Fired at close range, the containers blew apart, spewing a hailstorm of death. Unless a soldier hugged the ground, he was almost certain to be hit. For good measure, gunners often fired double canister, called "canned hellfire."

Brigade after brigade charged up the slope of Malvern Hill. Shot and shell were visible in flight, and those who saw them swore they were coming straight for them. Missiles whizzed, whirred, whooshed, whistled, zinged, hissed, howled, and banged. Cannonballs bounced along the ground, gouging the earth and smashing anyone in their path. Clouds of acrid smoke hung over the guns, bringing tears to the gunners' eyes. But once they settled into their routine, gunners could fire two shots a minute, with horrendous results. Bodies and fragments of bodies were flung about like rag dolls. Men were splattered with the blood of their comrades; flying pieces of bone and teeth did as much damage as shrapnel. Seeing his men falter, a Confederate colonel shouted: "Come on, come on, my men! Do you want to live forever?"[26] They surged forward with the Rebel yell, only to be mowed down. The Union line held.

When the last charge was broken, Confederate general D. H. Hill looked out over the hillside. He could hardly believe his eyes. Over 5,300 dead and wounded lay in every imaginable position. Some were writhing in agony, begging God to end their misery. Some had torn open their clothing to see if their wound was fatal; for example, no one could survive a shot in the stomach. "It was not war—it was murder," said Hill.[27] The Seven Days were over.

McClellan was five miles from Richmond when Lee began his campaign. The next week found his army bottled up at Harrison's Landing on the James, eighteen miles away, protected by the guns of Union warships. His losses numbered 9,735 killed, wounded, captured, and missing; a missing man was usually a dead man whose body had not been recovered. Lee's losses totaled 19,739, that is, more than twice his opponent's. There were so many dead that a girl visiting a Confederate cemetery exclaimed, "Why, the soldiers' graves are as thick as potato hills!"[28] Worse, Lee had either lost or been fought to a standstill in three out of four battles.

The Young Napoleon still had an enormous advantage in manpower and supplies. The difficulty was in his mind, not in his resources. Believing himself beaten and outnumbered, he stayed in camp, whining about how the original gorilla had betrayed him. President Lincoln promised reinforcements, but nothing he said had any effect. McClellan stayed put. Finally, in August, Lincoln ordered the Army of the Potomac back to the Washington area. Left behind were thousands of Union graves with crude wooden markers. A Rebel scribbled these lines on one marker:

> *The Yankee host with blood-stained hands*
> *Came Southward to divide our lands*
> *This narrow and contracted spot*
> *Is all this Yankee scoundrel got.*[29]

The Seven Days stunned Richmond. During the fighting, and for days afterward, casualties poured into the city. "Walking wounded" came on foot, under their own power. Serious cases arrived in springless wagons driven along rough country roads. There were also wagonloads of bodies heaped one on top of another. Mrs. Roger Pryor tried to avert her eyes from such ghastly sights. "I used to veil myself closely as I walked to and from my hotel, that I might shut out the . . . open wagons in which the dead were piled. Once I *did* see one of those dreadful wagons! In it a stiff arm was raised, and shook as it was driven down the street, as though the dead owner appealed to Heaven for vengeance."[30]

Homes, stores, churches, and schools became temporary hospitals. Richmond's women flocked to these places of suffering, anxious to help in any way they could. They brought bedsheets to be torn up for bandages, as well as food and ice; it was brutally hot, and nothing refreshed the wounded like a cool drink. Slave women worked alongside their mistresses. "Efficient, kindly colored women assisted us," a white woman recalled. "Their motherly manner soothed the prostrate soldier, whom they always addressed as 'son.'"[31]

But there were limits to what they could do. Being treated for gunshot was the supreme test of courage. The rifle musket made a ghastly wound. When the soft lead bullet hit an arm or leg, it did not make a neat hole, but tore away muscles and shattered bones. There was only one remedy: amputation. The surgeon had to remove the limb quickly or lose the patient to blood poisoning. The lucky ones were knocked out with ether or chloroform, medical "miracles" introduced in the early 1850s. These had been in short supply until Stonewall Jackson captured fifteen thousand cases of chloroform in the Valley. Nevertheless, there was not always enough to go around where needed. The patient had to be held down by the surgeon's assistants and a piece of wood put in his mouth to keep him from biting off his tongue. Then the surgeon began to cut.

Medicine was still very primitive. The only requirement for admission to medical school was the ability to pay tuition. A student went through a two-year course, the second year being a repeat of the first; he learned all that was known about medicine in just one year. Things we take for granted today did not exist in the mid-nineteenth century. There were no antibiotics, no X rays, no blood transfusions, no vitamins, no antiseptics, and no idea that germs cause infection. Surgical instruments were never sterilized. Bandages were taken from the dead and reused without being washed. Surgeons probed for bullets with dirty fingers. An Alabama private was on the right track when he said: "I beleave the Doctors kills more than they cour."[32] That was not what they intended, but they did not know any better. At least a third of the wounded died of infection, shock, and loss of blood.

Other battles would be costlier than the Seven Days, yet few would have such important results. The campaign was a personal triumph for Lee. Although he failed to destroy the Army of the Potomac, and took heavier casualties, he had upset the enemy's plans. That was enough to make his reputation. From then on, he was called "the First Captain of the Confederacy" and "the Savior of Richmond." Stonewall Jackson, who trusted few men, trusted Lee. "I would follow him blindfolded," he said.[33]

The Seven Days gave Abraham Lincoln much to think about. Had the Young Napoleon succeeded, the war might have ended quickly, allowing slavery to survive for at least another decade. Lincoln's aim had always been to save the Union. The Seven Days convinced him that this could not be done without changing the very nature of the war. The North would have to fight a total war, that is, mobilize all its human and economic resources for victory. Likewise, the Southern war effort would have to be crippled, even at the price of ruining its economy and impoverishing its people. The North must play for keeps. It must wage a war of conquest.

The slaves had a key role to play in this drama. Lincoln had not intended to free them; indeed, freeing them would violate his campaign promise not to touch slavery where it already existed. Yet the war had to be won. Not only was the slaves' labor essential to the South, they had also become a powerful symbol. Freeing them, Lincoln reasoned, would transform the war into a struggle for something far greater than union: a crusade for human freedom. That would ennoble the Union cause and spoil chances of foreign

An amputation outside a field hospital tent, Gettysburg, July 1863. Note the surgeon with his long knife and his assistant holding out the patient's leg.

intervention. As long as Northerners fought for union alone, Europeans could call them hypocrites and talk of aiding the South. But no European government, however hostile to the United States, dared ally itself with slavery against freedom.

On June 22 Lincoln told his cabinet about the Emancipation Proclamation. Unless the Rebel states returned to the Union before the year was out, their slaves would be freed "as a fit and necessary military measure." Note: as a military measure, not because slavery was wrong. Cabinet members advised against issuing the proclamation at once, as it would seem like a desperate effort to save a lost cause. The president agreed to wait until the Union won a decisive victory, in effect, a victory over Robert E. Lee.

The Civil War was becoming a contest between Lee the soldier and Lincoln the statesman. And no one could foresee the outcome during that summer of 1862.

IV ✦ BLOODY SEPTEMBER

All the country was flaming, smoking, and burning, as if the last great day, the Day of Judgment of the Lord, had come.

—Charles C. Coffin, *Boston Journal*, report of September 17, 1862

General Lee could not afford to rest on his laurels. After the Seven Days, it was urgent that he put his army into shape for the next round of fighting. Fortunately, with the Young Napoleon cooped up at Harrison's Landing, he had a few weeks to bring his forces up to strength. Unfit officers were reassigned and the army reorganized into corps under Jackson and Longstreet. If Lee was displeased with Stonewall's performance during the Seven Days, he never said so. Old Pete's achievements, however, won his admiration.

These changes were completed in the nick of time. By early August 1862, another threat had arisen. As McClellan began to evacuate the Peninsula, another Federal army was massing southwest of Washington. Named the Army of Virginia, it was led by Major General John Pope, an able soldier with victories in the West. Those victories, however, had gone to his head. He bragged about them constantly, and about how he was a tireless campaigner who made his headquarters in the saddle. He also claimed that westerners were better soldiers than easterners. His troops couldn't forgive the insult and were not willing to go all out for this "bag of wind," as they called him. Stonewall made his only recorded joke at Pope's expense: "I can whip any man who doesn't know his headquarters from his hindquarters."[1]

The Army of Northern Virginia numbered sixty-five thousand men. If Pope's army of forty-five thousand was joined by McClellan's ninety thousand, it might easily break through to Richmond. Lee could not stand idly by while two armies combined against him. Once again he vowed to strike first. The plan was to guard the capital with Longstreet's corps while Jackson swung northward, then eastward, to get behind Pope. When Lee was sure that McClellan was really leaving the Peninsula, he would come up with the rest of the army.

Lee sent Jeb Stuart to tear things up in the Yankee rear. Stuart did as ordered. He raided Pope's headquarters, took his dress uniform, and ran off with his papers. These were a real prize, because they revealed the exact positions of the Union armies.

Meantime, Jackson's foot cavalry went on a record-breaking speed march. Crossing the Bull Run Mountains at Thoroughfare Gap, they covered fifty-eight miles in two days. Caked with dust, sweating from every pore, they kept up a grueling pace; indeed, some died of sunstroke. Their general could not have been prouder. Once he reined in his horse to watch a regiment pass. He looked like a common soldier in a dirty uniform with a dirty cap pulled forward over his eyes. But everyone knew Old Blue-light, and cheered until staff officers were sent to keep them quiet. No matter; as they passed, they silently raised their hats and waved them around their heads. "Who could not conquer with such troops as these?" Stonewall asked, as proud of them as they were of him.[2]

After being defeated at Second Manassas, Union general John Pope was sent west, where he earned a reputation as a tough Indian fighter during and after the Civil War.

On August 26, he pounced on Pope's supply base at Manassas Junction. The Union troops thought they were safe, until twenty-four thousand Rebels seemed to burst out of the earth. Taken by surprise, they gave up or ran away.

Jackson's men ate what they wished, took what they liked, and burned the rest. Then they staged one of the most spectacular train wrecks in history. A barrier was built across the tracks to derail any train that came along. Three trains came! They came only minutes apart, and at top speed. The first slammed into the barrier, jumped the track, and flipped over on its side. The second plowed through the wreckage of the first, its cars overshooting one another before coming to rest. The third piled up against the second, its boiler exploding with a roar heard miles away. An engineer survived and was made a prisoner. Learning that his captors were Stonewall's men, he asked to see their commander. But when they pointed out a scruffy giant with a shaggy beard, he moaned, "O my God! Lay me down again!"[3]

Pope raced northward with his entire army, only to find Jackson dug in along the bed of an unfinished railroad at the edge of the old Manassas battlefield. The bluecoats were horrified at the scene. Civil War battlefields were poorly "policed"; the orderly cemeteries we see today came after the war. Exhausted by their efforts, the victors usually buried the dead in shallow graves, easily uncovered by rain or dug up by animals. As Pope's men took their positions, they found the ground littered with the skeletons of comrades who had died the year before. They fell silent, wondering if this was also to be their fate.

The Battle of Second Manassas (Second Bull Run) began at daybreak on August 29. Reinforcements had increased Pope's fighting strength to seventy-three thousand, and he was eager to use them. Despite furious attacks, however, the Rebels stood their ground. And all the while they wondered out loud: "Where is Longstreet? What could be keeping Old Pete?" Through it all, Stonewall rode among his men, urging them to hold on and promising that help was on the way.

By sunset, the Union dead were heaped in front of the railroad embankment. Johnny Rebs sat around blazing campfires, passing the word that Longstreet's corps had come at last. It was camped on their right, opposite the enemy's left flank.

Next day, Pope made a fatal error. Believing Jackson's corps to be on the verge of collapse, he ignored Longstreet to attack it with his full strength. It was touch and go for a couple of hours. The defenders' ammunition ran low, forcing them to strip the dead of their cartridge boxes. Confederates, running out completely, actually threw rocks at the attackers. But still no Longstreet!

Lee was with his staff, watching from a hilltop. Everyone was tense—everyone except the commanding general. Time and again, it seemed that Jackson would be overrun, but Lee was calm. Nor did he send a hurry-up order. He knew his old warhorse. Longstreet was a perfectionist. He was taking his time, waiting for the ideal moment to strike. And when it came, the blow was shattering. His artillery tore into the Union left, killing men and spreading confusion. Then his corps charged with the Rebel yell.

Pope turned to meet Longstreet on the left, but it was too late. Jackson hit him in front and on the right. Old Blue-light was in top form that day. Grabbing a battle flag, he led the counterattack in person. Those who saw him said he became a god of war, scattering all before him. "What officer is that, Captain?" a Union prisoner asked a guard. Told it was Stonewall Jackson, he got carried away by the excitement. He ran toward a Confederate regiment, waving a broken sword and shouting, "Hurrah for General Jackson! Follow your general, boys!" That made his guard weep with pride. Deciding that the Yankee was an all-right fellow, he let him go. "He saluted me with his broken sword and disappeared in an instant," the Rebel recalled. "I hope he escaped."[4] It was a strange war.

Second Manassas was Lee's greatest victory thus far. He had inflicted 14,462 casualties on the enemy at a cost of 9,474 Confederates. His reputation soared. Pope became a laughingstock in both camps. In Richmond, youngsters recited a rhyme:

> *Little Be-Pope, he came at a lope,*
> *The Rebels to find them.*
> *He found them at last, then ran very fast,*
> *With his gallant invaders behind him!*[5]

And when a Union officer said, "I don't care for John Pope one pinch of owl dung," he spoke for his comrades.[6] Pope was sent to fight Sioux Indians in Minnesota.

President Lincoln was bitterly disappointed—and scared. He had pinned his hopes on an all-out offensive, only to have another defeat. Worse, the victorious Army of Northern Virginia was barely thirty miles from Washington. Little did he know that Lee had no intention of going there, at least not right away.

Second Manassas solved nothing for Lee. His army could not stay where it was. Supplies were dangerously low, with little chance of obtaining more locally. The old saying was true: "A crop of soldiers kills out any other crop in the quickest possible time."[7] Union and Confederate armies had stripped northern Virginia of food until the next year's harvest; even local farmers had difficulty making ends meet. Thus, Lee must either advance or retreat. But advancing on Washington was out of the question, since fresh troops were pouring in to strengthen its defenses. Similarly, a retreat would throw away all his hard-won gains. The moment he withdrew, Union forces would return to his beloved Virginia.

Lee decided to take the war north by way of Maryland, a slave state that had remained in the Union. This move had several advantages. To begin with, it would draw Union forces away from

Virginia for the rest of the 1862 fighting season. Maryland also had thousands of Southern sympathizers who, Lee believed, were eagerly waiting for a chance to join his army. And that army would find plenty to eat in Maryland's prosperous countryside.

If all went well in Maryland, he intended to move into Pennsylvania to cut the Pennsylvania Railroad, a vital Union link with the West. This done, he would turn his attention to either Philadelphia, Baltimore, or Washington. Capturing any of these cities might well encourage France and Britain to enter the war on the Confederate side. So far, only Lincoln's cabinet knew he had prepared the Emancipation Proclamation with these same countries in mind. Thus, Lee had more riding on the invasion than he knew. If he failed, Lincoln would change the very nature of the war.

On September 4 the Army of Northern Virginia splashed across the Potomac at White's Ford, thirty-two miles north of Washington, where the river is half a mile wide and three feet deep. The army numbered fifty-five thousand men, mainly battle-tested veterans. Reaching the Maryland shore, Rebels cheered, tossed their hats into the air, and sang "Maryland, My Maryland!," the best known of all state songs:

> *Thou wilt not cower in the dust*
> *Maryland, my Maryland!*
> *Thy gleaming sword shall never rust,*
> *Maryland, my Maryland!*
> *Dear Mother! burst the tyrant's chain,*
> *Maryland!*
> *Virginia should not call in vain,*
> *Maryland!*

At least ten thousand soldiers did not sing; they deserted before crossing the Potomac or soon afterward. Some deserted because they had no shoes, and their feet were rubbed raw; leather was always scarce in the Confederacy, making shoes harder to get than any other type of clothing. The majority, it seems, deserted out of principle. Although they trusted Lee, they felt he was wrong this time. They had enlisted to defend their own soil, not to invade someone else's, and refused to take part in an operation in which they did not believe. Not that they left the army permanently. When the army returned to Virginia, they rejoined, since home always came first.

Meanwhile, Lee's troops marched along the Maryland roads, four abreast under the blazing sun, dust crunching between their teeth. They went at an average speed of two miles an hour, sharing the roads with the army's wagon trains and artillery. But since horse-drawn vehicles moved faster, the infantry had to move into the ditches as they passed. It was thirsty work, and canteens emptied quickly. Johnny Reb was not particular; he filled up from any pond or puddle along the way. "How many wiggletails and tadpoles I have drunk will never be known," a private wrote.[8] Dirty water caused all sorts of complaints, particularly diarrhea.

The infantryman took a lesson from Stonewall's foot cavalry. He stripped down to fighting weight, giving up his knapsack and tossing away everything but the essentials. These he rolled lengthwise in a rubber sheet, or "horse collar," which he slung over his left shoulder with its ends tied at the right hip. This distributed the weight evenly, while leaving his hands free. A veteran left this description of his comrades: "The private soldier, reduced to the minimum, consisted of one man, one hat, one jacket, one pair of pants, one pair of drawers, one pair of socks, one pair of shoes, and his baggage was one blanket, one gum cloth, and one haversack [for rations.]"[9] A toothbrush might also be stuck through a buttonhole like a flower, and a tin cup hooked onto the belt. The whole outfit weighed nine or ten pounds.

Marching soldiers sang patriotic songs and humorous songs with lines like this: "A pretty girl who gets a kiss and runs to tell her mother/ Does something that she should not do, and don't deserve another." And they joked, constantly. If, for example, a fellow mimicked a chicken, a cow, or a pig, his buddies would break into loud cackling, mooing, and oinking. If a marcher greeted a friend with "Howdy, Bill," his words rippled down the ranks of an entire brigade. Cavalrymen, whose horses raised clouds of dust, were heckled by the infantry: "Hey, mister, where's yer mule?"

The army's first stop in Maryland was the city of Frederick. Local people were shocked when the lead units appeared. They had never imagined, much less seen, such creatures. Dark-skinned, a blend of suntan and grime, the Rebels dressed like tramps and stank like mules. Yet these were Lee's veterans, the men who had defeated the flower of the Union army. A woman wrote to a relative:

> I wish, my dear Minnie, you could have witnessed the transit of the Rebel army through our streets. . . . I could scarcely believe my eyes; was this body of men moving smoothly along, with no order, their guns carried in every fashion, no

two dressed alike, their officers hardly distinguishable from the privates, were these, I asked myself in amazement, were these dirty, lank, ugly specimens of humanity, with shocks of hair sticking through holes in their hats, and dust thick on their dirty faces, the men who had ... driven back again and again our splendid legions ...? O, they are so dirty! I don't think the Potomac River could wash them clean.... There is not a scarecrow in our cornfields that would not scorn to exchange clothes with them; and so tattered! There isn't a decently dressed soldier in the whole army. I saw some strikingly handsome faces though, or rather they would have been so if they could have a good scrubbing.[10]

Dirty as they were, their rifles shone.

Their ragged appearance discouraged recruiting; Confederate sympathizers in Maryland talked big, but few joined the ranks. Most residents were loyal to the Union, and resented Lee's "traitors." Citizens would not speak to them. Merchants closed their shops. Girls pinned tiny American flags to their dresses, daring them to do something about it. The Johnny Rebs behaved like gentlemen, as Marse Robert had ordered. They knew the general meant business. Military police patrolled the town with clubs, ready to hit soldiers who misbehaved. Thieves could expect justice—swift, *permanent* justice. Outside the town, the columns passed two thieves strung up on the same tree.

The Rebels stayed at Frederick for three days, resuming their march on September 9. Their objectives had been set out in Lee's Special Orders No. 19. The army was to be divided and move westward. Lee would head for Pennsylvania with Longstreet's corps, while Jackson captured Harpers Ferry. The army would then reunite to seize Harrisburg, the Pennsylvania state capital, and cut the Pennsylvania Railroad. Lee's orders were so secret that his generals handled them with special care. Longstreet memorized his copy, then chewed it into a soggy pulp.

McClellan had no idea of Lee's plans or strength when his army reached Frederick on September 13. That afternoon, Corporal Barton W. Mitchell was resting at an abandoned Rebel campsite when he saw a thick envelope on the ground. Opening it, he found a paper wrapped around three cigars. After sharing the cigars with his friends, he idly read the paper. It was headed "HEADQUARTERS, ARMY OF NORTHERN VIRGINIA: Special Orders No. 19." Names like Lee, Longstreet, Jackson, and Stuart fairly leaped off the page. The mystery of how it got there has never been solved. Evidently, a Confederate officer dropped it while packing up. If he discovered the loss, he never admitted it. Who would?

Mitchell gave the paper to his captain, who sent it speeding up the chain of command. McClellan's questions were answered in a flash. Not only did he know Lee's strength, but the location of each of his divisions and their mission. He was elated, as he had a right to be. This was war-winning information! With it, he could slip between Lee's scattered units and defeat them separately. Waving the document, he cried: "Here is the paper with which, if I cannot whip Bobby Lee, I will be willing to go home."[11] Yet nothing had changed. McClellan was still the same man, timid as ever. Rather than speed ahead, he spent nearly a day in making his "preparations."

During that time, Lee somehow learned about the lost order. *He* acted instantly. On September 14 he sent messages to his field commanders. The invasion was off! All units must stop what they were doing and recross the Potomac! It had been a close shave, but the Confederates had lost nothing but time.

Meanwhile, D. H. Hill, one of the Confederacy's most aggressive generals, fought a delaying action at South Mountain, an extension of the Blue Ridge chain. Later that day, Stonewall Jackson sent word that Harpers Ferry was about to fall. Again Lee changed his mind. Fresh orders were issued: the army must gather at Sharpsburg, Maryland, without delay. Marse Robert meant to fight!

Sharpsburg lay between Antietam Creek, a quarter of a mile to the east, and a bend in the Potomac, which the creek joined a mile to the south. Nestled amid a patchwork of cornfields, pastures, and orchards, the town was home to thirteen hundred people. They were simple, devout folk, largely members of the German Baptist Brethren, or "Dunkers." So modest were they, that their one-room church lacked a steeple, which to them was a symbol of pride. Apart from the incidents of everyday life—births and deaths, planting and harvesting—nothing "important" ever happened in this quiet place. But that was about to change. For there, on a lovely September day, the fields and lanes would run red with blood. Rebels called this horror the Battle of Sharpsburg; Yankees knew it as Antietam. Whatever the name, it would change America forever.

Harpers Ferry fell on the morning of September 15. Union prisoners, over eleven thousand of them, could scarcely believe they had been defeated by an army of "tramps." But they could appreciate courage and good leadership. Upon seeing the Rebel commander, they treated him as a celebrity. Prisoners broke ranks, tossed their hats into the air, and cheered wildly. Stonewall rode up to the Ninth Vermont regiment, removed his hat, and said, "Boys, don't feel bad. You couldn't help it. It was just as God willed it."[12] The Lord, for Stonewall, was a Confederate.

News of Jackson's success made Lee's men happy, but did not fill their stomachs; they hadn't eaten a square meal since leaving Frederick. Those who could, ate green apples and ears of corn. Some were so hungry they chewed straws "merely," as one put it, "to keep their jaws from rusting and stiffening entirely."[13]

The Union army appeared east of Antietam Creek early that afternoon. As the day wore on, its ranks swelled into a blue ocean, flowing down the hillsides and spreading over the fields below. The Confederates watched in amazement, wondering how (or if) they would get out of this scrape. The situation was pretty grim.

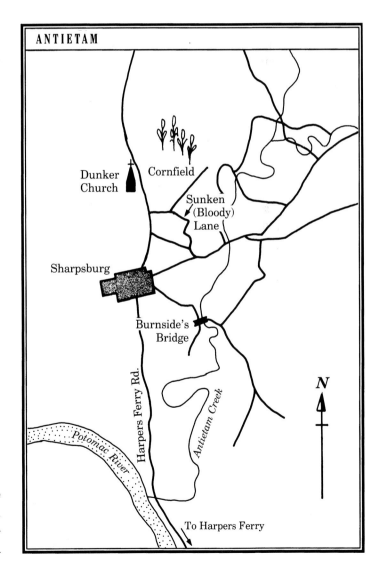

McClellan had at least sixty thousand men, with more arriving by the minute; Lee had barely nineteen thousand. It should have been easy to dispose of Lee and then go after Jackson. Again, McClellan hesitated. Lee, he insisted, had a hundred thousand men! Crazy as it seems, the Young Napoleon scared himself with a phantom army. Jackson arrived the next day, September 16, raising Confederate strength to thirty-five thousand. "Boys, it's all right!" soldiers yelled as they arrived. But McClellan's army had also grown, to eighty-seven thousand, giving him an advantage of over two to one. Still, he refused to attack until his preparations were "complete." Lee used the extra time to tighten his defenses.

The Confederates held a four-mile line west of Antietam Creek. Jackson commanded on the left, near a forty-acre cornfield bordered by a road with split-rail fences on either side; the ripe corn stood shoulder high, ideal for concealing troops. Longstreet commanded the center and right. The center was a country lane zigzagging east and south of the road. Years of use had worn the lane into a shallow trench, also bordered by fences; soldiers tore up the rear fence, piling the rails in front to form a low breastwork. The Confederate right was on a hill overlooking a stone bridge that crossed the creek south of town.

Lee had set up a do-or-die situation. Because he was fighting with his back to the Potomac, if his line broke, there could be no retreat. If he lost, his army must either surrender or be annihilated, thereby dooming the Confederacy. But he did not expect to lose. Here is where character and judgment became all-important. He had taken George McClellan's measure as a man, and found him wanting. Knowing McClellan to be timid, he counted on him to do something really stupid. He was not disappointed.

Those who saw Lee that evening found him calm, even cheerful. Nearly everyone else was jittery. Having been through several battles already, both armies knew what lay ahead. From private to general, most would have agreed that waiting was harder than fighting. Nervous pickets—guards posted in front of each army—shot at anything that moved, including skunks and rabbits. In the Union camp, a dog barked. A startled soldier sprang to his feet, knocked over a stack of rifles, and set the whole camp to shooting at shadows. A Rebel spoke for his comrades during those long hours: "I wished the battle was done." A gentle rain began to fall, turning into a downpour by midnight. The sleepless armies lay in mud, watching the sky brighten in the east.

Dawn, Wednesday, September 17, 1862. The rain stopped, leaving the fields shrouded in mist. Gradually, as the sun rose, the mist cleared. McClellan's guns began to roar, heralding the battle. His plan was perfect, on paper. It called for simultaneous attacks at both ends of the Confederate line, forcing Lee to pull reinforcements from the center. At the critical moment, a third attack would smash through the weakened center and destroy the Confederates. But Lee had guessed right: McClellan did something stupid. He ignored his own plan. Rather than fight a single coordinated battle, he fought three separate ones, allowing Lee to shift his forces as needed. Nevertheless, the Army of Northern Virginia barely escaped annihilation.

The Union First Corps led off against the Confederate left. Its commander, Major General Joseph Hooker, rode with the first wave. Passing through a patch of woods, he noticed flashes of light in the cornfield: the sun glinting off bayonets. Thousands of Rebels were standing in the corn, thinking themselves invisible. Hooker halted the advance and called for artillery support.

Three dozen cannons opened fire at once. The shelling was so intense that witnesses claimed to have heard one gun every second for fifteen minutes. The cornfield erupted with clods of earth, cornstalks, and human parts flung helter-skelter. A Union officer saw a cannonball strike a Rebel, and "an arm go 30 feet into the air and fall back again. . . . It was awful."[14]

Men in butternut ran to the rear, trying to escape the hail of death. Lee was nearby and saw some of them. Asked where he was going, one replied, "Goin' to the rear."

"Leave your comrades and your flag at such a time?" asked Lee.

"Look'ee here, General . . . I'm a leetle the durndest demoralized Reb you ever seen!"

Lee let him pass, but another man did not get off so easily. Seeing him dragging a stolen pig, Lee became furious. He sent him to Jackson under armed guard, with orders to have him shot at once. Stonewall, however, needed every man he could get. He put the thief in the front line, where he earned a pardon for bravery.[15]

The cornfield became a slaughter pen. Men lost control, some weeping, some screaming, and some bursting into hysterical laughter. Fighting at close quarters, soldiers went at one another with bayonets and clubbed rifles. They rolled on the ground, punching, biting, choking, scratching. Cannon smoke blanketed the area, covering the sweating men with an oily black film. It was so thick that you could not tell friend from foe a foot away; Rebel sergeants told their men to lie down and "look for the blue britches under the smoke." Good advice, only it did not always help. Union and Confederate regiments shot hundreds of their own men in the confusion.

No participant ever sees a battle in its entirety, nor even a small fraction of it. Battle is essentially a personal experience. The participant is not watching a sporting contest, but is in a "game" of life and death. Those who fought in the cornfield recalled it differently. What they recalled was highly personal and colored by emotion. It was not the "big picture" of the history books, but the small, human experiences that soldiers carry with them for the rest of their lives.

A private in the Sixth George regiment saw six cows stampede in his direction. "I remember I was more afraid just then of being run over by a cow than of being hit by a bullet," he wrote. Nearby,

John B. Gordon, a lawyer by profession, rose to become one of the finest corps commanders in the Army of Northern Virginia.

a Yankee dove for cover; moments later, a trembling puppy crawled into his shirt.[16]

Survival was purely a matter of luck. Men were hit by spent bullets, those that had lost their killing force but stung terribly. A shell ricocheted off the ground, passed between the seat of the pants of a Yankee horseman and his saddle, and kept going. A group of Rebels saw a shell land in their midst. They stood there, paralyzed with fear, watching the fuse burn. It burned out, but there was no explosion; the shell was a dud. A member of the Fifteenth Virginia regiment felt the wind of a bullet pass between his jaws as he gave the Rebel yell. "Boys," he cried, "I have to leave you. Going to the rear to look for that damned ball. Give 'em hell and my compliments."[17] A Yankee turned back when a bullet cut his belt, dropping his pants down around his ankles. He wore no drawers. Naked from the waist down, he hobbled along, while his regiment stood there laughing and bullets cracked overhead.

The battle seesawed back and forth, charge being met by countercharge. Finally, after three hours, the fighting ebbed. The Yankees held the cornfield, but it was no prize. Forty acres of corn had been trampled or blasted to bits. Bodies lay in heaps among the cornstalks. Bodies, largely Confederate, were draped over split-rail fences, shot while climbing over. Fleeing Rebels passed scores of their comrades lying on the ground in neat lines, all dead. In certain places, it was difficult to stand, since grass is slippery when soaked with blood. Asked the location of his division, Confederate general John Bell Hood looked over his shoulder and said, "Dead on the field!"[18] In all, over eight thousand men had been killed or wounded for nothing. History remembers this awful place as *the* Cornfield."

Major General Edwin V. Sumner ended the lull by hurling his Second Corps against the Confederate center. Moments before, a worried General Lee had ridden behind the sunken lane with some staff officers. As McClellan had predicted, Lee had weakened this position to reinforce his left. It now was paper thin.

Lee was near the Sixth Alabama regiment when its colonel, John B. Gordon, overheard him express concern. Not to worry, Gordon piped up. His men would hold the lane, or die trying. Lee nodded and rode off, hoping for the best. But for those who knew

Gordon, this was no idle boast. Thirty years old, he was a tall, wiry man with a goatee beard and a booming voice. A native of Georgia, he had begun the war as a captain, quickly rising to higher command; by the end, he would be one of Lee's most trusted field officers. Utterly fearless, Gordon was an inspiration in battle. "He's the most prettiest thing you ever did see on a field of fight," soldiers said. "It'ud put fight into a whipped chicken just to look at him."[19]

The Yankees got off to a bad start. Their lead division was advancing in parade-ground order, bands playing and flags waving, when it came to an apple orchard. Just then, a shell exploded amid a row of beehives, filling the air with angry insects. Bee stings had a greater effect than rifle bullets. "Rally to the flag, boys! Rally to the flag!" officers shouted. Few obeyed. Slapping their faces and flailing their arms, the attackers scattered. The attack came to an abrupt halt.

The Irish Brigade rushed in to fill the gap. Its four regiments, including New York's famed "Fighting 69th," advanced behind green battle flags decorated with golden shamrocks and harps. A magnificent sight, thought John Gordon. And what a pity to spoil it with bullets!

Proudly they marched, as if on Broadway. The defenders waited for them to come within range. "Steady, men, steady! Hold your fire!" Rebel officers cried. They were not to shoot until they could see the Yankees' belt buckles, and then to aim at these.

The Irish Brigade came closer, closer. One hundred feet. Sixty feet.

Fire!

Jets of orange flame lashed from the sunken lane. The advancing line was literally torn apart. Bullets struck with such force that soldiers were lifted off their feet and slammed to the ground. Some were hit seventeen times within a few seconds, riddled from head to foot with bullets. Gunners on both sides poured in a steady stream of solid shot and shells. In 1960 a boy searching the area for relics found a Confederate shell embedded nose to nose in a Union shell, proof of the fantastic firefight at the sunken lane.

Charge after charge was broken, only to be renewed by fresh units. John Gordon stood behind his regiment, shouting orders and encouragement. Cannonballs plowed the ground near him. Men fell on either side of him. But nothing touched him. "They can't hurt him," soldiers cried. "He's got a charmed life."[20] Then the first bullet went through the calf of his right leg, followed by one higher up. Since no bones were broken, he stood his ground, leaning on his sword. A third bullet pierced his left arm, and a fourth tore through his shoulder. He had done enough, men called, begging him to go to a field hospital. Gordon refused. He had given his word to General Lee and would fight as long as he could stay on his feet.

The Yankees were equally determined. Vowing to break through at any cost, the Fifth New Hampshire regiment put on "war paint." Smearing their sweaty faces with gunpowder, they gave an Indian war whoop and swept forward, joined by units from Pennsylvania and New York. Reaching high ground, they fired into the sunken lane below. It was like shooting fish in a barrel; the Rebels were jammed together so tightly that it was impossible to miss. A fifth bullet struck Gordon squarely in the face. *That* put him down. He fell forward, unconscious, landing with his face in his cap. He might have drowned in his own blood had a Yankee bullet not opened a drain hole in the cap.

Driven from their position after three hours, the Rebels retreated and regrouped closer to Sharpsburg. Union casualties numbered about three thousand. Confederate losses are unknown, but they were very high. A Yankee noted that dead butternuts lay so thick in the sunken lane that he could have walked its length on human flesh. After the battle, an old woman visited the site. Horrified, she asked God's mercy for those who lay in the "bloody lane." From then on, the sunken lane has been called Bloody Lane in memory of those who fell there.

Never before in American history was a war so close to being ended by one decisive blow. Having cracked the Confederate center, McClellan had the enemy at his mercy. Longstreet later admitted that ten thousand fresh Union troops would have destroyed the Army of Northern Virginia in an hour. McClellan had more than enough troops waiting in reserve. His generals urged him to use them at once. The Union rank and file knew the time had come, and said so; they wanted to go ahead and finish the job. But the Young Napoleon did nothing. He held back, claiming it would "not be prudent" to renew the attack in this sector.[21]

The action shifted to the Confederate right. To get at the defenders, Major General Ambrose E. Burnside had to cross the Antietam with his Twelfth Corps. That should have been easy. Although the creek is fifty feet wide, it is so shallow that troops could have waded across in several places. But no one thought to look for a ford, or to ask local farmers about an easier crossing downstream. Burnside decided to cross the stone bridge, which meant crowding his corps into a narrow space, making it an excellent target for those on the hillside across the way.

Each time the Twelfth Corps set foot on the bridge, it drew a withering fire. Confederate gunners, running short of cannonballs, fired fifteen-inch lengths of railroad track. These were plainly visible in flight, tumbling and twisting as they sped toward their destinations. After repeated tries, and heavy losses, Burnside's men finally stormed across. The Rebels fled toward Sharpsburg. It was no heroic retreat; far from it. "Oh, how I ran!" recalled Private John Dooley. "I was afraid of being struck in the back, and I frequently turned half around in running, so as to avoid if possible such a disgraceful wound."[22]

The Army of Northern Virginia was done for. Lee had no more reserves. His left was a shambles. His center was paper thin. His right flank had collapsed. Ammunition was short, and his men were groggy with fatigue. Lady Luck had given McClellan one last chance. All he had to do was support Burnside if called upon, as he had promised.

The Yankees were moving to the final assault when Major General A. P. Hill saved the day. One of Jackson's best officers, Hill

The bridge over Antietam Creek. On September 17, 1862, General Ambrose Burnside's Union troops tried to storm across the bridge several times, but the Confederates, dug in along the ridge in the background, threw them back with heavy losses.

had stayed behind to start the Harpers Ferry prisoners on their way to Southern jails. Knowing he was needed on the battle-field, Hill marched his division the seventeen miles to Sharpsburg at foot-cavalry speed. Burnside's officers saw them coming but mistook them for their own reinforcements. The Rebels wore blue, having exchanged their tattered uniforms for new Yankee ones; they even carried the Stars and Stripes. They came to within a few yards of the advancing Yankees, then cut loose with everything they had. Burnside fell back to the bridge and called for help. The Young Napoleon refused. The Twelfth Corps recrossed the bridge. The Battle of Sharpsburg (Antietam) was over.

General A. P. Hill was one of the boldest field officers in the Confederate service. Wearing his famous red flannel shirt, he saved the day at Sharpsburg, forcing Union general Ambrose Burnside to retreat across Antietam Creek.

The sun set, a blood red disk glowing in the smoky haze. In twelve hours of combat, Confederate and Union casualties totaled 22,712, of whom 1,546 Rebels and 2,108 Yankees died in action. There had never been anything like it before, nor has there since: September 17, 1862, is still the bloodiest day in American history.

Exhausted as they were, neither Johnny Reb nor Billy Yank slept soundly that night. Mostly, they sat around campfires, trying to calm down. Sometimes, they joined in a favorite song. It was a sentimental song, but it said what soldiers felt in their hearts:

> *Do they miss me at home, do they miss me?*
> *'Twould be an assurance most dear*
> *To know that this moment some loved one*
> *Were saying, 'I wish he were here';*
> *To feel that the group at the fireside*
> *Were thinking of me as I roam.*
> *Oh, yes, 'twould be joy beyond measure*
> *To know that they miss me at home.*

Those who nodded off for a couple of minutes might awaken screaming; the day's experiences haunted their dreams, and would do so for years afterward. Those out on official business had real-life nightmares. One of Jackson's aides, Colonel Henry Kyd Douglas, was on an errand for his chief. The scene burned itself into his soul. He rode over "a veritable field of blood, the dead and dying lay as thick over it as harvest sheaves. . . . My horse trembled under me in terror, looking at the ground, sniffing the scent of blood, stepping falteringly as a horse will over or by dead human flesh; afraid to stand still, hesitating to go on, his animal instinct shuddering at this cruel human mystery."[23]

The dead were lucky, if they went quickly. The ordeal of the wounded had only just begun. Altogether, 17,292 men had been wounded, and all required attention. The moment the guns fell silent, their shrieks and moans filled the night air. Some cried for help or water; losing blood makes you very thirsty. Others cried, "Mother! Mother!" or called for wives and sweethearts. Pickets on both sides arranged informal truces to allow stretcher bearers to pick them up.

The field hospitals were hellish. Surgeons, their clothes stained with blood, their sleeves rolled up to their elbows, worked by lantern light. There were so many wounded that they had to ration their time and energy. Those who could be helped waited, usually for hours, on stretchers outside the operating tents. All the while, they heard screams from inside and saw amputated limbs being taken away in buckets. At one hospital, a converted farmhouse, surgeons threw arms and legs out the window into the yard. The pile became several feet high, nearly level with the windowsill.

Wounded Rebels lay beside wounded Yankee prisoners, and vice versa. Surgeons did not discriminate, but helped everyone in need. As they waited their turn, enemies discovered their common humanity. Their causes were different, but underneath they had the same feelings and needs. They spoke of home, recalled past fights, and complimented one another's bravery. When one was thirsty, the other brought water, if he could move about. Soldiers held each other's hands, giving comfort despite their own pain. "We were no longer enemies," a Georgian recalled, "but American soldiers who believe in extending a helping hand to those in distress."[24]

Men with fatal wounds were put under trees to await the end. Some grew impatient. One fellow, told that he would be dead in a few hours, decided these were not worth living in pain; he shot himself. Or a soldier asked a comrade for a special favor. A member of the First Delaware regiment recalled how a lieutenant dealt with a comrade who begged, "for the love of God," to be put out of his misery. The lieutenant drew his pistol, put it to his friend's right ear, and pulled the trigger.[25] Such things happen in war. How often is uncertain, since there are rules against "mercy killings." But they do happen, and are not regarded as murder by the rank and file.

Women helped the wounded on both sides. In Sharpsburg, Rebel surgeons were assisted by local women, all loyal Unionists. On the Union side, Clara Barton arrived with thirty volunteers and a wagon loaded with medical supplies. Nicknamed "the Angel of the Battlefield," Barton was a trained nurse who went on to found the American Red Cross in 1881. At Sharpsburg, she acted as both nurse and surgeon. One soldier, for example, was in agony with a bullet in his jaw. She knelt down, cradled his head in her lap, and removed it with her pocketknife. Just like that, without anesthetic! Later, while raising a man's head to give him a drink of water, she felt a tugging at her left sleeve. A bullet had passed through her sleeve, into the man's chest, killing him instantly. That tragedy moved her deeply. She never patched the hole in her dress.[26]

Lee, too, was busy. At dusk, he called a council of war to discuss the situation. His generals were gloomy, knowing how narrowly they had avoided disaster. Each in turn reported on conditions in his sector and recommended a retreat before daybreak. Lee heard them out, then issued his orders. The dead were to be buried and the wounded evacuated. Shattered units were to be combined and the men given whatever food was available. But there would be no retreat. The army would stand its ground, and if McClellan wanted to fight, he would give him a bellyful in the morning. This was not just stubbornness on Lee's part. By holding on, he meant to show McClellan that his army still had plenty of fight in it. More: It would show his own men that they could take anything the Yankees threw at them.

Clara Barton was known as "the Angel of the Battlefield" because of the way she tended the wounded at Sharpsburg and elsewhere. She later founded the American Red Cross.

Both armies expected another battle. Johnny Reb was sure it would be his last. Billy Yank looked forward to finishing the job. The Young Napoleon was content to write letters about his marvelous achievement; he called the battle "a masterpiece of art."[27] September 18 passed without incident. Union soldiers grumbled; once again, their chief had not followed through. And, once again, their sacrifices had been in vain. "I have lost all confidence in him," a soldier wrote, echoing his comrades. "He is nothing but an imbecile, a coward, or a traitor."[28]

That afternoon, Lee gave the order to withdraw. Throughout the night, and far into the next day, the Army of Northern Virginia trudged toward the Potomac. It had crossed into Maryland with bands playing and flags waving. It left in a different mood. If anyone, even in jest, sang "Maryland, My Maryland," he was shouted down with "Damn My Maryland!" For those who still felt like singing, the favorite was "Carry Me Back to Old Virginny." Lee sat astride Traveller in midstream. As the last units started across, he heaved a sigh of relief and said, "Thank God."

Each side won something and lost something at Sharpsburg. The Rebels had performed magnificently. Yet, having beaten back a superior enemy, inflicting heavier losses than they suffered, they still lost the campaign. They had little to show for the invasion, save pride in themselves and hard-won experience. The Yankees halted the Rebel offensive, proving themselves the equal of Lee's veterans, yet failed to deliver the decisive blow. Nevertheless, Sharpsburg was enough of a victory to justify President Lincoln's next move.

Lincoln had been carrying the Emancipation Proclamation in his pocket since July. On September 22, five days after the battle, he met with his cabinet in the White House. During the Maryland campaign, he said, he had vowed that if God gave the Union a victory, he would take it as his signal to issue the proclamation. Well, Lincoln continued, "God has decided this question in favor of the slaves."[29]

Next day, the Emancipation Proclamation was printed in Northern newspapers. It declared that unless the Rebel states returned to the Union by January 1, 1863, their slaves "shall be then, thenceforward, and forever free." Lincoln's words promised much but delivered nothing; in fact, they were a proclamation without emancipation. The Emancipation Proclamation did not

President Abraham Lincoln and General George B. McClellan met at Sharpsburg soon after the battle. Lincoln tried to persuade McClellan to pursue Robert E. Lee's battered army, but the general always found fresh excuses for not moving.

free a single slave. Blacks in the loyal Border States—Maryland, Kentucky, Missouri—were not included, nor were those in enemy territory occupied by Union troops. In short, where Lincoln could have freed slaves, he did not. And where he wanted to free them, he could not.[30]

No matter. Black people did not care about the fine print. The moment the proclamation appeared, the slave "grapevine" spread the word. Slaves began to enforce emancipation by themselves. Jubilant blacks headed for the Union lines. They came on foot, carrying their belongings on their backs and leading their children by the hand. They came in the thousands on horseback, or in wagons "liberated" from their masters.

Black men began fighting for their freedom. Leaders like Frederick Douglass had demanded the right to serve ever since Fort Sumter. "Once let the black man get upon his person the brass letters, U.S.; let him get an eagle on his button, and a musket on his shoulder and bullets in his pocket," said Douglass, and "there is no power on earth that can deny that he has earned the right to citizenship."[31] The Emancipation Proclamation allowed precisely that. By the war's end, 186,017 blacks (131,111 of them former slaves) had served in the Union armies. Freedom, for them, was not a gift, but something they earned with their blood.

Southerners were outraged. Lincoln's proclamation, they believed, had carried John Brown's work a step further. It "proved" that black Republicans wanted a slave rebellion. "Lincoln the fiend" was accused of trying to stir up a civil war within the Civil War. For that, he belonged in hell. A poem, "Lincoln's Epitaph," reflected the white mood:

> *Beneath this stone, corrupt and stinking,*
> *Repose the bones of Abraham Lincoln.*
> *He freed the niggers, and for his pains*
> *His own soul is now in chains.*[32]

By a stroke of the pen, Lincoln strengthened the moral cause of the Union at home and abroad. In a way, he owed it all to the Rebel commander. Lee's invasion of Maryland had produced results far different than any he had imagined when he set out. He had fought well; he had humiliated the Union's leading general; but Sharpsburg proved that a battle's outcome cannot be measured purely in military terms. Without intending to, Lee helped seal the doom of slavery and allowed Lincoln to change the nature of the Civil War. Beginning that bloody September of 1862, it would be a war for the Union *and* a struggle for freedom.

V ✦ WINTER OF DISCONTENT

"Ain't you frightened,

General?" Old Pete asked.

"Wait till they come a

little nearer, and they shall

either scare me or I'll scare

them," Stonewall replied.

"Jackson, what are you

going to do with those people

over there?"

"Sir, we will give them

the bayonet!"

—Fredericksburg, Virginia,

December 13, 1862

(from *Gray Fox,* by

Burke Davis)

After recrossing the Potomac, Lee camped in the Shenandoah Valley west of Harpers Ferry. The next two months were spent in resting, resupplying, and reinforcing the Army of Northern Virginia. The army thrived, and soon was fit as ever. By the time the army would march again, it would number seventy-eight thousand men.

Those months were among the saddest in Lee's life. On October 26, 1862, his secretary delivered reports to his tent and left after a few minutes. The general was calm and businesslike, as usual, and the secretary had no reason to suspect that anything was wrong. He had not gone far when, realizing he had forgotten a document, he returned. Since Lee's aides never announced themselves, and no guards were posted, he walked in. What he saw took his breath away. The general was sitting on the edge of his camp bed, an open letter in his hand, crying. The secretary withdrew silently.

Lee had just learned that his favorite daughter, Annie, had died at the age of twenty-three. Only when he was alone was he able to break down. He revealed his feelings in a letter to his daughter Mary: "In the quiet hours of the night, where there is nothing to lighten the full weight of my grief, I feel as if I should be overwhelmed."[1] Still, one in his position could not afford to be overwhelmed. Too much depended upon him. Too many people looked to him for leadership. So Lee hid his grief, pulled himself together, and carried on.

Another kind of news came a week later. McClellan was out! Disgusted with his failures, President Lincoln had fired him; he would never hold another command. Lee had gotten to know the Young Napoleon so well during the last nine months that it was almost like losing a friend. "I hate to part with McClellan," he told Longstreet, "for we always understood each other so well. I fear they may continue to make these changes until they find someone I don't understand."[2]

The Army of the Potomac's next chief was surely not that man. Ambrose E. Burnside was a jolly fellow with fantastic whiskers; those whiskers, later called burnsides, or sideburns, are his only claim to fame. Although a West Pointer and a Mexican War veteran, he was not in the same league as Lee, Jackson, and Longstreet. And he was the first to say so. When told he was McClellan's successor, Burnside objected because he felt unsuited to high command. His appointment showed that President Lincoln still had a lot to learn about the military.

Nevertheless, Burnside had a pretty good plan. The idea was to mass 125,000 men opposite Fredericksburg on the Rappahannock River, midway between Washington and Richmond. This charming colonial city had been George Washington's boyhood home, where he supposedly cut down his father's cherry tree but could not tell a lie. Once across the river, Burnside would make a beeline for the Confederate capital, while Lee was still in the Valley. Even if Lee moved in time, he would be outnumbered and forced to fight in open country. Everything, therefore, depended upon speed. Any delay in crossing the Rappahannock would allow Lee to concentrate and dig in along the ridge behind Fredericksburg.

The first part of the plan went like clockwork. Burnside reached the northern bank of the Rappahannock during the third week in November. He had moved so

General Ambrose Burnside was famous for his whiskers, nicknamed "sideburns." Although an able soldier, he was not in the same league as Robert E. Lee and Stonewall Jackson.

quickly that Lee was taken completely by surprise. Burnside could have crossed in one night; there were several fords upstream, and a Union officer saw a cow wade across the river at one spot. But he decided to wait for the army's pontoons, wooden floats thirty feet long over which planks were laid to form a floating bridge. Unfortunately, his staff had no idea where the army's pontoons were, or where to look for them. Frantic orders went out from Burnside's headquarters. But by the time the pontoons were found and brought to the river early in December, Lee's army had arrived at Fredericksburg to defend the city.

Fearing the worst, townspeople left their homes. Refugees fled southward, clutching their meager possessions. Mothers carried little children in one arm and a bundle of food or clothing in the other, while the elderly hobbled along as best they could. Meanwhile, Union and Confederate pickets traded insults. A typical exchange went something like this:

"Hallo, Yank," a Rebel shouted from Fredericksburg.

"Hallo, Secesh!" a Yank answered from across the river.

"When you coming over, bluecoat?"

"When we get ready, butternut."

"What do you want?"

"Want Fredericksburg."

"Don't you wish you could get it!"[3]

Yankees laughed when a picket asked why Rebels looked like tramps. The Rebels laughed at the reply: "We-uns don't put on our good clothes to butcher hogs!"[4]

On the night of December 10, Burnside's engineers finally began to build three bridges. It was pitch dark, the river shrouded in fog. Unable to see beyond the tips of their fingers, the engineers worked slowly, anchoring one pontoon beside another. Lee had posted a brigade of Mississippi infantry along the waterfront for just this occasion. The Mississippians aimed "by ear," firing at the sound of hammering and sawing. Shots rang out, followed by a scream and a splash, then the patter of feet running on wood. A routine soon developed. Engineers dashed to the end of their bridge, worked feverishly for a couple of minutes, then raced back before the bullets got too close. This went on until daybreak gave the Rebels better targets.

Burnside ordered his heaviest guns into action the moment the fog lifted. Their mission: level Fredericksburg, and get those snipers!

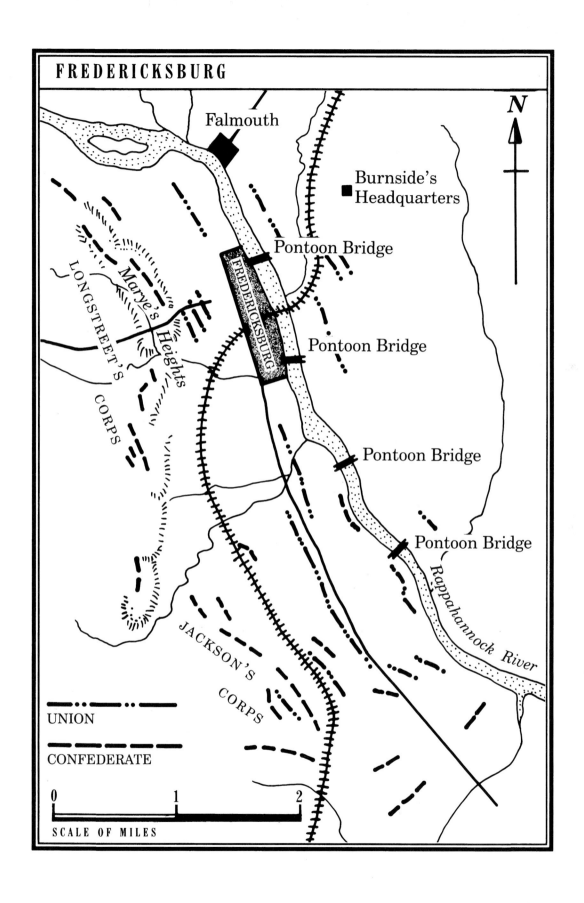

FREDERICKSBURG

Falmouth

Burnside's
Headquarters

N

Pontoon Bridge

FREDERICKSBURG

Marye's Heights

LONGSTREET'S

CORPS

Pontoon Bridge

Pontoon Bridge

Pontoon Bridge

Rappahannock River

JACKSON'S

CORPS

UNION

CONFEDERATE

0   1   2

SCALE OF MILES

Union shells tore the city apart. Fires raged, sending clouds of blazing cinders into the sky. Walls and chimneys collapsed into the streets. Chunks of mortar and pieces of wood flew about like shrapnel. Although most of the inhabitants had fled, a few remained behind, including an elderly woman. A Mississippian saw her calmly walking down a street, amid bursting shells and crumbling buildings. She seemed to find it all very interesting, peering through holes in walls and watching solid shot bounce along the street. Her lack of concern for her safety gave him courage. "I felt as if it really would not do to avoid a fire which was merely interesting, and not at all appalling, to a woman; so I stiffened my spinal column as well as I could and rode straight down the street."[5]

Sergeant Buck Denman, Twenty-first Mississippi Infantry, met an even more adventurous female. A giant of a fellow who hunted bears for a living, Buck was in his sniper position behind the corner of a house. He was about to pull the trigger when a girl of about three skipped out of an alley and began to chase a shell that was rolling along the sidewalk, its fuse hissing. Buck wiped his hand across his eyes, thinking he was seeing a vision of his own daughter. But no; there *was* a child about to grab a shell! Dropping his rifle, he ran out, scooped her up in his arms, and ducked around the corner in the nick of time.[6] Her name is lost to history. But, later, she was in the Confederate front line during the fiercest fighting.

The shelling had little effect, other than to wreck the city and drive the defenders underground. The moment it stopped, the Mississippians, who had hidden in cellars and rifle pits, continued their sniping. Finally, a company of bluecoats rowed across the river on the pontoons. As soon as they set up a beachhead, other troops followed. Among them was twelve-year-old Robert Hendershot, a drummer in the Seventh Michigan regiment; Civil War drummers were as young as nine.

"Get out; you can't go!" an officer yelled as Robert scrambled aboard a pontoon.

"I want to go," said the boy.

"No, you will get shot. Out with you."

Robert leaped overboard, but clung to the side and hitched a ride across, unseen. Coming ashore, he picked up a rifle near a dead soldier and rushed into town, where he found a wounded Confederate.

"Surrender!" Robert cried, pointing the weapon at his head. The fellow obeyed.[7]

By sundown, Robert and the others had flushed out all the snipers. What they did not know was that Lee never intended to hold Fredericksburg. He had moved to the hills above the town and ordered the Mississippians to withdraw gradually, letting the Union think they had won after a savage fight. But it was a trick to make them overconfident.

The bridges were completed by sundown. Then, and throughout the following day, December 12, the Yankees crossed the river, led by bands playing patriotic tunes. The instant they stopped, Southern bands on the hillsides welcomed them with "Dixie"; Rebels even threw their hats into the air in greeting. The one thing they did not do was open fire. Lee had over two hundred guns on the ridge overlooking the river. He could easily have bombarded the city once it was occupied. But he did nothing. Most Yankees thought he was low on ammunition, or about to retreat in the face of such heavy odds. An army old-timer disagreed. Pointing to the ridge, he said: "They *want* us to get in. Getting out won't be quite so smart and easy. You'll see if it will."[8]

Burnside's men completed the ruin of Fredericksburg that night. As officers watched, giving silent approval, soldiers looted private homes. Furniture was burned for heat and cooking.

Union pontoon bridges below Fredericksburg, Virginia, December 1862. Such bridges were made by anchoring flat-bottomed barges next to one another and laying a roadway of wooden planks across their tops.

Leather-bound books were trampled in the mud, and paintings slashed with bayonets. Drunks staggered along, holding stolen bottles of wine and whiskey. Laughing soldiers danced in women's dresses, or paraded in female hats and underwear, to the cheers of their comrades. For many, it would be their last fling.

December 13 dawned cold and damp. As they formed ranks, the Union troops realized what lay in store for them. Lee held a seven-mile line along the high ground west of town. Jackson and Stuart commanded on the right. The Confederate strongpoint, however, was on the left. There Longstreet's corps was posted on Marye's Heights, a steep hill crowned by artillery. At the base of the hill, facing the city across an open plain, was a sunken road. Unlike Bloody Lane at Sharpsburg, this road was deep and protected by a stone wall. Old Pete's men knelt five deep behind the wall, ready for anything. Burnside meant to assault these positions head-on. He apparently could not imagine what would happen to his men. But they could. "Boys, we are in for it now," they muttered.

The assault began on the Confederate right. The blue lines surged forward. The Rebels fired, dropping them by the hundreds. But they re-formed and came on again, and again. At last, they punched a hole in the Confederate line, only to be driven back by Stonewall's reserves. They ran for their lives, as the Southerners poured volley after volley into their backs.

Watching from a hilltop observation post, Lee knew it had been a close call. Several young staff officers, however, saw only the "glory." As the Yankees fled, they cheered and shook hands. Lee turned and uttered one of his best-known remarks: "It is well that war is so terrible, or we should get too fond of it." This did not reveal a newer, bloodthirstier side of his character. He was not smiling, nor did he mean that war was fun. The remark was a gentle put-down, his way of telling hotheads not to be so happy about killing.

Lee himself had a brush with death. He was peering through his field glasses when a cannon exploded nearby, killing its crew. A chunk of metal weighing about seven hundred pounds landed just behind him. Lee glanced at it for a moment, then calmly went about his business as if nothing had happened.

The action shifted to the Confederate left. At each assault, so many Yankees fell that the ground resembled a blue carpet. Lee became worried when he saw the attacks renewed with such determination. Longstreet reassured him. "General," he said, "if you put every man now on the other side of the Potomac on that field to approach me over the same line, and give me plenty of ammunition, I will kill them all before they reach my line."[9] He meant it.

Six times the Yankees charged Marye's Heights. Six times they were hurled back with dreadful losses. As they crossed the plain, Rebel artillery tore gaping holes in their ranks. Nearing the stone wall, they heard cries from unseen officers on the other side: "'Tention! Commence fi-ir-ing!" Johnny Rebs rose from behind the wall and blazed away. It was like a continuous burst of machine-gun fire, the men in the rear passing loaded rifles to their comrades in front. Old Pete said the Yankees fell "like the steady dripping of rain from the eaves of a house."[10]

Survivors hugged the ground, taking cover behind the dead. Some actually piled bodies in front of them, forming a wall of flesh. Passing through the wreckage of earlier assaults, fresh troops were urged to get down by the survivors. Some did, and lived, at least a little while longer. Most did not, and were literally blown away. Those who were pinned down had to stay put until sundown. Those hours dragged by like an eternity. To impress the Yankees with their marksmanship, snipers on the hillside shot at anything that moved, including stray chickens. Rebels taunted them with catcalls: "Take off them boots, Yank! Come out of them clothes; we're gwine to have them! Come on, blue-bellies, we want them blankets! Bring them rations along!"[11] That night, odd patches of white appeared on the battlefield. The Johnny Rebs, shivering in their rags, had stripped the enemy dead, leaving their naked bodies in the moonlight.

Buck Denman and the child he rescued were at the sunken road when the Yankees charged and throughout the battle that followed. Buck and his friends had their hands full with the enemy, but were equally concerned about her safety. Fierce fighters one moment, they became tender nursemaids the next. They passed her from hand to hand, taking turns patting her and comforting her amid the exploding shells. Afterward, at night, they wrestled with each other for the privilege of feeding her and keeping her warm under their blankets.

Fredericksburg was a Union catastrophe. The Army of the Potomac suffered 12,653 casualties, compared to 5,309 for the Army of Northern Virginia. Next day, Burnside became hysterical with remorse. His soldiers were calling him a "poppycorn general," a fool with less sense than a toad. Ranting about saving his honor, he vowed to lead a suicide charge against Marye's Heights. His aides persuaded him to order a retreat instead. On the night of

December 14–15, he recrossed the Rappahannock, taking his pontoons with him.

Only then did the Rebels return to Fredericksburg. To honor its gallant stand, the Twenty-first Mississippi was selected to lead the way back into the city. The men assembled, but stayed put; the regimental flag could not be found. Buck Denman stood with his company, the child in his arms. Suddenly he stepped to the front, held her over his head, and shouted: "Forward, Twenty-first, here are your colors!" The whole line sprang forward.

They were marching through the burned-out streets when a scream pierced the air. The next thing Buck knew, a young woman was fainting right in front of him. It was the child's mother, frantic with worry about her daughter. Buck caught her as she fell, set her down gently, and put the child on her chest. Then he collected his fee: "She was most the prettiest thing I ever looked at, and her eyes were shut; and—and—I hope God'll forgive me, but I kissed her just once."[12]

Buck's commanders were in no kissing mood. Lee was depressed. Confederate newspapers were hailing him as a military genius and his victory as the end of the war. Fredericksburg *was* a

Union army winter quarters along the Rappahannock River opposite Fredericksburg, 1862. Whole forests were cut down to build log cabins such as this one, called Pine Cottage by its inhabitants.

splendid victory; that he knew. He also knew it was a hollow victory. He had defeated the Army of the Potomac, but had not destroyed it. The war would continue.

Stonewall Jackson was furious when he saw the ruined city. His eyes blazed with that blue light his foot cavalry knew so well. "What shall we do, General?" an aide asked him. "Kill them," he growled, pointing across the river. "Kill them all, sir! Kill every man!"[13]

When Abraham Lincoln learned of Fredericksburg, he moaned: "If there is a worse place than Hell, I am in it."[14] But hell or no hell, he would not quit. The Union must be saved regardless of cost. He dismissed Burnside and started over again.

The armies settled into winter quarters. It was to be a winter of discontent.

The Rebels camped in the hills near Fredericksburg, the Yankees at Falmouth directly across the river. Those camps changed the face of the land. Both armies cut down whole forests for building materials and firewood. Soldiers lived in log cabins arranged in neat rows along company and regimental streets; Lee Boulevard was the main street in the Confederate camp. Cabins were furnished with handmade tables, chairs, and bunks; mattresses were sacks stuffed with straw. Bayonets driven into the ground served as candlesticks; if candles were scarce, soldiers used "slush lamps," containers of hog fat with a piece of rag for a wick. Lastly, a wooden signboard with the cabin's name was hung over each cabin door. Among these names were Swine Hotel, Hole in the Wall, Devil's Inn, Yahoos, and The House That Jack Built.

It rained constantly, turning the camp streets into rivers of red mud. Soldiers waded in mud, often losing their shoes in the ooze. Passing cavalry units splattered them from head to toe; more than one cavalryman was dragged from his mount and given an infantryman's view of the mud. Firewood was so damp that cabins filled with smoke, making the inhabitants cough and retch. "We are in a liquid state," Lee wrote his wife, "up to our knees in mud." A few days later, following another downpour, he corrected himself: "We have mud up to our eyes."[15]

Both armies likened the winter of 1862–1863 to that of 1777–1778, when the Continental Army suffered at Valley Forge, Pennsylvania. The Rebels saw themselves as George Washington's devoted men, with the Yankees as the British. With good reason. The enemy had plenty of supplies, eight hundred tons a day brought by railroad and wagon train. Rebels had nowhere near that amount. Northern Virginia had been picked clean of supplies, and the South could not produce enough to meet basic needs. Early in the war, Lincoln had clamped a blockade on all Southern seaports. Nevertheless, some things came through the blockade aboard swift "blockade runners," while others were landed in Mexico and carried across the Mississippi River. But however they arrived, imports were so expensive that only the wealthy could afford them.

Escaped prisoners gave vivid descriptions of life in the Rebel camp. Lee's men, one wrote, "are ill-dressed, ill-equipped, and ill-provided, a set of ragamuffins that a man is ashamed to be seen among, even when he is a prisoner and can't help it."[16] One in three had no shoes. Men wore "Longstreet slippers," bits of cowhide wrapped around their feet; unfortunately, ice formed on the bottoms, turning the slippers into ice skates. Blankets were made of carpets cut into strips. But even these were scarce, forcing three or four men to sleep together to share body warmth, and lice. Having not washed for weeks, due to a lack of soap, they also stank; yet everyone stank alike, so no one noticed. Men longed for the overcoats they had thrown away during the summer. Now, if a guard left his post, he gave his coat to his relief and ran to his cabin to escape the biting cold. Everyone, including generals, stuffed his shirt with newspapers for added warmth.

Hunger was the worst enemy. It was no accident that Johnny Rebel called his winter quarters Camp Starvation. The daily ration was steadily reduced, until it consisted of a pound of moldy flour and a quarter pound of rancid bacon; "coffee" was anything that turned water brown.

Johnny Reb became ravenous, willing to try anything to fill his belly. Members of the First South Carolina regiment killed rats—big fat ones—to see what they were like when broiled. Not bad, some said, claiming they "tasted like young squirrel."[17] Members of the Twenty-second Georgia regiment found more appealing game. Brigadier General William Mahone kept some turkeys in a pen outside his tent. They were for himself and visiting generals, not to be shared with common soldiers. His soldiers, however, believed in sharing. One morning, the pen was found empty. From then on, the question "Who stole Mahone's turkeys?" was always good for a laugh.[18]

Poor diet made for poor health. Doctors noted an increase in diseases like pneumonia, typhoid fever, and scurvy, caused by a lack of vitamin C found in fresh fruits and vegetables. Diarrhea claimed its share of victims every week.

Nevertheless, winter quarters was not all misery. Soldiers had lots of time on their hands, and they used it in countless nonmilitary ways. Off-duty hours were spent in bull sessions, discussing everything from the war to girls. Army slang was colorful and expressive. To be embarrassed, for example, was to be "squashmolished" or "flummoxed." A few Civil War words are still in use, having become part of the American language. Take the term "cool," used today for a steady person in control of their emotions. In 1862 a brave soldier was said to be "so cool water froze in his canteen."[19]

Soldiers read anything they could get their hands on. Many had Bibles, and used them; newspapers were always in demand. Their favorite reading, however, was letters from home. Mail was the soldier's only link to his loved ones. Receiving mail regularly showed that they still thought of him, still loved him though he was far away. The absence of mail was sheer torture. "Martha," an Alabamian wrote his wife, "I haint got nary letter from you for sometime when you fail to Rite . . . it ceeps mee uneasy all the time."[20] Although his spelling and punctuation leave much to be desired, his meaning is clear. Others advertised for wives in hometown newspapers. One soldier wanted a good woman

> *To calm his sorrows*
> *And soothe his woes,*
> *Cook his victuals*
> *And wash his clothes.*

She must be under fifty, have all her teeth, have feet smaller than size eleven, and be sweet-tempered.[21]

Things were tough, and a sense of humor was needed to make life bearable. A hearty laugh raised the spirits. Johnny Reb poked fun at everything and everyone, except Marse Robert. An officer with a big mustache might be greeted with: "Take them mice out o' your mouth! Take 'em out! No use to say they aint thar; see their tails hanging out!" But the infantryman's favorite target was a cavalryman in high boots. "Come up out o' them boots!" he would shout. "Come out! I know you're in thar; see your arms stickin' out!"[22] One way to cause excitement was to put a handful of cartridges in a cloth bag, lower it down the chimney of a log cabin at night, and wait for the explosions to drive the inhabitants into the cold. Or he could cover the chimney with boards and let the smoke do the rest.[23]

Soldiers in both armies enjoyed games that are today reserved for children. Letters reveal that Confederate soldiers played leapfrog, Johnny-on-the-pony, hopscotch, marbles, and blindman's bluff; and they spun tops. Adult activities included boxing, wrestling, and "hot jackets," in which opponents whipped each other with hickory switches. Some men liked bowling, with six-pound cannonballs. Baseball also had its fans. The ball was a walnut wrapped in wool yarn, the bat a tree branch cut to size. Unlike today's nine-man team, there was originally no limit to team size; the Ninth Louisiana regiment fielded a hundred men at a time. And instead of three bases, they used as few as two and as many as four.

But nothing compared to the snowball fights at Fredericksburg. Players turned out by companies, regiments, and divisions. Each had a knapsack full of snowballs that had been packed tight, sprinkled with water, and left out overnight. Led by their commanders, thousands advanced with the Rebel yell, while bugles blared and drums beat the long roll. Old Pete joined in, leading a regimental charge and taking his share of hits. Color and rank vanished as black slaves and white masters pelted one another with snowballs. Officers were pulled from their horses and their faces washed in snow. Not even the commanding general was immune. Once, while leaving his tent, Lee stepped into the middle of an all-army snowball fight. He was hit several times, but was unhurt. He was lucky. During that winter, one man lost an eye; black eyes, loose teeth, sprained ankles, and broken bones were common. This happened, a participant noted, "all in *fun!*" In Georgia, two men died in a snowball fight.[24]

One day, the armies gathered on the hillsides on either side of the Rappahannock to witness a musical battle. A Union band led off with "John Brown's Body," "The Battle Hymn of the Republic," and "The Star-Spangled Banner." A Confederate band answered with Southern favorites like "Dixie" and "The Yellow Rose of Texas." Each time their band played, thousands cheered and sang along. It went on like this until sundown, one band challenging the other, and no one firing a shot. Finally, a Union bugler played "Home, Sweet Home." Soldiers, 150,000 of them, tried to sing, but few could get out the words. "As the sweet sounds rose and fell on the evening air," a Yankee recalled, "all listened intently, and I don't believe there was a dry eye in all those assembled thousands."[25] The bugler finished, leaving both armies silently staring into the darkness.

At Fredericksburg, and elsewhere throughout the war, opponents had informal get-togethers. Johnny Reb and Billy Yank were

Soldiers everywhere spend a lot of time waiting. Here Union officers from Pennsylvania play poker.

still very much alike. They spoke the same language, took pride in the same history, and had the same ideas of fair play. Thus, it was not only natural, but sensible, for them to put the war aside whenever possible.

They made contact even with the Rappahannock flowing between them. It usually began with a "hollering" acquaintance. A picket would call out to ask if his opposite had anything to trade. Tobacco, scarce in the North, was plentiful in the South. Coffee and sugar were precious in the South, thanks to the blockade. But it is not easy to cross a wide river in wartime without getting shot. So, instead of going themselves, soldiers traded by remote control. They built hundreds of tiny boats, two to three feet long by six inches wide, complete with sails and rudders. On a breezy day, hundreds of these vessels could be seen gliding back and forth with their cargoes. The business was so reliable that Southern wives sent their men lists of things they needed: medicines, pocketknives, dressmaker's pins, sewing needles.

Enemies also met face to face. Rival officers once struck up a hollering friendship. The Confederates had invited some local girls to a dance, so a Rebel invited a Yankee acquaintance. He rowed him across the river after dark, lent him a suit of civilian clothes, and returned him safely before daylight. Another time, guards arrested two Yankees in civilian clothes and brought them to Colonel John B. Gordon. Technically, they were spies and could have been shot under the laws of war. Morally, however, they were under the protection of their hosts, who were honorable men. Having given their word that their guests would be safe, they could not allow an officer to break it. Gordon understood. He sent them back with a warning to stay away. Perhaps they did. But on several occasions, Rebels spent the night in the Yankee camp as officers' guests. If the guards knew of their presence, they kept quiet, or lied. One of their guard stations was known as "Outpost Liar."

Lee frowned on these doings, but never interfered. For the most part, they were harmless, and even did some good. His only objection was to a trade in Southern newspapers, which foolishly printed articles about his positions and troop movements. He, like his Northern foes, believed freedom of the press must be limited in time of war.

Napoléon said: "It is not men who make armies, but a man." The French emperor knew what he was talking about. Leadership is more than organizing armies and fighting battles. The man—the commanding general—gives an army its spirit and sense of purpose. If he is the right man, the army will try anything for him, serving against seemingly hopeless odds. If not, it will never perform to the best of its ability.

Robert E. Lee illustrates this simple truth. Not only did he lead the Army of Northern Virginia, he was also its father figure and friend. Lee had charisma, the ability to draw others to him by the magnetism of his personality. This did not come naturally, since he was a quiet, dignified person who some found cold and distant. But he worked hard at becoming the sort of man he knew his army needed.

We see him at his best during that winter at Fredericksburg. He deliberately chose to live simply as a way of building respect. No fancy uniforms for him! He wore no pistol or jeweled sword or silver spurs. Although any homeowner in Virginia would have been proud to have him sleep under his roof, Lee refused all invitations. He preferred his tent, even in the coldest weather. Once, an aide tried to get him indoors during a stormy night. No, Lee insisted, he

did not want to disturb the family. "It was entirely too pleasant for him, for he is never so uncomfortable as when comfortable," said the aide, dreading a night in the cold dampness.[26]

Lee's diet was as simple as his living quarters. His main meal usually consisted of fried bacon and boiled cabbage; sometimes, as a special treat, a cold sweet potato was added. If admirers sent gifts of food, these were given to the hospitals. His only luxury was allowing himself to be adopted by a stray hen. Each morning, she paced outside his tent until the flap was opened. She strutted in, laid an egg under his camp bed, and left, cackling proudly. When the army moved in the spring, she traveled in style, perched atop a wagon.

Lee seemed to thrive on hard living and little food. In letters to Mary, he said he had never felt better. But in March 1863 he caught a cold, followed by stabbing pains in his chest. That is when the doctors took charge, and forced him to go indoors. He wrote Mary, complaining they were "tapping me all over like an old steam boiler before condemning it."[27] He recovered. But what no one knew then was that he had probably suffered his first heart attack.

Like Napoléon, Lee had a fantastic memory for names and faces. He would sit astride Traveller, watching a regiment trudge through the mud. Recognizing a private, he waved or called him by name. The man straightened up, feeling himself grow ten feet tall in front of his comrades. A few well-chosen words could win over a

Robert E. Lee and his generals. From left to right are Wade Hampton, Jeb Stuart, Jubal Early, Joseph E. Johnston, John Bell Hood, Lee, A. P. Hill, Stonewall Jackson, James Longstreet, P. G. T. Beauregard, and John Hunt Morgan. From a lithograph done about 1865.

man for life. "Come in, Captain, and take a seat," he told a messenger who came to his tent. "I'm no captain, General; I'm nothing but a private," the fellow replied. Lee brushed the objection aside. "Come in, sir. Come in and take a seat. You ought to be a captain."[28]

Soldiers approached their commander freely. Once, a private broke ranks and came up to him. They had never met before, but they shook hands like old friends and fell into conversation. As the column passed, a soldier looked back to see his comrade, his hand resting on Traveller's neck, chatting with the general. Another time, a private sauntered over to Lee, saluted, and said he needed chewing tobacco. Lee never touched the stuff, but he did ask a member of his staff to give the fellow a chew.

Lee never spoke with bitterness, even of the enemy. The Yankees were always "those people," their commander always "that man." Johnny Reb, however, was addressed as "my boy," "my son," "my man," and "my friend."

Kind words got better results than sharp commands, Lee believed. There are many examples of how he acted on this belief. One is about a work detail digging a trench. "Good morning, my young friend. I feel sorry for you," Lee told the lieutenant in charge. "Why so, General?" "Because you have so much to do." Just like that: short and sweet. Speaking as a friend, he let the lieutenant know he expected a good day's work.[29]

Lee also knew that gestures could speak louder than words. Before one battle, he rode in front of the Confederate infantry. He gave no rousing speech; in fact, he said nothing. All he did was remove his hat, as if in church, or in the presence of someone he greatly respected. "*That* is the most eloquent address ever delivered!" a soldier said, turning to a comrade. Another advanced shouting, "Any man who will not fight after what Marse Robert said, is a damned coward!"[30]

Lee loved his men and showed it in countless ways. He tried never to expose them to needless danger. Once, while he was watching an artillery duel, a staff officer rode up. Lee ordered him away. When the officer protested that he could not go to safety while his general was in danger, Lee snapped: "It is my duty to be here. Go back the way I told you, sir."[31] Losing men was like losing his own children; it brought tears to his eyes.

Lee relaxed by taking long rides and visiting homes along the way. He especially liked to talk to women and play with children. Among his favorites was Janie Corbin, a vivacious five-year-old

with long blond curls. During one visit, he found Stonewall
Jackson at the house. As Janie climbed onto Lee's lap for a kiss,
she whispered she would like to kiss Jackson as well. When he told
Stonewall of her wish, he began "to blush like a schoolgirl."[32]
Jackson and the little girl soon became friends. The warrior would
sit on the floor and entertain her by cutting out paper dolls.
Sometimes he cut a series of dolls with their hands joined, telling
her they were the Stonewall Brigade, his best fighting unit.

Lee had a sense of inner peace that calmed those around him.
But he was no softy. He had a hot temper that he struggled to control all his life. If someone annoyed him, he grew silent as a stone.
His face reddened and his cheek muscles tightened. Then quietly,
but firmly, he put the offender in his place. Yet he regretted the
pain he caused, and quickly made amends. One time, for instance,
Lee spoke sharply to an army scout. Moments later, he had his
orderly prepare the best meal he could and place it on the table in
his tent. Then the general had the scout, a private, sit down in his
own chair, and Lee waited on him like a butler.

Soldiers worshiped Lee. We can read thousands of letters by
Confederate troops and never find a bad word about him. Their
nicknames for him were friendly, yet respectful. They called him
"The Old Man," "The Great Tycoon," and "Uncle Robert." Some
called him "Old Bob," but never to his face; he hated the name
Bob. Their favorite, of course, was "Marse Robert."

Soldiers never compared Marse Robert to other men. Jackson
and Longstreet and Stuart were great soldiers, to be sure; but they
could not hold a candle to Lee. No one could. His men regarded
him as a higher form of humanity. When he appeared before them,
he was sometimes cheered; mostly, though, they stood in silent
awe. "We loved him much, but revered him more. We never criticized him, never doubted him," a veteran recalled. "The rest of us
may be descended from monkeys," said another, "but it took God
to make Marse Robert."[33]

By the winter of 1862, he had become his soldiers' cause and
country. What they did, they did for him. What they suffered, they
suffered for him. And they suffered gladly. As a one-armed Rebel
said, shaking his empty sleeve: "I did it for Marse Robert, and by
God, I'd do it again!"[34]

Lee knew he was but a man, and could only do what was humanly
possible. Victory, after all, was not just a matter of brilliant generals leading heroic troops. The home front lay behind the fighting

front. There everything his army used, from beans to bullets to bandages, was produced. And there the South was losing the war.

Lee saw the evidence with his own eyes. Although retreating Yankees always left behind tons of supplies, they never seemed to lack anything. Northern newspapers, which he read constantly, told of the Union's economic vitality. "What a marvel is here!" wrote Chaplain A. M. Stewart, home on leave from his Pennsylvania regiment in the fall of 1862. "Something new under the sun! A nation, from internal resources alone, carrying on for over eighteen months the most gigantic war of modern times . . . yet all this while growing richer and more prosperous! And the *ladies*! They never looked more handsome . . . and surely never dressed finer and more fashionable—the war not withstanding."[35]

In Washington, the Patent Office had never been busier. At the height of the war, Northerners were inventing more things for civilian use than ever before. A tiny sample of these inventions includes passenger elevators, steam printing presses, flypaper, fountain pens, roller skates, stitching machines for shoes, and washing machines. Factories were sprouting like mushrooms after a rain. That marvelous invention, the sewing machine, was turning out record numbers of army uniforms and ready-to-wear civilian clothes. In agriculture, the increased use of reapers and mowers was allowing a woman to do more work in a day than three men working by hand. A visitor to Iowa was astonished to see "a stout woman whose sons are in the army, with her team cutting hay. . . . She cut seven acres with ease in a day, riding leisurely on her cutter."[36]

Meantime, Lee saw the Confederacy falling behind everywhere. Richmond, the Confederacy's gun-making center, turned out a hundred rifles a day. The North had thirty-eight rifle factories capable of producing five thousand a day. Southern rifles were made entirely by hand, one piece at a time. Northern rifles used interchangeable parts, the key to mass production.

The burdens of war weighed heavily upon the Southern people. The blockade created shortages, causing prices to spiral out of control. In less than two years, the cost of flour rose two and a half times, bacon eight times, and sugar fifteen times. Salt, essential to preserving meat, went from two dollars a bag in 1861 to sixty dollars within a year. We get an idea of what this meant by comparing the wages of a free black in Richmond and a Rebel soldier at Fredericksburg. Johnny Reb earned eleven dollars a month for risking his life; the free black ten dollars a day for shining shoes!

Essential items became scarce, triggering a search for substitutes. In this connection, the word *Confederate* came to mean anything second-rate and shoddy. Confederate flour was cornmeal, Confederate butter whipped sunflower oil. Confederate pins and needles were made of thorns; Confederate buttons were persimmon seeds with holes bored in them. Confederate clothes were anything that covered one's nakedness. The wife of one of Lee's aides told how "large women appeared squeezed into garments of smallest proportions—small women floating in almost limitless space; while women of tall stature dangled below [short] skirts, and others trailed about in fathoms of useless material."[37]

The heaviest burden fell on the farm woman; indeed, next to the soldier at the front, she suffered more than any other Confederate. She had to plant, plow, and harvest, and do so without machinery. In addition, she butchered the hogs, smoked the meat, cut the firewood, and made the soap. If a plow broke, it stayed broken, because there was no one to fix it and there were no spare parts. The experience of Mrs. Aaron Thomas, a North Carolinian with a husband in the army and several small children, was typical. "There were just not enough daylight hours . . . for her to do all the tasks that must be done and still cultivate her crop," a neighbor recalled. "She would get all the children to bed . . . and then go out to the fields to work at night by the light of the moon."[38]

High prices and scarcity brought hunger to Southern cities. Desperate people did desperate things. On April 2, 1863, hundreds of women gathered in downtown Richmond to demand food for their children. Jefferson Davis spoke to them, only to be silenced by shouts of "Bread! The Union! No more starvation!" A riot followed in which women looted government warehouses, stopping only when police threatened to open fire. There were similar riots in Macon, Georgia; Bladenboro, North Carolina; and Mobile, Alabama. Elsewhere, armed women held up wagon trains. A women's gang armed with "guns, pistols, knives and tongues" looted a flour mill near Lafayette, Alabama.[39]

Still, Southern women supported the war effort. They worked in hospitals, rolled bandages, prepared cartridges, and did thousands of other war-related tasks. In their gardens, they grew vegetables and poppies, from which painkilling opium was extracted. Everyone knitted socks and sewed clothing for soldiers. When the war began, Mary Lee fled to Richmond before Union forces seized Arlington. There she, her daughters, and their friends worked with their needles all day, every day.

Farm women had to take over all the chores when their husbands and sons went to war. Here some women in Virginia take time out to sew for their men.

Sewing was love. A wife wrote her soldier husband: "I have about finished your drawers. I love to sew for you. I have such sweet, loving thoughts about you. If your body is as warm when wearing these clothes as my heart is while making them, you will be very comfortable."[40] Girls put slips of paper with their names and addresses into their handiwork. One left a rhyme:

> *Apples are good but peaches are better*
> *If you love me, you will write me a letter.*[41]

Marse Robert praised the devotion of Southern women. Yet, he knew, one cannot live on devotion alone. Without the means, even these devoted people must reach their breaking point.

What was the Confederacy's breaking point?

When would it be reached?

Lee could not answer these questions. No one could. Only one thing was certain: Mr. Lincoln was not going to quit.

VI ⟡ LEE'S MASTERPIECE

The armies watched each other across the Rappahannock for four months. From December 1862 to April 1863, they waited, and suffered, and prepared to resume the killing.

The Union's Army of the Potomac was rebuilt during these months. The defeat at Fredericksburg had sent its morale to rock bottom. Desertions averaged two hundred a day, and the mails were full of packages containing civilian clothing, as relatives helped loved ones to desert. But thanks to Burnside's replacement, Major General Joseph Hooker, things began to improve early in the new year. This time, it seemed, Lincoln had found the right man.

Hooker, forty-eight, was a West Point graduate who had served in the Mexican War. Six feet tall, with blond hair and gray-blue eyes, he was said to be the handsomest man in the Union army. And one of the bravest, too. Nicknamed "Fighting Joe," he preferred to lead from the front, encouraging his men by his own example. He had distinguished himself in the Peninsula campaign, at Second Manassas, and at Sharpsburg, where he was carried from the cornfield with a bullet in his foot. A lover of whiskey, Hooker drank more than was good for him; a "hooker" is still slang for a shot of whiskey.

He was also a fast talker, and none too careful with his words. President Lincoln, he said, was a nice man but no war leader; what

Despite heavy odds in his favor, Union general Joseph Hooker lost his nerve and was defeated by the Confederates at Chancellorsville.

America needed was a military dictator. Lincoln learned of the remark and wrote the general a stinging letter: "I have heard . . . of your recently saying that both the army and the government needed a dictator. Of course it was not *for* this, but in spite of it, that I have given you the command. Only those generals who gain success can set up dictators. What I now ask of you is military success, and I will risk the dictatorship."[1] Still, Lincoln had confidence in Hooker's fighting ability. He would put up with his big mouth for the sake of the country.

Hooker rose to the challenge. That he was an able soldier became clear from the moment he took charge. There was more food, and better food, than the army had ever seen before. Furloughs were given, so that men could go home for a week or two; homesickness was greatly reduced, and many deserters returned of their own free will. To build team spirit, each corps received a special insignia: a diamond, a shamrock, a star, or other design. Each division within a corps got a colored badge to be worn on the cap: red for the first division, white for the second, blue for the third. Hooker was convinced that idleness hurt morale, so troops were kept busy with drill, maneuvers, and parades. His efforts were appreciated. Wherever the general rode on his snow white stallion, he was greeted with a cheer and a song:

> *For God and our country*
> *We're marching along.*
> *Joe Hooker is our leader;*
> *He takes his whisky strong.*[2]

Fighting Joe had returned to the army what it needed most: its self-respect. Or, as a soldier put it: "Under Hooker, we began to *live.*"[3]

Lincoln visited the army on April 5, 1863. Since his son, Tad, wanted to see real live Rebels, they went down to the river opposite Fredericksburg. They saw Rebel pickets at their posts and gunners manning their weapons. A Confederate artillery officer watched them through his spyglass; he recognized the president, and could easily have sent shells in his direction. But that would not have been sporting, and he was a gentleman. So he removed his hat and bowed to the Yankee chief.

The president walked through the camps and visited the field hospitals. Along the way, he passed shacks inhabited by runaway slaves. Most had come from the surrounding area, although some had swum the river by clinging to pieces of driftwood. Blacks welcomed him with shouts of "Hurrah for Massa Linkum!" His wife, Mary, the daughter of a Kentucky slaveowner, wondered how many black children were named Abraham Lincoln; she called them "those pickaninnies." The president also wondered. "Let's see," he said. "I should say that of all those babies under two years of age, perhaps two-thirds have been named for me."[4]

The main reason for his visit was to discuss the spring offensive with Hooker. Such an offensive, the president believed, was bound to be difficult. Hooker commanded 135,000 men, more than double the 62,000 available to Lee. (Longstreet had taken two divisions for special service south of Richmond.) But Lee was still the king of spades. He had used the winter to build a twenty-five-mile defense line along the Rappahannock. Attacking such defenses head-on would be suicidal. Lee might also use his defenses aggressively, as in the Seven Days campaign. He could hold any part of his line with a small force, while moving his main force to counter a threat elsewhere.

Hooker designed an excellent plan of his own. He intended to ease Lee out of his defenses and fight him in the open. To hold Lee's attention, 40,000 men would cross the river five miles below Fredericksburg. Hooker would then move swiftly, and secretly, northward with an 80,000-man strike force. His destination was Kelley's Ford, twenty-five miles above the Union camp. Crossing the river, he would swing southward past Chancellorsville, a crossroads tavern in the Wilderness of Virginia, seventy square miles of dense forest, tangled underbrush, and winding streams. This would put him behind Lee at the exact moment a "demonstration," or false attack, was distracting him at Fredericksburg. Menaced on three sides—right, left, and rear—Lee must leave his defenses or be trapped in them. Either way, the Army of Northern Virginia was doomed.

Lincoln liked the plan. His only advice was to throw in every man at once, avoiding McClellan's error at Sharpsburg. Hooker, however, needed no advice. He reminded the president that he led "the finest army on the planet." He could easily whip Lee's ragged crew and take Richmond. "My plans are perfect," he said, "and when I start to carry them out, may God have mercy on General Lee, for I will have none."[5]

Hooker's attitude troubled Lincoln. Before saying good-bye, he drew him a lesson from nature. "The hen," he observed, "is the wisest of all of the animal creation, because she never cackles until the egg is laid." It was a good lesson, and a proper caution against arrogance.[6]

The Yankees began to break camp on April 28. Before dawn, cavalry patrols ordered local people to stay indoors or be arrested for spying. Hooker had no intention of allowing Virginians to warn Lee at the last moment.

The roads had dried out and the army moved quickly. Arriving at Kelley's Ford, soldiers threw pontoon bridges across and crossed to the opposite bank. By dawn of April 29 the army was at Ely's Ford on the Rapidan, a branch of the Rappahannock. The Rapidan is rapid, a fast-flowing stream with shoulder-deep water. All day, and far into the night, the Union columns plunged into the cold water. Soldiers stripped off their uniforms, held their gear above their heads, and waded across. Huge bonfires, casting a reddish glow on the water, were lit on each bank to guide them. Scores of men lost their footing on the slippery rocks and were swept downstream. Several drowned. Cavalry patrols rescued the others with ropes.

Everyone was in high spirits. Billy Yanks crowded around the bonfires, warming themselves and singing merrily. "Hurrah for Old Joe!" they cried whenever Hooker appeared. They had reason to be happy. They had crossed two rivers without a hitch. All they had to do now was finish the job.

Fighting Joe was overjoyed. Lincoln's point about cackling chickens had made no impression on him whatsoever. As far as he was concerned, the battle had already been fought and the war won. "I have the rebellion in my breeches pocket," he told a group of officers, "and God Almighty himself cannot take that away from me."[7]

His remark sent chills up his listeners' spines. There he was, without having fired a shot, putting himself above the Lord. "I do not like that sort of talk on the eve of battle," an officer whispered to a neighbor. "There is no sense in defying the Almighty when you are fighting General Lee."[8]

Hooker's plan was unraveling as he spoke. At first, Lee believed the troops crossing below Fredericksburg were the real attack force. But their failure to advance aroused his suspicions. These were confirmed by Jeb Stuart. As the Yankees crossed the Rapidan, Stuart's patrols took some prisoners in the Chancellorsville area. They were wearing the insignia not of one corps, but of *three*. Clearly, the northern, or left, wing of the Confederate army, was Hooker's objective.

What to do? Lee seemed to have only two choices, both equally bad. Retreating toward Richmond would expose him to a combined attack from the north and south. Turning to meet the threat from Chancellorsville would open him to attack from behind via Fredericksburg.

Lee decided to do neither. If "Mr. F. J. Hooker," as he called him, wished to fight, he would show him a thing or two. Once again he must divide his army, as Lincoln feared he might. A skeleton force of ten thousand would hold the Fredericksburg defenses, while the rest marched to Chancellorsville.

Stonewall Jackson's corps was to lead the way. "Tell your good general that I am sure he knows what to do," Lee told one of Jackson's aides. "I will meet him at the front very soon."[9] He was calm as he spoke. During the past year, he and Stonewall had become more than partners. They had become close friends who could almost read each other's minds. They thought alike, and even had the same gut feelings about a situation. If Stonewall was ready to follow Lee blindfolded, Lee could trust him with anything.

Friday, May 1, 1863. May Day. Stonewall's veterans halted near

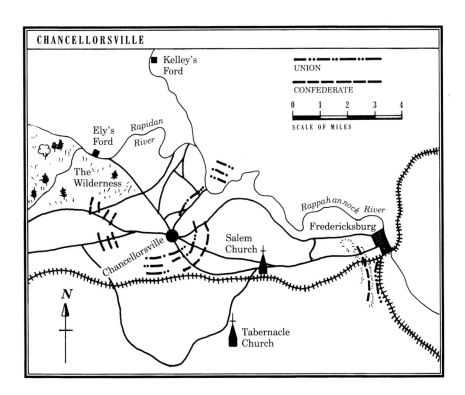

the southern edge of the Wilderness after another speed-march. They were not alone. Waiting for them was a tiny Confederate covering force, which had dug shallow rifle pits the night before.

Union troops began to pour out of the Wilderness, fanning out across the open country beyond. This was a critical time for Hooker, because the faster he moved, the better his chances of victory. The Wilderness was too overgrown for him to maneuver his superior infantry and artillery to full advantage. Soldiers were lucky to see twenty yards ahead in that jungle, let alone fight a coordinated battle. In certain places the trees grew so close together that a man had to flatten his body to glide between them. Going into open country, however, allowed Hooker to bring his entire force into play. His gunners could easily support the advancing infantry, while smashing Rebel counterattacks.

Only Jackson barred the way. Outnumbered four to one, had he chosen to hold his ground, the Yankees would have rolled over his force. Stonewall, however, was like Lee: When pressed, he attacked. Ordering his men out of the rifle pits, he charged the oncoming Yankees. What they lacked in numbers, the Confederates made up for in noise and fighting spirit; they literally "hollered" themselves across at the enemy. Such a tactic could never have halted a determined army. And it would not have halted those Billy Yanks, either; they knew they had the advantage and wanted to avenge Fredericksburg. But it was enough to faze Fighting Joe Hooker.

His plan had taken everything into account—everything except Marse Robert. He *should* have retreated in the face of such heavy odds. When he did not, something snapped inside of Hooker. Rather than push ahead, he ordered everyone back to Chancellorsville. The attack was called off. The army must dig in and await a Confederate attack. Later, to explain this strange action, rumor had it that he was drunk. He had a simpler reason: "Well, to tell the truth, I just lost confidence in Joe Hooker."[10]

His generals were stunned. Everything had turned topsy-turvy. One moment they were advancing to victory. The next moment they were retreating into the Wilderness. Upon receiving the order, three corps commanders sent word that Hooker *must* let them go forward as planned. He refused.

That refusal was the turning point in the battle. From then on, according to a Union general, his chief "was a whipped man."[11] Hooker knew it. His generals knew it. His troops knew it. And Robert E. Lee knew it, too. Once Fighting Joe flinched, Lee felt he could take any risk and stand a good chance of success.

Late that night, Lee and Jackson sat on wooden boxes, their heads close together, holding their hands up to a crackling fire. Stonewall described the situation. The Union front lay in the Wilderness, protected by trenches and felled trees, their branches sharpened and pointing outward. Its left was anchored on the Rappahannock shore. Both generals wanted to attack, but not against these strong positions. Just then, Jeb Stuart rode up with the latest reports. A cavalry patrol had located the Union right. It was "in the air"; that is, it rested on no natural obstacle, but gradually faded into the woods. It was wide open.

Lee smiled. Bending over a map, he swung his finger to the left, bringing it down on the enemy's weak spot. "Jackson, how can we get at those people?" he asked.[12] The question was enough. Before turning in, Stonewall sent scouts to find a way around.

Saturday, May 2, 1863. When Lee awoke before dawn, Jackson was already back at the fire, studying a sketch made by his mapmaker. The scouts had done their duty.

"General Jackson," said Lee, getting down to business right away, "what do you propose to do?"

"Go around here," Stonewall answered, tracing a line on a map with his finger.

"What do you propose to make this movement with?" Lee asked.

"With my whole corps."

"What will you leave me?"

"Two divisions!"

Lee drew a deep breath. Stonewall wanted to take twenty-eight thousand men, leaving him with a mere thirteen thousand. *That* was spreading things pretty thin—so thin that Lee's troops would be six feet apart in certain places.

"Well, go on," said Lee calmly.[13]

Lee had thrown away the rule book. Not only was he redividing his army, this time into thirds; he was putting it in grave danger. Dividing an army means weakening it numerically. Dividing it in the face of a vastly superior enemy is to risk annihilation. Stonewall was to march west and then turn north. For most of its fourteen miles, his route lay directly in front of the Union positions. An alert enemy could drive a wedge between the parts of Lee's army before Stonewall got into position to attack. Still, it was worth the gamble. Lee trusted his friend absolutely, and had absolutely no respect for Mr. F. J. Hooker.

The strike force left shortly after sunrise. Lee watched it from his command post. Stonewall rode over for a final briefing. Then he rejoined his men.

It was their last meeting.

The day grew hot. Most of the soldiers were hungry. All were thirsty. Jackson set a terrific pace. Riding from regiment to regiment, he told their colonels that he expected a maximum effort: "Keep the column closed. . . . Permit no straggling. . . . Press on, press on!"[14] Stragglers were to be prodded with bayonets; if necessary, an officer could hit a straggler over the shoulder with the flat of his sword. Every minute of daylight was precious. Not only must Jackson take the Yankees by surprise, he had to finish them off before sundown. Anything less than a total victory would enable them to recover during the night.

The foot cavalry marched as never before. The usual jokes were told. The usual remarks were made about officers. "Here's one of Jack's little boys," soldiers laughed as a young staff officer rode past. "Let him by, boys! . . . Have a good breakfast this morning, sonny? . . . Better hurry up, or you'll catch it for getting behind. . . . Tell Old Jack we're all a-coming. . . . Don't let him begin the fuss till we git thar!"[15] The aide rode on, blushing from ear to ear.

Lee tried to mask Jackson's movements as best he could. Jeb Stuart was sent to form a moving cavalry screen along the column's right side. His own troops were ordered to act as if they were preparing for an all-out assault. Throughout the day, Lee's artillery boomed and his riflemen fired into the Union lines near Chancellorsville. Nevertheless, the enemy realized something was wrong; or at least some of them did. Union pickets actually saw Jackson's column and shot at it with their rifles. Their reports to headquarters only encouraged Hooker. It so happened that the road Jackson was using bent slightly southward, before turning west. Southward, toward Richmond! Fighting Joe decided that Lee was in *retreat*. Not even God Almighty could save him now!

Union pickets took several prisoners, boastful fellows who told all they knew. "You'll catch hell tonight," said one as they led him away. A Georgian told his captors: "You think you've done a big thing just now, but you wait until Jackson gets around on your right."[16] Such warnings were promptly reported to headquarters— and promptly ignored. It went on like that for hours. Even sightings by frontline commanders were disregarded. The colonel of the Seventy-fifth Ohio regiment, for example, was laughed at when he reported in person. "You are frightened, sir," a senior staff officer told another colonel, snickering. Headquarters had decided that Lee was retreating; that's all there was to it. Anyone who disagreed was either a fool or a coward, or both.

At two o'clock in the afternoon, a scout guided Jackson to the top of a low hill. Below them, a few hundred yards away, was the Union right.

Soldiers of the Eleventh Corps, Major General Oliver O. Howard commanding, stood around in groups, laughing, talking, and smoking their pipes. Soldiers sat by campfires, cooking supper, their rifles neatly stacked outside their tents. To their rear, army butchers were slaughtering cattle, which had been driven along to provide fresh meat. Although Howard had been informed of Rebel troop movements, he felt perfectly safe. Yes, he had heard gunfire in the direction of Chancellorsville. But that was miles away—not his problem.

Jackson watched without changing his expression. But those eyes of his told everything. "His eyes burned with a brilliant glow, lighting his sad face," an officer recalled. Old Blue-light was mentally fighting his supreme battle.[17]

Jackson massed his infantry in the woods for a mile on either side of a narrow wagon road called the Turnpike. Three lines of troops, one behind the other, formed the crossbar of a T, with the road stretching ahead of them. In those woods, it took hours to form the lines, and Jackson grew impatient. He constantly glanced at his watch, then at the lengthening shadows. At 5:15 P.M. he could wait no longer. Less than two hours of daylight remained. Although the attack lines were still incomplete, he decided to act.

Turning to Robert E. Rodes, an aide, he asked: "Are you ready, General Rodes?"

"Yes, sir."

"You can go forward, then."[18]

A bugle call echoed through the woods. Back came the sound of other bugles from the right and left, as the signal was passed from regiment to regiment, division to division.

The attack lines surged forward, gathering momentum as they went. Brush and thorns tugged at the troops every step of the way. By the time they fired their first shot, scores of Johnny Rebs had had their clothes torn off; they fought the battle naked except for their boots and drawers.

A Billy Yank sat on the ground, his boots off, rubbing his aching feet. Suddenly, frightened deer bounded through the camp. Wild turkeys ran out of the woods, flapping their wings and gobbling madly. Swarms of birds took flight, chirping and twittering. A rifle cracked in the woods nearby. Someone said a picket was emptying his weapon before returning to camp. Nothing to worry about.

Then it happened.

Jackson's men burst from the woods with a whoop and holler and a bloodcurdling yell. *Yip-yip-yip-e-e-e-e-e-e-e! Yah-ah-ah-yah-e-e-e-e-e-e-e!*

"Johnnies! Johnnies!" a private screamed, scarcely able to believe his eyes. The Rebels were swarming "like flies on a dead horse." This was not supposed to be happening, but it was. Leading each regiment was a red battle flag with the Southern cross.[19]

Yankee soldiers did what any sensible people would have done. They ran. Overcome by fear, they threw away their gear to gain speed; they even cut the straps of their knapsacks as they ran. Eyes blazing, Old Blue-light led the first wave on horseback. Time meant everything just now, and it was slipping away. If only he could hold the sun in place for a few more hours!

"Press on! Press on!" Jackson cried. Leaning forward in the saddle, he extended his open palms outward, as if to push the attack with his own body. At times he stopped to raise his eyes upward, calling upon God's favor. His men swept onward, cheering as they went. When the cheering grew especially loud, Jackson lifted a hand to heaven, his lips moving in silent thanksgiving, for this was the Lord's doing. Whenever he came to a cluster of fallen Rebels, he stopped and raised a hand again, blessing their souls. Then he repeated his battle cry: "Forward, men, forward! Press forward!"

The Yankees surrendered in droves. Many were found huddled in rifle pits, speechless, teeth chattering, in a state of shock. Four men and a lieutenant of the Seventh North Carolina regiment charged into the midst of the 128th Pennsylvania. Thinking quickly, the lieutenant demanded their surrender before Jackson had them all shot. The entire regiment gave up meekly. Those responsible for the disaster were in a panic. General Howard tried to rally his shattered corps. "Halt! Halt!" he called, frantically waving a pistol. "I'm ruined, I'm ruined! I'll shoot you if you don't stop. I'm ruined, I'm ruined!"[20]

Stonewall was dissatisfied. He had delivered a stunning blow, but not the death blow he and Lee wanted. Slowly but surely, the shock was wearing off. As night fell, the Eleventh Corps was pulling itself together. Union infantrymen were fighting back. Union artillerymen were firing salvos down the Turnpike and raking the woods on either side. By morning, the whole Army of the Potomac would be up in force. There was only one thing to do: finish the job with a night attack.

At nine o'clock Jackson and his staff rode out in front of the Confederate line to study the enemy positions. It was a dark night, made still darker by clouds of drifting gunsmoke. Thousands of jittery men were firing at any sound, any movement, any shadow. In the confusion, two Union outfits almost blasted each other to kingdom come; a group of Yankees actually surrendered to comrades from the same unit.

Shots from Union pickets forced Jackson's party to turn back. Mistaking them for enemy cavalry, members of the Eighteenth North Carolina regiment opened fire at a distance of fifty feet. Horses reared, throwing their riders to the ground. Three bullets slammed into Jackson's left arm, severing an artery and shattering the bone. The arm would have to be amputated. "My own men," the general groaned as aides carried him to safety.[21]

Lee had turned in for the night when a messenger arrived. He had good news and bad news. The good news was Jackson's victory, though incomplete. The bad news was Jackson's injury. Lee was stunned. "Ah! Captain," he said, his voice quivering, "any victory is dearly bought that deprives us of the services of Jackson even for a short time." The messenger then tried to describe how Jackson had been carried to a field hospital, but Lee cut him short. "Ah, Captain, don't let us say anything more about it; it is too painful to talk about."[22] Lee was so upset that, in order to be able to think clearly, he had to drive any thought of his friend from his mind.

His first move was to have Jeb Stuart take over Jackson's corps. Stuart's orders were to continue the assault at daybreak. Lee would also attack at the same time. His aim was to unite both wings of his army at Chancellorsville and drive the enemy into the river.

There was no reason for Hooker to accept any of this; indeed, victory was still possible, even likely, if only he had the willpower. His battered troops had been reorganized and resupplied during the night, as Jackson had feared. Manpower was abundant, too. He had three corps standing by in reserve, and they were fresh, having taken no part in the day's fighting. Had he wanted to, Hooker could easily have thrust them between the wings of Lee's army, destroying each in turn. But the idea of a counterattack seems never to have entered his mind. Rather than throw in every man as President Lincoln advised, Fighting Joe was keeping the reserves to cover his retreat.

Sunday, May 3, dawned clear and warm. At first light, Stuart seized a hill overlooking a key Union position. Then, under the cover of thirty heavy guns, he sent his men forward. They all knew of Jackson's wounding, and advanced with his name on their lips. "Charge! and remember Jackson!" they cried. "Charge! and remember Jackson!" Stuart led the way, relishing every moment. Overcome by the thrill of battle, he sang, "Old Joe Hooker, will you come out of the Wilderness!"[23]

Union gunners replied with a hail of hot iron. Stuart's men fell in droves. Private Nick Weeks, Third Alabama regiment, recalled with horror:

> *The biggest trees offered no protection. One might as well have been in front as behind it. Limbs and the tops were falling about us as if torn by a cyclone. We were enveloped, as it were, in a dense fog, the flashing guns could be seen only a few feet away. . . . What a din. What a variety of hideous noises. The ping of the [bullets], the splutter of canister, the whistling of grape, the 'where are you,' 'where are you' of screaming shells. . . . [I saw] an arm and shoulder fly from the man just in front, exposing a throbbing heart. Another's foot flew up and kicked him in the face as a shell struck his leg. Another, disemboweled, crawled along on all fours, his entrails trailing behind, and still another held up his tongue with his hand, a piece of shell having carried away his lower jaw.*[24]

Weeks screwed up his courage and kept going.

The shelling proved too much for hundreds of his comrades. They hugged the ground, refusing to rise even when a colonel ordered his regiment to walk right over them; he personally drove a fellow colonel's face into the ground with his boot. A fleeing Rebel saw a rabbit darting ahead of him. But it was every man—and every rabbit—for himself. "Get out of my way, Mr. Rabbit," the soldier yelled, "and let somebody run who knows how!"[25]

There was yet another reason for running: forest fires. Exploding shells had ignited the brush in many places. Flames sped along the ground, creating whirlwinds of hot cinders. These settled in treetops, turning them into torches sixty feet high. Stacks of ammunition boxes caught fire, their contents "cooking off" with a rapid *pop, pop, pop*. Rifles lying on the ground blew up when fire touched them, as did the cartridges in dead men's pockets. The dead were fortunate; they were beyond suffering. Those too badly injured to crawl to safety were roasted alive. Their terrified screams, cries of pain, and pleas to be put out of their misery rose above the din of battle. Veterans recalled the smell of Chancellorsville as well as its sights: burned wood and burned gunpowder mixed with burned flesh.

Rebels and Yankees put aside their anger to save the wounded. A Union private was working frantically, dragging away members of both armies, when two Rebels came to lend a hand. "We were trying to rescue a young fellow in gray. The fire was all around him. The last I saw of that fellow was his face. . . . His eyes were big and blue, and his hair like raw silk surrounded by a wreath of fire. . . . I heard him scream, 'O, Mother! O, God!' It left me trembling all over like a leaf. After it was over, my hands were blistered and burned so I could not open or shut them; but me and them Rebs tried to shake hands."[26]

Stuart's guns finally beat down all resistance. While his infantry advanced, Lee threw his own line forward. Both wings of the Confederate army united to form a continuous front. At last they reached the Chancellorsville House, which Hooker had used as a headquarters and field hospital. The Yankees were gone, and the house was enveloped in flames. Rows of Union dead lay in the yard under canvas sheets. Confederate dead and wounded covered the ground for hundreds of feet.

Lee rode at the head of his army. To his right, the woods were ablaze, sheets of flame and plumes of smoke reaching skyward. A deafening noise, more like an animal roar than a human cheer, met him as he stopped in front of the burning house. Thousands of men, their faces blackened with soot, waved and threw their hats into the air. Marse Robert had done it! He had given them their greatest victory of the war! Deeply moved, Lee lifted his own hat by the crown and held it over his head. It was a silent "speech," his way of saying thanks. The soldiers went wild. "What a head, what a head!" they yelled. "See that glorious head! God bless it, God bless it!"[27]

We do not know how Lee felt, since he was tight-lipped about his feelings. But if he was happy, the feeling passed quickly. The cheers were still echoing in his ears when an aide arrived with a note from Stonewall. He was in a field hospital to the west, but had been following the battle by the noise. Now he wanted to congratulate his friend on a brilliant achievement. Lee's face became a mask of sorrow. His voice cracking with emotion, he gave his reply: "Say to General Jackson that the victory is his, and that the congratulation is due him."[28] At the pinnacle of his military career,

Marse Robert refused to take any credit for himself.

Lee was about to renew the attack when another messenger arrived. He came from Fredericksburg, ten miles away, and he had startling news. The Yankees were finally attacking. They had begun with a replay of Burnside's assault, only this time it worked. Bluecoats had scrambled over the stone wall, cleared the sunken road with the bayonet, and surged up to the crest of Marye's Heights. Pausing to catch their breath, many of them in tears, they swarmed down the other side of the hill. Now they were heading for Lee's rear at Chancellorsville. Lee canceled the attack and sent part of his force to halt the advance. For the rest of that day, and most of May 4, it fought a savage holding action at Salem Church. By the time the battle ended, Hooker was safely back across the Rappahannock.

Chancellorsville was Lee's masterpiece. If there is such a thing as a perfect battle, this was it. Lee had done everything right. After dividing his army twice, he went after an enemy twice his size. He out-generaled Hooker, defeated him, and humiliated the Army of the Potomac. Besides driving the invader away, he captured 19,500 rifles, tons of ammunition, and mountains of supplies. But the

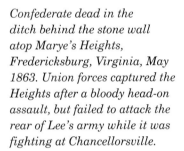

Confederate dead in the ditch behind the stone wall atop Marye's Heights, Fredericksburg, Virginia, May 1863. Union forces captured the Heights after a bloody head-on assault, but failed to attack the rear of Lee's army while it was fighting at Chancellorsville.

"butcher's bill," as they called it, was very high. Lee lost 13,156 men—killed, wounded, missing—or 22 percent of his army. Hooker's losses were 16,845, that is, 13 percent of his force.

Abraham Lincoln was devastated by the news. The color drained from his face, and it became "French gray," like the wallpaper on the walls of the Oval Office. He paced up and down the room, head bowed, hands clasped behind his back, muttering: "My God! My God! What will the country say! What will the country say!" Secretary of War Edwin M. Stanton believed he meant to commit suicide, and was afraid to leave him alone at night.[29]

Lee, too, was depressed. Although victorious, he had failed to achieve his main objective. The Army of the Potomac was still intact, and would return. Worse, he had lost Stonewall Jackson.

Jackson seemed to rally after losing his arm. Then he developed pneumonia. Nowadays, he would have been given antibiotics from the outset; but these wonder drugs would not exist for another eighty years. Thus, even minor infections became life threatening, and pneumonia is anything but minor. Once it took hold of his weakened body, his days were numbered.

Lee refused to believe that Jackson was dying. He went down on his knees, begging God to spare his life. He told an aide to give him his regards, adding, "He has lost his left arm, but I have lost my right."[30] It was no use. Jackson died on May 10.

Being a general was dangerous work, particularly if one led from the front. People were not surprised when a general lost his life. Seventy-eight Confederate generals died during the Civil War; only one American general died in combat during eight years of fighting in Vietnam. But Jackson's loss had an effect unlike any other's. For Northerners, it was almost worth a battlefield disaster to be rid of him. For Southerners, it was an omen of things to come. After Chancellorsville, there would be no more smashing victories for the Army of Northern Virginia, and no more crushing defeats for the Army of the Potomac.

The morning after Jackson's death, Marse Robert wrote his son, Custis: "It is a terrible loss. I do not know how to replace him."[31] He never found the answer, for Stonewall Jackson was irreplaceable.

VII ✦ GETTYSBURG

This battle was to decide not only the future character of the war but of the nation. . . . The common soldier recognized dimly that this was the pivotal battle of the war, and hence every man's hand was nerved to do his best.

—Private Warren Goss,

U.S. Army

Lee's first task after Chancellorsville was to reorganize his army. Jackson had been such a military giant that it took two men to fill his boots. His corps was split in half, and each put under an experienced officer. One corps was led by A. P. Hill, who had saved the day at Sharpsburg. A peppery little fellow who wore a bright red flannel shirt in battle, Hill had a superb combat record; his division was considered the best in the army. The other corps went to Richard S. Ewell, a hero of Jackson's Valley campaign. Nicknamed "Bald Dick" because of his shiny hairless head, Ewell had bulging eyes and a long, pointy nose. A superb horseman, he had lost a leg at Second Manassas, and from then on had to be tied to his mount. If both men together did not equal one Stonewall Jackson, at least they were battle-tested veterans. Anyhow, they were the best Lee had.

On May 16 Lee met with the Confederate cabinet in Richmond. Another threat was looming in the West, a vast territory vital to the Confederacy. Here lay the railroad yards of Chattanooga, Tennessee; the machine shops of Atlanta, Georgia; and the docks of New Orleans, Louisiana, the South's largest city. Here, too, was Texas, with its herds of longhorn cattle and its long border with Mexico, across which European supplies flowed to the states of the Upper South.

Things had been going badly out West for over a year. In the spring of 1862 Union fleets seized New Orleans and Memphis, Tennessee, on the Mississippi River. The Union's western armies were led by a team like that of Lee and Jackson. Ulysses S. Grant and William Tecumseh Sherman had kept Kentucky loyal to the Union, conquered nearly all of Tennessee, and were about to lay siege to Vicksburg, Mississippi. Vicksburg was the Confederacy's last stronghold along the "Father of Waters." Its loss would give the enemy control of the entire river, cutting the Confederacy in half and opening its eastern states to attack from behind.

The cabinet had to decide how to handle this menacing situation. One solution was to send part of Longstreet's corps to Vicksburg, as Old Pete had been urging for weeks. But Lee objected. This plan, he argued, would weaken the Army of Northern Virginia at a critical time. As they spoke, Hooker was receiving large reinforcements from the North; all his losses were being made up, and then some. Immigration from abroad guaranteed that the Union would always have the advantage in manpower. The South, however, could not replace its losses.

Lee gave the cabinet an arithmetic lesson. At Chancellorsville, an invading army of 135,000 had lost nearly 17,000 men; Lee's army of 62,000 lost over 13,000 men. This was nothing to cheer about. Four such battles would wipe out Lee's army, while leaving the enemy with as many men as Lee had at the outset. Time, and arithmetic, were against the Confederacy. If the war went on much longer, defeat was a certainty. It followed, therefore, that sending troops to Vicksburg would only postpone the inevitable. The South, Lee insisted, must act decisively while it still had the manpower to take the initiative. Conclusion: The North must be invaded a second time.

As in 1862, Lee hoped to do several things at once: feed his army, upset the enemy's plans for another year, disrupt railroad traffic, and take Philadelphia or some other key Northern city. Such a move would also force Lincoln to withdraw troops from the West, relieving the pressure on Vicksburg. But Lee did not want another victory. He wanted *the* victory. Like Napoléon, whom he admired, he believed in the war-winning stroke, a massive blow to annihilate the enemy. And he had precisely the weapon to do it: the Army of Northern Virginia. Lee admired his men as much as they admired him, perhaps more. "Our army would be invincible if it could be properly organized and officered," he said. "There were never such men in any army before. They will go anywhere and do anything if properly led."[1] The cabinet agreed to the invasion.

The army began to move during the first week in June of 1863. Leaving a small rear guard at Fredericksburg, it headed westward, toward the Blue Ridge Mountains. Lee planned to march down the Shenandoah Valley, keeping the wall of the Blue Ridge between him and the Union army. He would then cross the Potomac near Harpers Ferry and continue northward through Maryland into Pennsylvania. The Johnny Rebs did not, of course, know the details of the plan. But they could figure things out from the landmarks and the direction in which they were moving. Morale was high. Everyone had contempt for an enemy they had so often beaten. Even Marse Robert, a colonel recalled, "believed his army could whip anything on the planet."[2]

On June 8 the Confederates camped at Culpepper, Virginia. Nearby, at a place called Brandy Station, Jeb Stuart held a review in Lee's honor. Hour after hour, twelve thousand horsemen swept past the commanding general. At the end, they fought a mock battle, charging artillery with their gleaming swords. Next day, they fought for real.

Scouts had informed Hooker that the enemy was pulling out of Fredericksburg. This time he did put in every man. The entire Union cavalry corps, ten thousand strong, was sent to find out what they were up to. After fording the Rappahannock north of Brandy Station, the corps gave Stuart the shock of his life.

What followed was the largest cavalry battle in American history. Twenty-two thousand mounted men clashed at breakneck speeds. It was no wild free-for-all, but a coordinated action, a sort of ballet on horseback in which large units acted together. Choosing its target, a regiment would move forward at a steady walk. As it drew near, it increased its pace to a trot, then to a gallop, and finally to a hell-for-leather charge.

The plain echoed to the sound of pounding hooves, clanging steel, and shouting men. Horses and riders went down in a welter of dust and blood. Wild-eyed horses, their bellies torn open and trailing their guts, ran in every direction. Opponents slashed at each other's heads with swords. Troopers, shot from the saddle with pistols, were dragged along the ground when a boot became caught in a stirrup. Yankee casualties totaled 866 killed, wounded, and missing. Rebel casualties were 523, among them Roonie Lee, shot through the leg. The Yankees were driven away, but it had been a close call and no credit to Stuart.

Brandy Station confirmed that Lee was on the march. On June 13 Hooker broke camp at Falmouth. Both armies were now heading north along a parallel course on either side of the Blue Ridge.

The temperature soared, making the roads oven hot. Clouds of choking, blinding dust rose beneath the soldiers' feet. Men fell out of line exhausted, their faces flushed, gasping for breath. In a Texas brigade, five hundred men collapsed with sunstroke, and several died.

The Rebs found the waters of the Potomac a blessing. Beginning on June 16, it took nine days for Lee's seventy-five thousand men to cross. Regiments plunged in naked, holding their clothes over their heads. Now and then, girls strolling along the riverbank saw them; actually, they would not take their eyes off them. "Well, boys, I've been seceding for two years and now I've got back into the Union again!" said one fellow as he stepped onto the Maryland shore. Another told a group of sour-faced Union women: "Here we are, ladies, as rough and ragged as ever but back again to bother you."[3]

Lee's army drew cheers from onlookers in Maryland, where there were still Confederate sympathizers. Not in Pennsylvania. That state was solid for the Union. Pennsylvanians, particularly women, told the invaders exactly how they felt. They did so not only out of love for their country, but because they knew they would not be harmed. Marse Robert had cautioned his men about respecting civilians, and they knew he meant business. So, when a woman shouted, "Look at Pharaoh's army going to the Red Sea," they passed by without a murmur.[4] Then there was the girl who wrapped herself in Old Glory and called out: "Traitors—traitors—traitors, come and take this flag, the man of you who dares!" Nobody dared. General Pickett whipped off his hat, bowed, and saluted the flag. Every one of his men then raised his hat and cheered the spirited youngster.

No one taunted Marse Robert. He must have been some sight, tall and dignified astride his magnificent Traveller. Upon seeing him, a girl waved an American flag and burst into "The Star-Spangled Banner." Ever the gentleman, Lee raised his hat and kept going without changing his expression. A woman watching from a nearby window cried: "Oh, I wish he was ours!"[5]

Meanwhile, the North prepared. State governors mobilized militia units as far away as New York. In Pennsylvania, many of those directly in the invaders' path either fled or hid their valuables. Farm families took to the hills, driving their horses and cattle to safety. Refugees from the Cumberland Valley fled northward in wagons piled high with boxes and bundles and household goods of every description. Citizens of Harrisburg and other cities turned out with picks and shovels to dig trenches. Blacks, who had lived in

Pennsylvania for generations, pitched in alongside their white neighbors.

For many blacks the worst fear was not of death, but of being returned to slavery. And with good reason. We cannot be sure of the exact number, but it appears that hundreds of black people were seized and marched south. Farmers along the way saw them and heard their weeping. Some Rebels, however, did not have the heart for such cruelty. "We took a lot of Negroes yesterday," Private William Christian wrote his wife. "I was offered my choice, but as I could not get them back home I would not take them. In fact my humanity revolted at taking these poor devils away from their homes. They were so scared that I turned them all loose."[6] Pete Longstreet approved of the kidnappings. If Marse Robert was aware of the kidnappings, he kept his opinion to himself.

Lee had to know his opponent's strength and location at all times. Jeb Stuart, therefore, was sent to scout east of the Blue Ridge and report on Hooker's movements. He failed miserably.

Stuart had been angry with himself ever since Brandy Station. Never before had he been taken by surprise. Never before had he been so criticized for carelessness. Now he would set things right. After setting out on June 25, he went on a rampage. His hard-riding cavalry captured 150 supply wagons, burned a railroad bridge, and pushed to within sight of Washington. It was a glorious adventure, and it made Stuart feel better. But by going so far behind enemy lines, he lost contact with his own army. In effect, he rode right out of the campaign. When he returned a week later, he found Lee in the midst of the greatest battle ever fought on American soil.

Lee was blind without Stuart. A commander can only be as good as his information. Not knowing the enemy's location made Lee's every movement a step in the dark. And that made him frantic. Aides saw him pacing outside his tent, his hands clutching his hair, waiting for word from Stuart. "Where on earth is my cavalry?" he would ask passersby. "Have you any news of the enemy's movements? What is the enemy going to do?"[7]

Toward midnight of June 28, a spy known only as Harrison reported to Confederate headquarters. He had spent the past few days walking along the Pennsylvania roads. Wherever he went, he saw Union troop columns and wagon trains heading north. He also learned that Fighting Joe was out, replaced by one of his corps commanders, George Gordon Meade. A somber, no-nonsense soldier, Meade, aged forty-eight, had a quick temper; his men called him "a damned goggle-eyed old snapping turtle."[8] Lee had been his friend in the old army and respected his ability. "General Meade," he warned his staff, "will commit no blunder on my front, and if I make one he will make haste to take advantage of it."[9]

The spy's other news was electrifying. The Union army had crossed the Potomac and was moving toward the passes of the Blue Ridge. Stuart's silence had led Lee to believe that Union forces were still on the Rappahannock. This news changed everything. The Yankees must be kept east of the mountains, away from the Valley and the roads that linked Lee's army to Virginia. If those roads were cut, he would be trapped in Pennsylvania.

Orders to halt the advance went out to all corps commanders. The army was to cross the mountains and assemble near a town called Gettysburg. The place had a population of twenty-four hundred and a small college, a seminary for training Protestant ministers, and a school for young ladies. It had no military importance, other than being at the intersection of five roads. Lee had no intention of fighting a battle there. All he wanted was to gather his forces and figure out where to go next. Yet it was already too late. By the time his orders arrived, matters were speeding out of control.

Shoes were the reason. Thousands of Johnny Rebs were barefoot, as usual. That mattered little on the dirt roads of Virginia and Maryland. Pennsylvania's roads, however, were often macadamized, that is, paved with layers of crushed stone. These were murder on bare feet.

The commander of a North Carolina brigade had heard about a large supply of shoes in Gettysburg. On the morning of June 30, he went to get them. But as he approached the town, he ran into a Union cavalry brigade. Normally, that would not have stopped him; cavalry alone were no match for infantry firing from behind rocks and trees. What troubled him were the distant drumbeats. Yankee infantry! *That* meant trouble, especially since there were no Confederate cavalry to tell him how many infantry the enemy had or where they were. Wisely, he returned to camp. A. P. Hill, his corps commander, decided to send in a full division next morning. What Hill did not know was that Major General John Buford, the Union cavalry leader, had already sent an urgent message to Meade. The Rebels were near! Come quick, and bring up the whole army! Thus, both sides were blundering into the Battle of Gettysburg.

General George Gordon Meade. A hard man with a quick temper, Meade led the Army of the Potomac to victory at Gettysburg in July of 1863.

WEDNESDAY, JULY 1, 1863.
THE FIRST DAY

Gettysburg is located in a valley, amid rolling fields and patches of woodland. Two parallel ridges run in a north-south direction. Seminary Ridge, named for the seminary on its crest, lies a half mile west of the town. Cemetery Ridge begins a mile south of town and runs for about two miles, ending at two rocky hills called Little Round Top and Big Round Top. This ridge takes its name from Cemetery Hill, the site of a graveyard at its northern end, overlooking the town. A place of peace, the graveyard had a sign over its gate: All Persons Found Using Firearms in These Grounds Will Be Prosecuted with the Utmost Rigor of the Law. That meant paying a five-dollar fine for each shot fired. Had the law been enforced during the next three days, Gettysburg would have become the richest town in America.

The Confederates came by way of Seminary Ridge. Outnumbered and outgunned, Buford's troopers hung on as best they could. They were joined by a local man, John Burns, a seventy-year-old veteran of the War of 1812. Burns was angry at the Rebels, who had stolen or milked his cows, and he wanted to get even. At first, he was told to go away; fighting was young man's work. Just then a shell exploded nearby, and the young men ducked. But the old-timer stood erect, saying "Tut! tut! tut! I've heard that sort of thing before."[10] They let him stay until, four bullet wounds later, he ended up in a field hospital. He lived.

By midmorning, the Union troopers were in bad shape. Between shots, one fellow looked over his shoulder and gave a loud cheer. Approaching from the south were masses of men in blue uniforms and black sombreros. It was the "Iron Brigade," spearhead of the First Corps and supposedly the roughest outfit in the Union army. The Rebels thought so. They stopped in their tracks, shouting, "There are those damned black-hatted fellows again! 'Taint no militia. It's the Army of the Potomac!"[11] The Iron Brigade and the units that followed captured two enemy regiments and a brigadier general.

But Confederate reinforcements were also arriving in force. While A. P. Hill kept up the pressure in front, Bald Dick Ewell slammed into the Union right. The line cracked like an eggshell. Fugitives ran through Gettysburg, toward Cemetery Hill, the Rebels at their heels. Frightened townspeople offered their men food and coffee, anything to make them rally to save their homes.

It was no use. Those who could not escape hid in houses and stables. Rebels searched these places from cellar to attic. In one house, they found thirteen men in the closets, under the beds, and behind the piano. In all, five thousand Yankees were captured in and around the town.

Their comrades climbed Cemetery Hill. Exhausted and demoralized, they knew they could not withstand a fresh assault. And if they lost the hill, the Army of the Potomac would be unable to fight at Gettysburg. Lee knew it, too. Watching the retreat from Seminary Ridge, he sent word that Ewell should take the hill "if practicable." The gentlemanly Lee preferred to suggest actions to his subordinates, not give direct orders, which might have seemed harsh. That was an error. Lee wanted that hill—badly. But rather than order Ewell to take it without fail, he let him do as he saw fit.

Ewell had done enough fighting for the day. His men needed rest. Taking the hill was too dangerous, he said. His advance units were ordered to pull back to Gettysburg. Isaac Trimble, one of his generals, protested.

"Give me a division, and I will take that hill," Trimble begged.

Ewell refused.

"Give me a brigade and I will do it."

Ewell refused.

"Give me a regiment and I will . . . take that hill."

Ewell refused.

Trimble threw down his sword and stalked away, insisting he could not serve under Bald Dick.[12]

Onlookers were shocked; they never expected such timidity from this experienced officer. A colonel turned to a comrade and said sadly, "Jackson is not here." The other nodded in agreement. Stonewall, they knew, would have needed no encouragement to go for Cemetery Hill. Lee believed he would have won at Gettysburg had his friend been there.[13]

Toward evening, Longstreet joined Lee on Seminary Ridge. After studying the valley through his field glasses, he offered a plan of action. The best thing to do, he said, would be to move around the enemy left, slipping between the Union army and Washington. The Confederates could then take up a strong position and wait to be attacked, as at Marye's Heights. Old Pete had seen what the rifle musket could do in the hands of determined veterans. So had the Union commander. Meade later said that a repeat of Marye's Heights was exactly what he feared most.

Lee rejected the advice. Without his cavalry, he had no way of

General Winfield Scott Hancock "Hancock the Magnificent" rode in front of the Union lines to cheer up his men during the massive Confederate bombardment at Gettysburg on July 3, 1863.

knowing Meade's strength or location. Such a move might actually draw him into a trap. He would deal with the problem before him and not venture into the unknown. "If the enemy is there tomorrow," he said, "we must attack him."

Longstreet replied angrily: "If he is there, it is because he is anxious that we should attack him—a good reason, in my judgment, for not doing so."

"No," Lee snapped, showing his own anger. "They are there in position, and I am going to whip them or they are going to whip me."[14]

There was no point arguing once Marse Robert made up his mind. He had committed himself to a do-or-die, all-or-nothing battle. It was a decision he would regret.

Lee stayed up half the night, making plans and issuing orders. Across the valley, the Union chief was pulling out all the stops. Meade sped reinforcements to the front. Although he could not join them right away, he put them in good hands. Their leader was Major General Winfield Scott Hancock of the Second Corps. Hancock, aged thirty-nine, was one of the finest soldiers the United States has ever produced. Nicknamed "Hancock the Magnificent," he was a tall, strapping fellow with brown hair and a goatee beard. A born leader, he always seemed to be in the right place at the right time. The instant he appeared on Cemetery Hill, the troops took heart. Work parties were organized and sent to dig trenches. Five-gun artillery batteries sped across the graveyard, toppling tombstones and taking positions on top of graves.

THURSDAY, JULY 2, 1863. THE SECOND DAY

President Lincoln had been following the telegraph reports with growing anxiety for a week. On the second day of Gettysburg, he awoke early and, still in his nightshirt, went down on his bony knees to speak to the Almighty: "You know I have done all I can. Oh, God, give us a victory!"[15] Confederates, too, knew the stakes were high. As they prepared for battle, chaplains held prayer services in which they asked God's favor.

Lee's plan called for three separate attacks. Two attacks were to be diversions to keep the enemy off balance while the main blow struck home. A. P. Hill was to hit the Union center to keep reinforcements from being sent to either end of the line. Ewell was to pin down the defenders on the Union right. Longstreet, meantime, would spring into action. His men would storm the ridge on the Union left, near the Round Tops, and sweep along the crest until the Yankees were driven off it. Timing was everything. The attacks were to come at the same moment and at sunrise.

The trouble, again, was Lee's way of giving instructions. His desire for an early attack, like his desire for Ewell to take Cemetery Hill, was stated as a suggestion, not as a direct order. Longstreet chose not to follow the suggestion. One reason was anger over Lee's rejection of his own plan. The other was that getting things right was more important to Old Pete than sticking to a timetable. At dawn, he was still missing a division. It was on the way, but he refused to start until it was in position. Or, as he put it, "I never like to go into battle with one boot off."[16] By the time he was ready, at 4:30 P.M., the entire Army of the Potomac was on Cemetery Ridge.

With cannons booming and bands playing polkas and waltzes, Longstreet attacked. The Union's Third Corps was waiting in the fields just west of the ridge. It was in an exposed position, and the Confederates hit it like a runaway express train. At places like the Peach Orchard, the Wheatfield, and Devil's Den, Rebels and Yankees tore into one another with savage fury. Rifles became so hot they burned their owners' hands. After the battle, nearly twenty-eight thousand loaded rifles were collected from the field. Experts found that half had two bullets in the barrel, and six thousand had from three to ten bullets; one had twenty-three bullets. In the excitement, soldiers forgot to shoot and then, forgetting their weapons were loaded, rammed in bullet after bullet.

The Union's Third Corps was hurled back with heavy losses. Longstreet's next move was to send a division straight for the Round Tops. Although its attack was broken, two Alabama regiments nearly won the day. Led by Colonel William C. Oates's Fifteenth Alabama, they started up Big Round Top. The hillside was steep and treacherous, covered with huge moss-covered boul-

A Confederate sniper, killed in the Devil's Den, Gettysburg, July 2, 1863

ders. With enemy bullets zinging overhead, the Alabamians clawed their way up, holding on to bushes and rock ledges. It was unbearably hot. Scores of men, who hadn't eaten since dawn, and then only a mouthful of corn bread, fainted.

Their comrades clambered over the crest of the hill, driving the defenders down the other side. Colonel Oates looked through the trees. What a sight! Below him, across a shallow ravine, stood Little Round Top. Cemetery Ridge stretched northward, crowded with Union troops. It was a gunner's dream come true. He knew that within half an hour he could turn Big Round Top into a fortress that could hold out against ten times the number of men he had. By placing cannons on the hill, he could fire down the length of the Union line; it would be impossible to miss. Oates's superior, however, had different orders. He was to go on to Little Round Top right away.

Four Union regiments defended Little Round Top. The Twentieth Maine, an outfit made up of loggers and fishermen, held the extreme left. Its colonel, Joshua Lawrence Chamberlain, was a college professor with a talent for war. As the enemy swarmed up the hillside, Chamberlain rallied his troops. "Stand firm, ye boys from Maine, for not once in a century are men permitted to bear such responsibilities for freedom and justice, for God and humanity, as are now placed upon you."[17] It was a professor's speech, but it touched something deep inside of them.

Each time the Alabamians charged, the boys from Maine shot them down. Finally, their ammunition nearly gone, Chamberlain gave a desperate order: "Fix bayonets! Charge bayonets! Charge!"[18]

Rising as one, the Twentieth Maine began a wild downhill run, gaining momentum with each step. The effect was devastating. Oates saw a soldier fall, cry, "O, God! that I should see my mother," and die. "While one man was shot in the face, his right-hand or left-hand comrade was shot in the side or back. Some were struck simultaneously with three or four balls from different directions. . . . My dead and wounded . . . literally covered the ground. The blood stood in puddles in some places on the rocks; the ground was soaked with the blood of as brave men as ever fell on the red field of battle."[19] The Alabamians were fine soldiers— the best. But, they declared, in future they wanted nothing to do with Josh Chamberlain's boys.

The sun set. The moon rose. Everyone was exhausted, but nobody got much sleep that night. The wounded lay out on the battlefield in their thousands, moaning. Union stretcher parties ventured as far as the Wheatfield. Black servants combed this area as well, searching for their masters. Field hospitals filled to overflowing; there were three thousand men in one Union hospital alone. Gettysburg, normally a quiet place where a broken leg was big news, became a Confederate hospital. Surgeons took over every church and school, along with scores of private homes. "Wounded men were brought into our houses and laid side by side in our halls and first-story rooms," wrote housewife Jennie McCreary. "In many cases carpets were so saturated with blood as to be unfit for further use. Walls were bloodstained, as well as books that were used for pillows. . . . Into all the hospitals our women went freely and gladly to help in the care of the wounded, showing kindness alike to all, seeming to forget that any were enemies."[20]

Jeb Stuart arrived that night. Where had he been? Why hadn't he reported? Didn't he know the army was blind without his cavalry? Lee spat out the words with an icy fury that made staff officers cringe. Stuart, an officer recalled, "wilted." He explained his actions, but his chief only grew more indignant. Then, remembering what they were at Gettysburg for, Lee calmed down. "Let me ask your help," he said. "We will not discuss the matter longer."[21] There was a battle to be won, and he needed the cavalry.

Lee had risked everything on the invasion of Pennsylvania. But instead of winning the war with a bold stroke, the campaign had been a failure up to this point. He could not—*dared* not—admit defeat. Never again would he have more men than he had at that moment. Going back empty-handed would not halt the manpower drain. Sooner or later, the Army of Northern Virginia would be worn down to nothing. He had to gamble once more.

The fighting around Cemetery Hill and the Round Tops had forced the Union army to strengthen its right and left by weakening its center. Lee's next objective, then, was the center of the enemy line on Cemetery Ridge. Ewell would make a diversion on the Union right, while Stuart's cavalry swung around the Union rear to block reinforcements. At the same time, the artillery would swing into action. It had a three-part mission: silence the enemy's guns, demoralize his troops, and blast a hole in his line. Infantry would then swarm through the hole, turn, and destroy the Yankees from behind. Lee had absolute confidence in his troops. Officers might blunder, but the common soldiers had never let him down. He saw no reason why they should fail at this critical time.

Out on Cemetery Ridge, Meade had called his corps commanders to a war council. They met at Union headquarters, a one-room cottage with bare, whitewashed walls. Thirteen generals, plus their aides, leaned against the walls, sat on the floor, or lounged on a bed that occupied half the room. It was a hot night, and the room filled with strong odors. The windows were open, but everyone was sweating and smoking cigars. From outside came the sounds of marching troops and horse-drawn artillery.

Meade wanted the generals' suggestions about tomorrow. They offered three courses: to retreat, to attack, or to stand and fight. They argued back and forth, making a case for each option. Meade listened patiently, then told them what he had intended to do all along. Lee's attacks on both ends of the Union line had failed. He knew Lee. If his friend struck again, as he surely would, it would be at the Union center. And the Army of the Potomac would be waiting.

F R I D A Y ,   J U L Y   3 ,   1 8 6 3 .
T H E   D A Y   O F   D E C I S I O N

That morning, as the troops moved into their assault positions, Old Pete tried to change Lee's mind for the last time. "General, I have been a soldier all my life," he said. "I have been with soldiers engaged in fights by couples, by squads, by companies, regiments, and armies, and should know, as anyone, what soldiers can do. It is my opinion that no fifteen thousand men . . . can take that position."[22] The attack was bound to be a costly disaster.

Lee was not at his best that morning. Passing soldiers noticed that his face was drawn, as if he were deeply troubled; actually, he had a severe case of diarrhea and was constantly going into the woods to relieve himself. He brushed Old Pete's remark aside. "The enemy is there, General Longstreet, and I am going to strike him," said Lee bluntly.[23]

A stone fence three feet high ran along the crest of Cemetery Ridge. Peering over the fence, Union soldiers saw rolling fields and pastures stretching toward the base of Seminary Ridge. The ridge itself was alive with the Rebels' horse-drawn artillery and ammunition caissons. Rebel gun batteries appeared along the edge of the woods and on the slope in front. There were 220 guns, more than the Yankees had ever faced at one time; they had only 172 guns on this part of their line. The guns glistened in the sunlight, their barrels trained on the Union center.

Brigadier General George E. Pickett led his division in a disastrous charge of Union forces on Cemetery Ridge.

Three divisions, from thirteen thousand to fifteen thousand men, were to make the assault. Brigadier General George E. Pickett commanded the lead division. Pickett, aged thirty-eight, was a dandy who wore his perfumed hair down to his shoulders. He had been born in Richmond, but as a young man he had gone to Illinois to study law in his uncle's office. There he became friendly with another lawyer, one Abraham Lincoln by name. Told by Pickett that he wished to be a soldier, not a lawyer, Lincoln helped him get an appointment to West Point. Pickett always spoke warmly of his friend, and Lincoln's strongest term for this Rebel was "the rascal."

The Rebel assault troops waited in the woods behind the crest of Seminary Ridge. The sun beat down, the trees cutting off the circulation of air and raising the temperature. They knew they faced an awesome task. They would have to cross fourteen hundred yards of open ground, climb Cemetery Ridge, and fight those men behind the stone fence. No Civil War troops had ever attacked over such a long distance in the open. Veterans all, they were as frightened as rookies; *more* frightened, perhaps, because they knew what lay ahead. "I tell you, there is no romance in making one of these charges," wrote Private John Dooley. "I tell you the enthusiasm of ardent breasts in many cases *ain't there,* and instead of burning to avenge the insults of our country, families and altars and firesides, the thought is most frequently, *Oh,* if I could just come out of this charge safely how thankful *would I be!*"[24] Their only hope was the artillery: If their guns could clear the way, they might be able to get across with minimum loss. If not, it would be Fredericksburg in reverse.

To ease the tension, Rebels pelted one another with green apples. Many ate the apples instead. They were hungry, few having had enough, if indeed any, breakfast. Sergeant June Kimble, Fourteenth Tennessee regiment, thought more of his honor than his stomach. He sat among his men, silent and solemn, growing more agitated by the minute. Suddenly he leaped up and asked aloud, "June Kimble, are you going to do your duty today?" The answer, heard by everyone, was, "I'll do it so help me God."[25]

Things got off to a bad start. The diversions Lee had planned came to nothing. Bald Dick Ewell capped his string of failures by attacking too early and being driven back. Jeb Stuart was beaten off by Union cavalry under "Old Curly," George Armstrong Custer, at twenty-three the youngest general in the Union army.

All was quiet along Cemetery Ridge. After lunch, most Yankees took a siesta. They sprawled on the ground, sleeping soundly or dozing with eyes half-closed. It was so still you could hear the hum of bees going from blossom to blossom. At precisely 1:07 P.M. a sharp *boom* echoed across the valley from Seminary Ridge. Men, opening their eyes, actually saw a shell flying through the air. It came slowly, lazily, a black dot against a blue sky. It burst in a ball of orange flame and white smoke over the Union line. A minute passed. Another *boom,* and another explosion. Then every Rebel gun went off in a colossal roar.

A hurricane of iron lashed Cemetery Ridge. Artillery caissons exploded. Field hospitals were riddled with shrapnel. A shell went through six horses hitched side by side, blowing them to bits. Another horse galloped along on three legs. At a Second Corps encampment, officers were finishing a meal of fried chicken and pickled cucumbers. An orderly was serving butter when a cannonball cut him in half. Officers died as they stood up, some with cigars still between their teeth or pieces of food in their fingers. A shell splinter split open a colonel's cheek, knocking out two teeth. Asked if he was hurt, the colonel growled, "No, sir; just had a tooth pulled."[26] Veterans of bombardments from Malvern Hill to Chancellorsville swore they had never seen anything like it. Past bombardments, they said, were Fourth of July celebrations by comparison.

Officers set an example of courage and devotion. General Alexander Webb, for example, stood in the open, calmly leaning on his sword and smoking a cigar. General Abner Doubleday, supposedly the inventor of baseball, munched a sandwich while watching the bombardment from an exposed position. When a shell exploded nearby, covering him with dirt, he said, "That sandwich will need no pepper!"[27]

But for cold-blooded courage, nobody outdid Hancock the Magnificent. While passing behind his lines, on his way to the ridge, he met a six-year-old girl dragging a rifle larger than herself. Seeing Hancock, she cried, "My papa's dead, but here's my papa's gun."[28] The general was tight-lipped as he went on to join his men.

Men were hugging the ground in fear, when they heard the sound of hoofbeats *in front* of the stone fence. Raising their heads, they saw Hancock and a color-bearer carrying the clover-leaf flag of the Second Corps. An aide came up to ask if a corps commander should be exposing himself in this fashion. Yes, he should, Hancock replied with a snort. "There are times when a corps commander's life does not count."[29]

Their generals' defiance stiffened the soldiers' courage. So did the fact that Rebel gunners were overshooting their targets. Gradually, the surprise wore off. The Billy Yanks settled down; some even fell asleep. Others joked about enemy marksmanship. "What do you think of this?" asked John Gibbon, Hancock's second-in-command. "Oh, this is bully," men answered with a laugh. "We are getting to like it." "We don't mind this."[30]

The Union artillery had already swung into action. With so many guns firing, the rising smoke turned the sun into a huge scarlet disk. The heated atmosphere played tricks with sound. It was quiet at Chambersburg, 25 miles across the Blue Ridge, but people 150 miles away heard the explosions clearly.[31]

Shells overshot the crest of Seminary Ridge and burst among the huddled Rebels, killing about three hundred of them. As Marse Robert rode by, an explosion shook the ground. The men yelled at him to go away, but he raised his hat, nodded in appreciation, and went about his business. A soldier sang to calm himself:

Backward, roll backward, O Time in thy flight:
Make me a child again, just for this fight!

A fellow nearby chimed in, "Yes; and a *gal* child at that."[32]

One by one, the Union batteries ceased fire and were pulled back. By 2:55 P.M., all were silent. Meade had taken the guns out of action to save ammunition and allow them to cool. The main reason, however, was to lure the Confederates into the open. If they believed the guns were disabled, they would send their infantry across the field. The only question was: Would they take the bait?

Not if Old Pete had anything to say about it! Believing the attack to be doomed, he could not bring himself to give the go-ahead order. Twice he told his artillery chief, Colonel E. P. Alexander, to give the signal when the Union fire slackened. Alexander refused each time, saying Longstreet was in charge and should give the order himself. Critics later accused him of trying to shirk his duty. Perhaps so. Most probably not. We cannot be sure. Alexander was a gunnery expert, and Longstreet knew that Lee respected experts. He also knew that Lee had refused to listen to him. It is possible that he was trying to coax Alexander into saying he was running out of ammunition (which was true) as a way of persuading Lee to cancel the attack.

Pickett was with Longstreet when the Union guns fell silent. Alexander sent word that he had better come quick, since his ammunition was so low that he could not support an attack for more than a few minutes. Pickett asked if he should go ahead. Longstreet could not speak. "I saw tears glistening on his cheeks and beard," Pickett wrote his fiancée. "The stern old war horse, God bless him, was weeping for his men."[33] All he could do was nod. Pickett returned to his division. No tears for him; he was happy at this chance for "glory."

Longstreet rode over to Alexander's artillery only minutes later. When the gunner confirmed that his ammunition was nearly gone, Longstreet became frantic. "Stop Pickett immediately and replenish your ammunition," he cried. "I do not want to make this attack. I would stop it now but that General Lee ordered it and expects it to go on. I don't see how it can succeed."[34] But it was too late. No words could halt "Pickett's Charge."

As Longstreet spoke, the assault troops were scrambling to their feet and taking their places in line. Some fainted from heat and fear. Yet, even then, there were touches of humor. A Yankee shell exploded in the bushes near one regiment and sent a rabbit hopping away. A private called out, "Run, you little ol' hare! If I was a little ol' hare, I'd run too!"[35] His comrades laughed, but they envied the little animal. There was no way out for them.

Officers rode along the line with last-minute instructions. Advance steadily. Advance quietly. No shooting and no Rebel yells until you are just a few yards from the Yankee line. Stay together and follow your flags. Good luck!

"Up, men, and to your posts!" Pickett shouted. "And don't forget that you are from old Virginia."[36]

Farther down the line, General James J. Pettigrew called to his North Carolinians: "Now . . . for the honor of the good Old North State, forward!"[37] No commander mentioned the Confederacy.

Three divisions stepped out of the woods. As they left the shade, the bright sunlight hurt their eyes and made them squint. Hearts pounding, they came down the slope, past Anderson's guns, and into the field below. On they went, through shimmering heat waves, knee deep in ripening grain.

The men on Cemetery Ridge had never seen anything like this. A human wave rolled onward with perfect discipline. The enemy marched elbow to elbow, at 105 steps a minute, their officers leading with drawn swords. "Here they come! Here they come! Here comes their infantry!" a bluecoat blurted out, unable to contain his excitement.[38] Some of his comrades were terrified, others awed by the spectacle. "Beautiful, gloriously beautiful, did that vast array appear in the lovely little valley," an officer recalled.[39]

Lieutenant Frank Haskell wrote a classic description a few days after the battle. He wrote in the present tense, as if the action were still unfolding before his eyes:

> To say that none grew pale and held their breath at what we and they saw would not be true. . . . None on that crest now need be told that the enemy is advancing. Every eye could see his legions, an overwhelming, resistless tide of an ocean of armed men sweeping upon us! Regiment after regiment, brigade after brigade, move from the woods and rapidly take their places in the lines forming the assault. . . . The first line, at short interval, is followed by a second, and that a third succeeds. . . . More than half a mile their front extends; more than a thousand yards the dull gray masses deploy, man touching man, rank pressing rank, and line supporting line. Their red flags wave; their horsemen gallop up and down, [their rifles], barrel and bayonet, gleam in the

Confederate dead at Gettysburg. Note that the man in the foreground is wearing a Union jacket. The Johnny Rebs were usually so hard up for clothes that they wore Yankee uniforms taken from captured supply dumps or stripped from the bodies of the dead.

sun, a sloping forest of flashing steel. Right on they move as with one soul, in perfect order . . . over ridge and slope, through orchard and meadow and cornfield—magnificent, grim, irresistible.[40]

Without waiting for orders, the Billy Yanks rose from behind the stone fence, rested their rifles on the fence, and pulled back the hammers. A metallic *click, click, click* rippled along the crest of Cemetery Ridge. Artillerymen wheeled their guns back into position, loaded them, and took aim. Officers slid pistols from holsters.

The tension grew by the minute. In a New York regiment, a color-bearer leaped onto the fence, waving his flag and shouting for the Rebels to hurry up and get it over with. Nearby, a gunner cried, "Come on, Johnny! Keep on coming!"[41]

Closer and closer the Rebels came. "Easy, men, easy. Hold your fire," Yankee artillery officers called.

The Rebel lines grew larger.

"Fire!"

Every Yankee cannon roared at once. But it wasn't the blast of gunfire eyewitnesses remembered. They remembered, first, the gut-wrenching moan that went up from the lines of gray and butternut. Then, through the drifting smoke, they saw men falling in batches. Some crumpled to the ground like sacks of potatoes, some staggered a few yards before dropping. Soldiers spun around and literally came apart in pieces. An observer recalled, "Arms, heads, blankets, guns, and knapsacks were tossed in the air, and the moan from the battlefield was heard amid the storm of battle."[42]

The lines faltered, steadied, and pressed forward. As the distance closed, Union gunners changed their ammunition. For long distance, they had used solid shot and explosive shells. For close-in work, they switched to shrapnel and canister. The effect of these was horrendous. Entire companies fell as if cut down by a scythe. "Close up! Close up!" Rebel officers shouted. Captain M. P. Spessard, Twenty-eighth Virginia regiment, passed his dying son. Leaning over, he kissed the boy's cheek; then he raised his sword and kept going. General Lewis Armistead stuck his hat on the tip of his sword and pointed toward Cemetery Ridge. A young lieutenant cried, "Home, home, boys! Remember, home is over beyond those hills!"[43]

On they came, the ranks thinning with every step. The men behind the stone fence saw their faces clearly, saw the whites of their eyes.

"Fire!"

Thousands of rifles barked. Whole regiments fell, riddled with bullets and torn by shrapnel. But by now the Rebels were climbing

General Lewis A. Armistead put his hat on his sword and led his men forward during the closing stage of "Pickett's Charge," July 3, 1863. Moments after the scene depicted here, Armistead fell, mortally wounded, over the gun in front of him.

the slope toward the stone fence. Men pulled their hats down over their eyes so as not to see the flaming rifles up ahead. The fire was so intense that many bowed their heads as if walking against a hailstorm. Yet it was more than even they could take. Although a handful leaped over the fence, wounding Hancock the Magnificent, they were all killed or captured. Lew Armistead fell as he touched a Union cannon. The rest turned and ran for their lives. Pickett's Charge was over. It had lasted twenty minutes from start to finish.

"By God, boys, we've got 'em now," a Yankee shouted. "They've broke all to hell!"[44]

Never before had Lee's men fallen back in such confusion. It was fantastic, glorious, a sight to gladden a Union man's heart. A victory cry echoed from Big Round Top to Cemetery Hill.

"Fredericksburg! Fredericksburg! Fredericksburg!" soldiers chanted, raising their rifles above their heads. Bands struck up "The Star-Spangled Banner" and men sang "John Brown's Body." A division commander kissed his bearded aide. George Meade rode up with his son, a member of his staff. Seeing the Confederates retreat, he shook his fist and shouted *"Thank God!"* followed by "Hurrah!"[45]

The survivors' ordeal was not over yet. As they recrossed the field, the Union artillery opened fire again. Fearing a shot in the back was bad enough. What made things worse was having to pass through nearly a mile of smoking ground covered by dead and wounded comrades. Many survivors were in tears. Others were numb with shock at the realization of what they had been through.

Marse Robert was waiting for them. His generalship had failed terribly. But as a man, this was his finest moment. Dismounting from Traveller, he walked toward the oncoming men alone, reaching out to them with open arms. On the way, Lee passed a wounded Yankee prisoner lying on the ground. "Hurrah for the

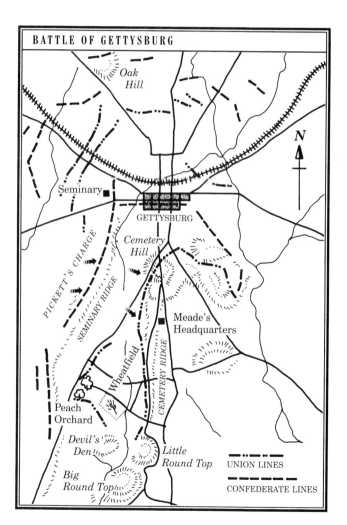

BATTLE OF GETTYSBURG

Oak Hill

N

Seminary

GETTYSBURG

PICKETT'S CHARGE

SEMINARY RIDGE

Cemetery Hill

Meade's Headquarters

Wheatfield

CEMETERY RIDGE

Peach Orchard

Devil's Den

Little Round Top

Big Round Top

UNION LINES

CONFEDERATE LINES

Union!" the Yankee shouted. He was scared when Lee stopped, turned, and came back toward him. But instead of killing him, as he expected, Lee took his hand and said, "My son, I hope you will soon be well." The surprised Yankee remembered his sad expression and the warmth of his voice. "As soon as the General left me I cried myself to sleep there upon the bloody ground."[46]

Now came the hard part; facing his own troops. There was no whining, no blaming others for his mistakes. He was the commanding general and, as such, bore full responsibility. He tried to encourage the survivors, saying, "All this will come right in the end . . . but, in the meantime, all good men must rally."[47] Then he said something that was both an admission and a plea for forgiveness: "It's all my fault! I thought my men were invincible!" He repeated it again and again: "My fault! . . . My fault! . . . The fault is mine!"[48]

Gettysburg was a Confederate disaster. In three days of fighting, the Army of Northern Virginia had suffered 22,638 casualties, compared to 17,684 for the Army of the Potomac. Pickett's Charge accounted for 6,467 killed, wounded, and captured. Some historians believe only 10,500 men made the charge, not 13,000 to 15,000

Confederate prisoners at Gettysburg. Although defeated, these men were certainly not "whipped." They pose for the camera standing proudly, indeed arrogantly. The fellow in the center is wearing a "horse collar" over his shoulder, rather than a heavy backpack. All three are wearing civilian clothes, since uniforms were hard to come by in the Army of Northern Virginia.

as was thought at the time. If this is so, then 62 percent of the attacking force was lost. Abraham Lincoln appreciated courage, even in Rebels. It was reported that before delivering the Gettysburg Address four months later, he looked out across that awful killing field, toward Cemetery Ridge. Turning sadly, he said: "I am proud to be the countryman of the men who assailed those heights."[49]

Lee bore no grudge against Longstreet; he remained his old warhorse, trusted, and deserving of trust, to the end. Military experts agree that Old Pete had been right to oppose an assault on the Union center. Almost a century later, President Dwight D. Eisenhower took British field marshal Sir Bernard Law Montgomery on a tour of the Gettysburg battlefield. Eisenhower had led the Allied armies to victory against Germany in World War II; Montgomery had been his top field commander. Looking toward Cemetery Ridge, Montgomery shook his head in dismay. It was, he said, "a monstrous thing to launch this charge." Pickett's Charge, he repeated, was "a monstrous thing." Eisenhower agreed. Longstreet's idea of moving around the Union left had been correct, he believed. "Why [Lee] didn't go around there, I'll never know."[50]

Early on Saturday, July 4, 1863, General John B. Imboden sat under a tree near Lee's headquarters tent. Lee had sent for him to discuss certain cavalry movements. But since the chief was busy elsewhere, he had been waiting for several hours. All was still. Everyone was asleep, even Lee's staff.

At 1:00 A.M., a lone rider approached. It was Marse Robert. In the moonlight, he seemed the saddest, weariest, loneliest person on earth. After a few words about the battle, Lee fell silent, lost in his private thoughts. Then he blurted out these agonized words: "Too bad! *Too bad! Oh! Too Bad!*"

Then, turning to Imboden, he said: "We must now return to Virginia."[51]

VIII ✧ THAT MAN GRANT

July 4, 1863, was a black day for the Confederacy. In the East, at Gettysburg, a cold, driving rain washed the blood from the grass. Toward evening, the retreat began. The Confederate army slogged toward the Potomac, a wagon train seventeen miles long carrying the wounded. There had not been time to treat most of them, so that every turn of the wagon wheels was agony. Men lay on the bare wooden floorboards, bouncing as the springless wagons lurched over rough roads. Canvas offered no protection, and everyone was soaked and shivering. "Oh God!" a man would cry. "Why can't I die? Will no one have mercy and kill me?"[1] A thousand miles to the west, the defenders of Vicksburg were raising the white flag of surrender over the city hall. There, at least, the prisoners—thirty thousand of them—were fed and cared for by the conqueror.

Gettysburg had been Robert E. Lee's first major defeat, and he took it hard. In August he offered Jefferson Davis his resignation. He was not well, he explained, adding that it would be best if a younger, abler man took his place. Davis frowned. Nobody, he insisted, could replace Marse Robert. Now, more than ever, the Confederacy needed his services.

Abraham Lincoln could not have agreed more strongly. Gettysburg and Vicksburg proved that it was no longer possible for the Confederacy to win the war militarily. But it was still possible for the Union to lose it. Lee was a fast learner, unlikely to make the same mistake twice. Unless he was checked, the war promised to go on for years, ending, if not in a Union battlefield defeat, in a negotiated settlement recognizing Southern independence; in effect, a defeat at the conference table. Lincoln, then, recognized Lee as the man to beat. But how? He had whipped four Union commanders—McClellan, Pope, Burnside, and Hooker—in less than a year. Meade, the victor at Gettysburg, had not pressed his advantage, allowing the Confederates to escape.

Lincoln studied the numbers. War is, after all, really a numbers game. The numbers involve many things: weapons, factories, supplies, ships, railroad mileage. But most of all they involve men's lives. A few days after Fredericksburg, he had made the same point as Lee would after Chancellorsville. In every major battle, he told a White House aide, the Union lost more men than the Confederacy. Yet the Union could always replace its losses, while the Confederacy could not. Therefore, "if the same battle were to be fought over again, every day, through a week of days, with the same relative results, the army of Lee would be wiped out to the last man, the Army of the Potomac would still be a mighty host, the war would be over, the Confederacy gone." The problem, he continued, was one of character. "No general yet found can face the arithmetic, but the end of the war will be at hand when he shall be discovered." [2]

Face the arithmetic. Here was the answer! Lincoln needed a general who would hammer away without counting the cost. True, Union losses would be frightful, a prospect that brought tears to his eyes. Still, in the long run, heavy losses might be a blessing in disguise. That was the cruel arithmetic of war. It was better, the president thought, to lose men to end the war quickly, than to fight, lose men, retreat, and have to repeat the process over and over again. That strategy cost more lives in the long run, and with no benefit whatsoever. The men in the ranks were beginning to understand this, too. Not that they heard the president speak of it; they knew it by instinct. The call was heard throughout the Army of the Potomac: "Abraham Lincoln, give us a man!"[3]

By early 1864 Lincoln had his man. Ulysses S. Grant was as stubborn and single-minded as the president himself. An observer said he always looked as if he had decided to drive his head through a brick wall and was on the verge of doing so. He *was* tough!

Born in Ohio in 1822, Grant stood five feet eight inches tall, weighed 135 pounds, and had brown hair, a short beard, gray-blue

eyes, and a deep voice. After graduating from West Point, he served
with distinction in the Mexican War. The war over, he was promoted to captain and sent to frontier posts, duty he hated because it
kept him from his family for years at a time. Like Marse Robert, he
was a warm, caring father. In 1854, while Lee was superintendent
of West Point, Grant resigned from the army to avoid charges of
being drunk on duty. By 1860, when Lee was military commander
of Texas, Grant was dreading the future. Having failed as a farmer
and a real estate salesman, he was reduced to selling firewood,
dressed in a faded army uniform. He finally took a low-paying job
as a clerk in his father's leather goods store in Galena, Illinois.

The Civil War gave Grant his big chance. Rejoining the army,
he rose rapidly through ability, daring, and luck. Early in 1862, as a
brigadier general, he captured two enemy forts on the Tennessee
and Cumberland rivers. The North, sick of bungling generals, was
thrilled by his message to the Rebel commander: "No terms except
an unconditional surrender can be accepted."[4] The phrase was electrifying. From then on, he was "Unconditional Surrender" Grant.

Success followed success. Grant defeated the Confederates at
Shiloh on the Tennessee River, took Vicksburg, and stormed
Missionary Ridge outside of Chattanooga. These victories stirred
up jealousy among less able commanders, and rumors (false) that
he was an alcoholic. Abraham Lincoln put an end to such talk.
"No," he said, "I can't lose this man. He fights."[5] On March 9,
1864, he named Grant general-in-chief of the armies of the United

General Ulysses S. Grant (left),
*seated opposite General John
Rawlins, his close friend and
chief of staff, at Cold Harbor,
Virginia, 1864*

States. It was a critical move. For the first time a general could make a plan and apply it to the war as a whole, something Lee was never able to do.

There was a scruffy, rumpled look about Grant. Unlike most generals, North and South, he disliked fancy uniforms. His usual outfit consisted of muddy boots, a private's pants and shirt, and a weather-beaten hat. The only sign of rank was the three stars of a lieutenant general pinned to his shoulder straps. Nothing fazed him, not even being awakened at three o'clock in the morning with news of an enemy breakthrough. Once he sank his teeth into a problem, or an enemy, he never let go. Yet he was squeamish. The sight of blood sickened him; he demanded that his meat be cooked until crisp.

Grant found his army camped at Brandy Station. The troops did not know what to make of him. "He's a little 'un," they muttered as he rode by, a cigar clamped between his teeth; he smoked two dozen cigars a day. Before long, however, the "little 'un" showed who was in charge. Veterans drilled for hours, then spent more hours at target practice. Supplies and reinforcements arrived by the trainload. Incompetent generals left for parts unknown. Soldiers noticed these changes, and approved. "The boss," they said, was not afraid to call a fool by his correct name.

But Grant had still to prove himself where it counted—on an Eastern battlefield. Despite its victory at Gettysburg, the Army of the Potomac lacked confidence. Soldiers had fallen into the habit of failure. Gettysburg was a fluke, they believed, an error that Lee would remedy the first chance he got. Grant's longtime aides found this attitude hard to understand; after all, the general had given *them* the habit of success out West. "Don't you believe in Grant at all?" a colonel asked his aides. "Yes, we believe in Grant," one replied, "but we believe a great deal more in Lee and in the Army of Northern Virginia."[6] Enlisted men held the Rebel leader in awe. They called him "Bobby Lee" and the "Gray Fox"; for them, he was a hero larger than life.

Grant was not afraid of Marse Robert's reputation. His mother once asked if he was worried about going up against the Southerner. "Not at all," he said. "I know Lee as well as he knows himself. I know all his strong points, and all his weak ones. I intend to attack his weak points, and flank [get around] his strong ones."[7] Deep down, he felt himself to be more than a match for Lee. This feeling had nothing to do with arrogance. It was based on a string of victories that even Southern generals admired.

General Philip Sheridan, chief of cavalry, Army of the Potomac. Known as "Little Phil," Sheridan was the brilliant, and ruthless, officer who cleared the Confederates out of the Shenandoah Valley in 1864.

Grant did not concern himself with small details. That was Meade's job; he still commanded the Army of the Potomac and saw to its day-to-day operations, freeing Grant to direct overall strategy. Several trusted aides had come with him from the West. The best of them was his cavalry chief, Major General Philip H. Sheridan. "Little Phil" was five feet five inches tall, had short black hair, dark eyes, and a hair-trigger temper. He was nothing like Jeb Stuart, his Confederate opposite. For Stuart, fighting on horseback was romantic. For Little Phil, however, the horse soldier was "only an infantryman with four detachable legs." Cavalry, he insisted, should not be used for guard duty or small-scale raids, but in masses to crush the enemy cavalry. Grant admired Sheridan, as did Lincoln, who said: "General Sheridan, when this peculiar war began I thought a cavalryman should be at least six feet four high; but I have changed my mind—five feet four will do in a pinch."[8]

Part of Grant's genius was his ability to see beyond the battlefield. Like Stonewall Jackson, he wanted to hurl "thunderbolts of war." This meant striking two targets simultaneously. One was the enemy home front. If civilians supported the Confederate war machine, then, he felt, they became legitimate targets. Not that he meant to harm them physically, much less kill them. But he would make them feel the war during every waking minute. Whatever kept Southern society going, from farms to factories to railroads, was fair game in his eyes. Lowering the standard of living would destroy people's willpower, spreading fear and hopelessness. Grant gave no name to this strategy; today, we call it "total war."

Grant's second target was the Rebel armies. He and Lincoln saw eye to eye on this question. He forgot about taking this city or that town. Places were worthless in themselves; their only value was as transportation and supply centers for enemy forces. Grant was out for blood. He would inflict the heaviest casualties possible, even if that meant taking heavy losses in return. No longer would there be separate eastern and western fronts, in effect two separate wars. There would be one war, each action fitting into an overall scheme with one man, himself, in control.

Grant told his generals what all this meant in practical terms. Meade, with the boss peering over his shoulder, was to target Lee's Army of Northern Virginia. If Richmond fell in the process, that would be a special bonus. But Richmond was a sideshow. "Lee's army will be your objective point," he told Meade. "Where Lee goes, you will go also."[9] Meade must hammer away without letup, killing Lee's men and preventing him from shifting forces to other trouble spots. Meanwhile, William Tecumseh Sherman was to invade Georgia from Tennessee. Advancing southward, "Uncle Billy," as his men called him, must destroy anything of value to the Rebel war effort. Lee would be stuck in Virginia, facing Grant, while Sherman demolished the Confederacy from behind. Terrible battles lay ahead. But Grant had a winning strategy. It was a brutal strategy, but no more so than war itself.

Grant's plan for 1864 was almost an exact copy of Hooker's. He meant to cross the Rapidan and slip between Lee and Richmond, easing him out of his trenches and forcing a showdown in the open. Since his army numbered 122,000 men to Lee's 66,000, the odds were heavily in his favor. Fighting Joe, of course, had enjoyed a similar advantage, and failed. But Grant was no Hooker; come hell or high water, he meant to press forward. Told that Union pontoons had been lost, Grant did not bat an eyelash. "If I beat General Lee," he said, "I sha'n't want any pontoons; and if General Lee beats me I can take all the men I intend to take back across the river on a log."[10]

Lee had an observation post on Clark's Mountain south of the Rapidan. Peering through his field glasses, he had a clear view of the river and the Union camps beyond. Common sense told him that Grant would come by way of Germanna and Ely Fords, then through the Wilderness. He and his generals knew the area well, but it was strange ground to Grant. He would let the Yankees get entangled in the Wilderness, then crush their right flank, as Stonewall Jackson had done. But this time he would cut their supply line, giving Grant two choices: dig in and starve, or beat a hasty retreat and lose most of his army along the way. It would be another Chancellorsville, only bigger and better. The very idea raised his spirits. "Colonel," he told an aide, "we have got to whip them; we must whip them, and it has already made me feel better to think of it."[11]

Longstreet was hopeful, yet cautious. Members of his staff had treated Grant's appointment as a joke. He was, they said smirkingly, simply another bluebelly with an inflated reputation. Old Pete put them straight. He knew Grant better than any Southerner. A cousin of Grant's wife, Julia, he and Grant had been friends since their student days at West Point. They had spent countless hours together, talking, joking, and playing brag, a card game similar to poker. "I was in the corps of cadets with him at West Point for three years," he said. "I was present at his wedding, I served in the same army with him in Mexico, I have observed his methods of warfare in the West, and I believe I know him through and through; and I tell you that we cannot afford to underrate him and the army he now commands. We must make up our minds to get into line of battle and stay there; for that man will fight us every day and every hour till the end of this war."[12]

And so he did.

On May 4 the Army of the Potomac splashed across the Rapidan. In addition to its men, the army had 274 cannons, 56,000 horses and mules, 835 ambulances, 4,300 supply wagons, and thousands of head of cattle to be slaughtered en route for fresh meat. Newsmen estimated that the wagons alone, if arranged in single file, would have stretched seventy-five miles.

All went well—*too* well. Grant knew Lee was nearby, and had expected to fight his way across the Rapidan. But not a shot was fired. The only signs of the enemy were cavalry patrols making observations and galloping away when challenged by Union cavalry. That worried Grant.

His men were worried *and* nervous. The Rapidan held bad memories. Almost a year ago to the day, they had crossed this same river on the way to Chancellorsville. Grim sights awaited them at the famous crossroads. Camping around the burned-out house, they could feel the spirits of the dead. A rumor went from campsite to campsite: Stonewall Jackson's left arm lay buried nearby. Just the thought of him gave them the creeps.

The dead had been buried in shallow graves, but winter rains had washed away the earth. Private Warren Goss was horrified at

Skulls found in the Wilderness in the spring of 1864. All of the skulls shown here belonged to men killed during the Battle of Chancellorsville the previous year.

the scene. "Weather-stained remnants of clothing, rusty gun-barrels and bayonets, tarnished brasses and equipments, with bleaching bones and grinning skulls marked this terrible field. In the cavity of one of these skulls was a nest with the three speckled eggs of a field bird. In yet another was a wasp nest. Life in embryo in the skull of death!"[13] Goss's comrades swallowed hard. They knew a big fight was coming and that this was what might become of them.

Next morning, Lee hit them with everything he had. It was not a battle in the sense that armies faced each other and fought in an organized fashion. Once the shooting began, it became a gigantic brawl among the blind. In that hellhole of the Wilderness, all formation vanished. Smoke settled over the area, making it impossible to see more than a few yards in any direction. Men pointed their rifles into the smoke and fired, they hoped, at the enemy. Even veterans of Chancellorsville were astonished. A Confederate compared the armies to maddened beasts: "Two wild animals were hunting each other, when they heard each other's steps they sprang and grappled. . . . Here, in blind wrestle as at midnight, did two hundred thousand men in blue and gray clutch each other—bloodiest and weirdest of encounters."[14]

Grant kept cool. Where Hooker had panicked, he sat under a tree writing orders in his neat handwriting. Send reinforcements here! Rush artillery there! Regroup and go forward everywhere! Hit them hard, and keep on hitting! So it went throughout the day. Every Rebel attack was met by a Union counterattack. The Army of the Potomac shook off its surprise and fought as never before. At sundown, as if by mutual agreement, the guns gradually fell silent.

Again, as in 1863, the woods caught fire. Flames lit the sky, while the wounded suffocated or burned alive. Again, enemies discovered their common humanity. Men helped one another as best they could, pulling victims to safety and sharing the precious water in their canteens. It was much appreciated. Union chaplain A. M. Stewart found a wounded Rebel sitting with his back to a tree.

"Well, friend, how are you getting along?" Stewart asked.

"Wall, stranger, bad enough," the Rebel replied.

"Got any water?"

"Nary a drop since yesterday."

The chaplain poured some into his cup from his canteen.

"Got a wife?"

"Yes, yes; and a whole lot of children, away in North Carolina; and oh, if I was only with Mammy now."

Stewart asked stretcher bearers to carry the Rebel to a field hospital. That was too much even for this veteran. He began to cry. Then, puzzled by his own reaction, he exclaimed, "Wall, now, this does beat all!"[15]

Next morning, May 6, both sides attacked at precisely five o'clock. No one had planned simultaneous assaults, but the effect was like armies of tanks speeding toward each other in a fog. The larger one, however, prevailed. Hancock the Magnificent, recovered from his Gettysburg wound, slammed into the Confederates and sent them reeling. Lee was on Traveller, watching them stream past in confusion. His line was broken and he had no reserves. Only Longstreet could save the day. He was on the way, but there was no telling if he would arrive in time.

Just then, men in butternut swarmed out of the woods. They were the Texas Brigade, the spearhead of Longstreet's corps.

"Who are you, my boys?" Lee called.

"Texas boys," they yelled.

That was the best answer Lee could have heard. He'd had a warm spot in his heart for Texans ever since his days on the frontier. Now he told them so. "Hurrah for Texas!" he shouted, shaking his fist in the enemy's direction. "Texans always move them!"

Those words were a compliment and a challenge. The Texans swept forward, determined to prove themselves to Marse Robert. But as they did, so did he. "Charge them!" Lee cried. "Charge! Charge, boys!" The excitement of battle had taken over, and his blood was up. He was leading the charge himself.

The Texans were astonished. Not only did they love him, they

Union wounded during the Wilderness campaign. The soldier on the stretcher seems to have lost his right foot. After surgery, patients were placed on the bare ground to recover under the trees.

knew that his death spelled final defeat. The same words came to hundreds of men at once, as if they were reading one another's minds. "Lee to the rear! Lee to the rear!" they roared. "Go back, General Lee! Go back! We won't go on unless you go back!"

Longstreet had the last word. Old Pete rode up to Lee and ordered him, politely, either to take over his corps or get out of the way. "If my services were not needed I would like to ride to a place of safety, as it was not quite comfortable where we were." Lee came to his senses. He turned around, shouting, "Charge them!"[16]

The Yankees were pushed back. Longstreet was a marvel, dashing about, waving his sword, and shouting for his men to push on. Then history repeated itself. He was about to break the enemy line when, like Stonewall Jackson, he was shot by his own men. A bullet went into his throat with such force that it lifted him from the saddle. Although he survived, nearly choking on his own blood, he would be out of action for five months. Word of the accident spread like wildfire; rumor had it that he was dead. The Confederate advance ground to a halt by the afternoon. There were some more attacks, but they accomplished nothing. Both sides had had enough. The Battle of the Wilderness was over.

Two capitals waited in suspense for news from the front. In Richmond, early reports indicated another Chancellorsville. In Washington, nobody had the slightest idea of what was happening. Grant had broken contact with the capital, and Lincoln himself was in the dark. "You see," he told a visiting congressman, "Grant has gone to the Wilderness, crawled in, drawn up the ladder, and pulled in the hole after him, and I guess we will have to wait till he comes out before we know what he's up to."[17]

Lee knew. The Wilderness had been a bloodbath. Grant's losses totaled 17,666, compared to 7,750 for the Confederates. Old Pete had been right: Lee was going to have his hands full with "that man" Grant. True, Lee had won a *tactical* victory; that is, he hurt the enemy worse than he had been hurt. But casualties are only one measure of success. *Strategically,* that is, considering the effect of an action on the war as a whole, the battle had been a defeat. Grant had taken Lee's best shot and come back swinging. He had held Lee, fixed him, and kept banging away. No one had ever done that before. The Wilderness, not Gettysburg or Vicksburg, was the true turning point of the Civil War. For it was there that Marse Robert lost the initiative. From then on, Grant would be making the moves and Lee would have to respond. As Lee told his staff: "the Army of the Potomac has a head."[18]

May 7 was spent in caring for the wounded and burying the dead. That night, the Army of the Potomac hit the trail again. The ordinary Billy Yank did not realize the significance of the Wilderness. All he knew was that he was leaving thousands of comrades behind in freshly dug graves. Grant, he snorted, was another in a long line of failures. Having bled the army for two days, he couldn't stomach another "to-do" with Bobby Lee. The enlisted man, as usual, seemed to have paid the price of a commander's bungling.

Coming to a familiar fork in the road, the Yankees expected to turn left, back toward the Rapidan fords. They didn't. The columns turned right, heading south. They were not retreating. Grant was taking them deeper into enemy territory. Their sacrifices had not been in vain after all. "Our spirits rose," a soldier recalled. "We marched free. The men began to sing."[19] They sang "Yankee Doodle," "John Brown's Body," and a black spiritual: "Ain't I glad to get out ob de wilderness!" They sang so loud that officers had to quiet them, lest Stuart's scouts detect their movements.

Lee, however, already knew their destination. Even before the scouts reported, he knew Grant was "sliding" to the left, trying to slip around the Confederate right; that is what he would have done, had the situation been reversed. Grant's destination was Spotsylvania Court House, a crossroads ten miles southeast of the Wilderness. Light-Horse Harry Lee had once spent some time there.

Marse Robert rode among his troops, urging them to move quickly. He set a strenuous pace, one that left soldiers panting. One fellow, not recognizing him in the dust and darkness, told him off. "Well may you order us to move on, move on, when you are mounted on a horse," he said. The general ignored the remark. After a while, however, he was recognized. The mood changed instantly. "Marse Robert!" men called. "Yes. Marse Robert, we'll move on and go anywhere you say, even to hell!"[20]

Lee won the race to Spotsylvania. Grant arrived to find the Rebels waiting in a deep trench fronted by breastworks. But that did not stop Grant. He ordered Hancock the Magnificent to drive his Second Corps through a place in the line called the "Mule Shoe" because it bulged outward like an upside-down U. After splitting the Confederate position down the middle, he would strike each part from the rear.

On May 12, at 4:30 A.M., Hancock advanced under cover of a fog so thick that division commanders needed compasses to find their way. But find their way they did. Within an hour, they had broken into the Mule Shoe and were closing in for the kill.

Lee, on Traveller, was in a clearing behind the line. As the demoralized Rebels rushed past, he cried, "Shame on you, men; shame on you! Go back to your regiments; go back to your regiments!"[21] They kept running.

Fortunately, a reserve division was posted nearby. Once more Lee tried to lead a counterattack in person, only to be turned back by soldiers shouting "Lee to the rear!" Nevertheless, he had a close call. Traveller, usually so calm in battle, began to rear when shells burst nearby. And a good thing, too. For a cannonball passed directly under him as he reared. Had all four feet been on the ground, his rider would have been killed.

Hancock's men fell back to the tip of the Mule Shoe and took cover in the captured trench. Regrouping, they counterattacked, determined to break through. The Rebels were equally determined not to give an inch; Lee was building another trench line in the rear, and the men in front had to hold out until it was finished. The irresistible force had met the immovable object.

The worst fighting was at a bend in the trench known as the "Bloody Angle." So many men were in action that it was impossible for those in the rear to get a clear shot; all they could do was pass their loaded rifles to the front ranks. But few in the front lived for more than a couple of minutes anyhow. "The conflict had . . .

become the closest and fiercest of the war," one of Hancock's aides wrote. "Amid a cold, drenching rain, the combatants . . . fired directly into each other's faces; bayonet thrusts were given over the entrenchments, and men grappled their antagonists across the piles of logs and pulled them over, to be stabbed or carried to the rear as prisoners."[22] When a group of twenty to thirty Rebels tried to surrender, they were shot by angry comrades.

The battle raged until midnight, when the new trench was finished and the Rebels gradually withdrew. Lee was shaken by the casualty figures. He had lost at least five thousand men to the enemy's sixty-eight hundred. Worse, he received word that Jeb Stuart had been shot in the stomach that afternoon. The wound was mortal, and he could not live through the night. Already Phil Sheridan was making his mark on the eastern front.

On May 9 Little Phil had set out on a campaign within a campaign. Twelve thousand cavalrymen, riding four abreast, formed a column thirteen miles long. Their mission: Lure Stuart into an uneven fight by threatening the railroad lines north of Richmond.

The opponents met at Yellow Tavern, just seven miles from the Confederate capital. All of Stuart's past mistakes were wiped away by this action. Outnumbered three to one, he charged again and again. Such courage gave Richmond's defenders time to man the trenches and save the city, but cost Stuart his life. "He never brought me a piece of false information," said Lee, tears filling his eyes. "I can hardly think of him without weeping."[23]

Those tears might also have been for the Confederate cause. Marse Robert had lost his first team. Stonewall Jackson dead. Pete Longstreet badly wounded. Jeb Stuart shot down at thirty-one. And still "that man" refused to turn back.

After two weeks of testing Lee's defenses, Grant repeated his slide to the left. By late May his men were on familiar ground. Passing Mechanicsville and Gaines's Mill, veterans remembered the Seven Days. This time their destination was Cold Harbor, a crossroads north of the Chickahominy and ten miles east of Richmond.

Marse Robert was waiting. Another forced march had brought him to Cold Harbor only hours ahead of the enemy. The Confederate defenses lay along a chain of low hills and were designed to hit an attacker in front and from both sides at the same time. Yankees marveled at the enemy's ingenuity and grit. Although aided by slaves, the Confederate soldiers did most of the digging themselves. A Union colonel, an expert engineer, wrote in his diary:

It is a rule that, when the rebels halt, the first day gives them a good rifle pit; the second, a regular infantry parapet with artillery in position; and the third a parapet with an abatis in front and entrenched batteries behind. Sometimes they put this three-days' work into the first twenty-four hours. . . . Lee is not retreating. He is a brave and skillful soldier, who will fight while he has a division or a day's rations left. The Rebels are not half-starved—a more sinewy, tawny, formidable-looking set of men could not be. In education they are certainly inferior to our native-born people, but they are usually very quick-witted, and they know enough to handle weapons with a terrible effect. Their great characteristic is their stoical manliness: they never beg or whimper or complain but look you straight in the face. . . .[24]

Cold Harbor was Grant's worst blunder. On June 3 he flung three corps at Lee's entrenchments, as if he had never heard of Marye's Heights or Cemetery Ridge. The Yankees advanced in formations twenty-eight feet deep. The Rebels mowed them down. In less than an hour the Army of the Potomac lost seven thousand men, compared to the Confederates' fifteen hundred. In the past Lee's troops had cheered after such a victory. Not today. They had little sense of accomplishment. They, too, could count. Each battle, they knew, cost men who could not be replaced, while the blue ranks were quickly refilled. "What's the use of killing these Yankees?" Rebels muttered. "It is like killing mosquitoes—two come for every one you kill."[25]

Grant was frustrated. Every time he moved, Lee kept a step ahead of him. Now he decided to take a giant step forward. He would take the army from just northeast of Richmond to Petersburg, a railroad center twenty miles south of it. By seizing the town, he would cut off Lee's supplies from the south and west, forcing him to abandon the capital. The only problem was time. He must leave Cold Harbor and cross the James River, a half mile wide and fifty feet deep, before Lee moved to block the path.

The Army of the Potomac left Cold Harbor on the night of June 12. Screened by Sheridan's cavalry, it crossed the Chickahominy and headed for the James. The Fifth Corps, however, broke away from the main force and headed for Richmond. It was a trick, and Lee fell for it. Thinking Grant was up to his old game, he pulled out of Cold Harbor and moved to cover the capital. Grant was in the clear!

Union engineers put a pontoon bridge across the James in eight hours. A plantation with many slave cabins stood near the landing place. Among the slaves was a man said to be 108 years old. He had been waiting a long time for the freedom army, he said. Asked what value freedom could have for one so old, he replied: "Well, massa, isn't a hundred and eight years long enough to be a slave?"[26]

An advance force practically ran all the way to Petersburg. Arriving on June 15, it found the trenches manned by a handful of Rebel troops. Petersburg was just waiting to be taken. But the Union commander, Major General William F. "Baldy" Smith, held back. Fearing a trap, he decided to dig in and await reinforcements. By then, however, Lee had realized his mistake. That night, his advance units rushed to Petersburg in the best foot-cavalry tradition. Thanks to Smith's caution, the war would last another ten months.

Grant was through with frontal assaults. Petersburg became a siege like Vicksburg, only on a larger scale; if anything, it resembled the trench warfare of World War I fifty years later. Both sides dug in for a long siege. Forts with names like Fort Hell (Union) and

Taking a break; Union soldiers in the trenches before Petersburg, 1864. Such trenches were to be seen again, on the western front in France, during World War I.

Fort Damnation (Confederate) dotted the landscape. The forts were linked to one another by trenches strengthened by logs and lengths of railroad track covered with earth. Explosive mines were buried to halt infantry, and pointed wooden stakes set at angles to stop cavalry. To supply his army, Grant turned the sleepy river town of City Point into a vast supply base, complete with a seven-mile railroad to the front lines.

Artillery thundered and snipers pecked away at the opposing trenches. It was suicide to show oneself for even an instant, much less charge into the no-man's-land between the lines. Yankee sharpshooters, using telescopic sights, could put a bullet between a man's eyes. On July 30 engineers set off four tons of gunpowder in a tunnel dug under a Confederate fort. The fort was demolished, but the Union infantry became confused and failed to push through the gap in the enemy line. Hundreds wandered into the crater, where they were at the Southerners' mercy. White troops, where possible, were captured; black troops were slaughtered.

Entrance to the mine dug by Union soldiers to blow a hole in the Confederate line at Petersburg, Virginia, in 1864. The mine did its job, but the attack failed due to poor planning and coordination on the part of Grant's forces.

Three weeks earlier, Lee had sent a force to threaten Washington by way of the Shenandoah Valley. It was an effort to take the pressure off Petersburg, and it backfired. Not only did the Washington defenses hold firm; Grant decided to have done with the Valley once and for all. Little Phil was sent to burn it from end to end. Houses, barns, stables, mills, silos, storage sheds, and farm equipment went up in flames. The Valley people were driven from their homes, becoming refugees in their own country.

Still the casualty lists grew. Fighting on the defensive, Lee lost about 30,000 men from May 4 to June 15, when the Yankees reached Petersburg. Grant lost about 65,000 men, an average of 1,512 per day and nearly the total of Lee's entire force at the start of the campaign.

The Union was in a state of shock. "Maniac," "lunatic," "murderer," "beast": Grant was called these names, and worse. He was bleeding the nation white, said a New York newspaper, and had "provided either a cripple or a corpse for half the homes of the North." Mary Lincoln was furious. "Grant is a butcher, and is not fit to be at the head of an army," she told her husband. "Yes, he generally manages to claim a victory, but such a victory! He loses two men to the enemy's one. He has no management, no regard for life. I could fight an army as well myself. Grant, I repeat, is an obstinate fool and a butcher."[27]

Abraham Lincoln continued to support his general. The president was a humane person who hated violence. He was also a realist who saw war for what it is. He knew that war is butchery, nothing more or less, and that the road to peace is paved with bodies. It was all a question of "the arithmetic"—that infernal arithmetic. Given this view, he was sure of his course. Grant must continue as before, he insisted. His advice was simple: "Hold on with bull-dog grip, and chew & choke, as much as possible."[28]

Grant was not nearly the killer he was accused of being. If anything, Lee, who called his men his sons, was the real "butcher." This had always been the case, even before Grant came on the scene. In five major battles—Seven Days, Second Manassas, Sharpsburg, Chancellorsville, and Gettysburg—Lee lost on average 22.2 percent of his troops, compared to his opponents' 14.4 percent; only at Fredericksburg did he lose a lesser percentage, 6.4 to 10.9 percent. In all his battles, Grant lost an average of 18.1 percent; and from the Wilderness through Cold Harbor, he lost 41 percent to Lee's 45.7 percent.[29] Since Grant took the offensive, and the attacker usually suffers more than the defender, his average losses were not especially high—cold comfort to the victims and their families.

Lee felt Grant's losses in a personal way; in fact, they came to his very doorstep. His wife's estate, Arlington, had been occupied by Union troops early in the war. In time, it became a military headquarters and a hospital serving the Army of the Potomac. Roads were cut through the woods and earthen forts built near the house. Congress eventually passed a law taxing Rebel property held by Federal forces. The owner, to pay the bill, had to appear in person, and be arrested if he was a Confederate soldier. The taxes on Arlington House were $92.07. Since Mary Lee was in Richmond, and could not appear, the estate was seized for nonpayment of taxes. But that was only the beginning.

The day after the Bloody Angle, Lincoln visited the wounded at Arlington. Alongside Mary Lee's garden, he found dead soldiers in their coffins. A message had just come, saying that Washington's only military cemetery had run out of space. The president immediately ordered the dead buried in the garden. Still the wounded kept coming, and dying. When the garden filled, the lawns became a graveyard: Arlington National Cemetery. Mary was heartbroken. Her husband blamed Yankee spitefulness.

The siege of Petersburg continued.

IX ✦ TO THE BITTER END

Summer's heat gave way to autumn's cool winds. Then came another winter of discontent, the Confederacy's last.

Each day brought its share of sadness, so that Southerners grew fearful of opening their newspapers. On September 2 Atlanta fell to Sherman's army. On November 8 Lincoln won election to a second term, assuring the continuation of the war. On November 16 Sherman left Atlanta in flames and began his march to the sea. Moving against weak opposition, he could do much as he pleased. Day by day, mile by mile, he smashed his way across Georgia. His men, proudly calling themselves "bummers," burned towns, tore up railroads, and took whatever they wished from the people, destroying everything else of value. Reaching the sea at Savannah by Christmas, he rested his army before invading the Carolinas early in 1865. His destination: Virginia.

Ordinary Southerners felt the war in countless ways. Families lived in constant fear for their loved ones at the front. Tragedy seemed to stalk certain families, like the widow who lost six sons in battle. Life became a never-ending struggle as Confederate money lost value. Prices continued to soar. By the end of 1864, a felt hat cost $125 Confederate, a man's suit $1,500, and a lady's bonnet $250. Even beggars raised their requests from a penny to a dollar. Food costs were outrageous. A Rebel private now earned $18 a month, but with flour at $1,200 a barrel in Richmond, hams

HEADQUARTERS ARMY
OF THE POTOMAC

April 7, 1865

General R. E. Lee

GENERAL:—*The result of the last week must convince you of the hopelessness of further resistance on the part of the Army of Northern Virginia in this struggle. I feel that it is so, and regard it as my duty to shift from myself the responsibility for any further effusion of blood by asking of you the surrender of that portion of the Confederate States army known as the Army of Northern Virginia.*

U. S. GRANT,

Lieutenant-General

Southern refugees fleeing advancing Union forces in 1864. As the war progressed, more and more Southern civilians fled their homes either to avoid the enemy or because soldiers of both armies had looted their farms and they were hungry.

at $350 apiece, and a turkey at $100, his family had to be ingenious to make ends meet. President Davis offered a suggestion to meet the crisis: "I don't see why rats, if fat, are not as good as squirrels."[1] There is no evidence that his family went hungry during the war.

At Petersburg things went steadily downhill. Johnny Rebs took to calling themselves "Lee's Miserables," after *Les Misérables*, a novel by the French author Victor Hugo. The name fit. They *were* miserable, as badly off as the wretched Parisians described in Hugo's book.

The Army of Northern Virginia had grown accustomed to hardship. But Petersburg was in a class by itself. Everything seemed to be falling apart at once. There was only so much you could do to a uniform with needle and thread. There reached a point where it was so worn that even patches would not hold. "In this army," a Texan wrote, "one hole in the seat of the breeches indicates a captain, two holes a lieutenant, and the seat of the pants all out indicates that the individual is a private."[2] Shoe leather, always scarce in the South, was virtually unobtainable by 1865. Civilians were driven to wearing shoes of dog or squirrel skin. Soldiers wore wooden shoes without socks, a sure way to get bruises, blisters, and splinters. A lucky Texan got hold of a few strips of rawhide, which he fashioned into shoes; his feet, he claimed, "looked as big as two 20-pound . . . hams."[3] Comrades envied him nevertheless; they went shoeless, leaving bloody footprints in the snow.

Slowly but surely, Lee's troops were starving. The daily ration consisted of a cup of cornmeal and a tiny strip of fatty bacon, often spoiled. No matter. Men became ravenous, willing to put anything into their bellies, even spilled corn gathered from under the horses' feet; the really desperate sifted horse manure for kernels of undigested corn. Lack of food brought malnutrition, malnutrition brought disease. The Confederate soldiers suffered from a host of preventable illnesses. Scurvy and night blindness decimated the ranks. Tiny scratches refused to heal, becoming life-threatening infections. Diarrhea was rampant. Men who had speed-marched with Stonewall Jackson now tired easily. Not only was marching difficult, a soldier digging a trench had to rest between each shovelful.

Soldiers from both sides still found time to trade with one another. The trenches, in certain sectors, were only seventy-five yards apart, making contact easy. During lulls in the shelling, a fellow would put his hands to his mouth and call:

"Billy Yank! O—B-i-l-l-y—Y-a-n-k!"

"Well, Johnny R-e-b?"

"Don't shoot! It's a truce."

"All right."[4]

Blue and gray stepped into no-man's-land to trade and talk. Although such meetings were forbidden, the common soldier had his own ideas. Lookouts cried "Rats to your holes!" if an officer appeared.

They still kept their sense of decency and fair play. There were exceptions, of course; but most obeyed the rules as they understood them. If ordered to open fire, soldiers might yell: "Look out, Johnny!" or "Hunt your holes, Billy, I'm going to shoot!" Even enemy officers might be spared. When, for example, Union general Samuel W. Crawford stood on a parapet to examine Rebel positions, a stone bounced into the trench behind him. Tied to it was a note reading: "Tell the fellow with the spy glass to clear out or we shall have to shoot him."[5] Only a brute, they said, would shoot someone in cold blood; it was especially wrong to target a poor fellow squatting over a latrine. These rules, however, did not apply to blacks wearing blue. The Rebel soldiers hated black soldiers, and sometimes murdered them after their surrender in action. It is not known how Marse Robert felt about such behavior.

A favorite pastime for commanders was scanning the enemy

General Robert E. Lee in fighting trim, probably late in 1864. Although wearing a pistol and a sword, he never used either weapon in battle.

line to identify fellow West Pointers. Grant had been Pickett's friend before the war, and would be his friend afterward. Having since married his fiancée, Pickett became a proud papa during the siege of Petersburg. Upon hearing the news, Grant and two brother officers sent a silver cup and a note under a flag of truce: "To George Pickett: We are sending congratulations to you, to the young mother and the young recruit."[6] Grant had also met Lee during the Mexican War. One day, he sent Marse Robert a message saying that he kept in such close touch with him that he knew what he ate for breakfast. Lee answered that he knew as much about Grant's dinners as he knew about his breakfasts. It was a polite way of saying that each had spies in the other's camp. Despite harsh conditions, Lee's health improved with the cold weather. His cheeks were ruddy, but his hair and beard had turned snow white. "He seemed made of iron," a visitor wrote, "and would remain in his saddle all day and then at his desk half the night without apparently feeling the fatigue."[7] He lived simply, refusing, as usual, to sleep indoors or eat better than his men. Mary, hungry in Richmond, asked him to send any food he could spare. He sent a dried-up lemon found in his luggage and a basket of green apples. Three little girls once gave him eggs, pickles, and popcorn. He begged them to bring him nothing but kisses and keep the food for themselves.

His men loved him more than ever; indeed, they idolized him. He was the only steady, reliable thing in their lives. The world might be collapsing around them, but they could always count on Marse Robert. He was kindness, courage, and genius rolled into one. If he was nearby, they felt safe; he was always in control, always knew what to do. "Howdy do, Dad," soldiers called as he rode through the camps. "Howdy do, my man," he'd reply. Once, after he passed, a soldier turned to a comrade. "God bless Marse Robert!" he said, deeply moved. "I wish he was emperor of the country and I was his carriage-driver!"[8]

Lee seemed to be the Confederacy's last hope. On February 6, five days after Sherman turned north into the Carolinas, he was named commander of all Confederate forces. But it was an empty title, carrying no real authority. Politicians controlled the war effort, and they were a sad lot.

Nothing hurt Lee more than his inability to improve his men's living conditions. States' rights had become a fatal disease by 1865. The Confederate States of America was merely the name of a country, not of a true nation. The states were jealous of their rights, unable to see beyond their own narrow interests. Governors hoarded supplies, or ordered that they be used only by state units under Lee's command; the governor of Georgia threatened to secede from the Confederacy if he didn't get his way. Planters refused to send their slaves to work on fortifications, claiming the work was too hard and would lower their value. Lee's hatred of slavery did not prevent him from requesting slave laborers.

His worst grievance was against the Confederate government. Jefferson Davis, a self-styled military expert, sent reinforcements not to Petersburg, where they were urgently needed, but to places of little or no value. The Confederate Congress had become a debating society, filled with do-nothing politicians who gave long, flowery speeches that said nothing. Early in 1865 Lee spent a few days with his family in Richmond. While Custis, home on leave, read a newspaper, his father paced the room, his jaws set, his eyes fixed on the floor.

Before becoming president of the Confederacy, Jefferson Davis was a United States senator from Mississippi and secretary of war. A graduate of West Point, he thought he knew more about fighting a war than he actually did.

"Well, Mr. Custis," he snapped. "I have been up to see the Congress and they don't seem to be able to do anything except eat peanuts and chew tobacco while my army is starving."

Custis kept quiet.

"Mr. Custis," Lee continued, his anger rising, "when this war began I was opposed to it, bitterly opposed to it, and I told these people that unless every man should do his whole duty, they would repent it; and now . . ." Lee paused.

"And now they will repent."[9]

The army was melting away as he spoke. One reason was battle casualties: Grant was killing Rebels faster than they could be replaced by draft calls. Things grew so bad that men were being drafted up to the age of fifty. Few went willingly. In Richmond military police arrested pedestrians and hustled them off to army barracks. Nevertheless, one group was spared under the so-called Twenty Nigger Law, which excused anyone owning twenty or more slaves from military service. Ordinary citizens were outraged. They denounced the Confederate cause as "a rich man's war and a poor man's fight."

Grant made things worse by his stand on Confederate war prisoners. Traditionally, prisoners were paroled if they signed a pledge not to fight for the duration of the war or until they were exchanged. Captives might be exchanged man for man, or at a fixed number of men per officer, according to rank. Grant halted these when parolees were recaptured in later battles and because of the South's refusal to treat blacks as prisoners of war. Rebel leaders, Lee included, wanted former slaves captured in Yankee uniforms returned to their home states for such punishment as the laws allowed, up to and including the gallows.

Confederate violations, bad as they were, were a convenient excuse. Grant's real purpose was to wear down enemy manpower by any means possible. This made sense, according to "the arithmetic." Union prisoners in Confederate hands were so many extra mouths to feed at a time when its own soldiers were starving. As Grant put it: "It is hard on our men held in Southern prisons not to exchange them, but it is humanity to those left in the ranks to fight our battles. Every man we hold, when released on parole or otherwise, becomes an active soldier against us at once either directly or indirectly."[10] All prisoners, therefore, must suffer in order to shorten the war. That was too bad, Grant thought, but winning the war came first.

Yankee captives were kept in places like Richmond's Libby Prison, Belle Island on the James River, and Andersonville in south-central Georgia. Among the largest Union prisons were Point Lookout in Maryland, Johnson's Island on Lake Erie, and Fort Delaware on Pea Patch Island in the Delaware River. All were disgusting. Neither side deliberately set out to harm prisoners, but they suffered nonetheless. Prisoners later told hair-raising stories of hunger, disease, and filth.

Thousands perished who might otherwise have returned to their families. Of the 194,000 Yankees held by the South, 30,218 died. Of the 214,000 Rebels kept in the North, 25,976 died. Although the numbers are not that far apart, the greater blame rests with the Union. It had the resources to care for its prisoners, but failed due to inexperience, inefficiency, and plain stupidity. The South, scarcely able to feed itself, found it impossible to feed war prisoners properly. Things became worse after Grant crossed the Rapidan, and large numbers of captives flooded the system. In any case, neither side had much to brag about in its treatment of prisoners.

The collapse of Rebel morale cost Lee's army more than any campaign. Southerners, civilians and soldiers alike, lost faith in their cause. Women were as effective as Yankee guns in putting soldiers out of action. Their letters, once so important in keeping up morale, now destroyed it. Every day thousands of "paper bullets" told fighting men how bad things were at home and how they must return before it was too late. The letter an Alabamian received from his wife was typical: "We haven't got nothing in the house to eat but a little bit o meal. . . . Try to get off and come home and fix us all up some. . . . If you put off a-coming, 'twont be no use to come, for we'll all hands of us be out there in the garden in the graveyard with your ma and mine."[11]

Such pitiful letters demanded that a man choose between his duty to his loved ones and his duty as a soldier. Thousands chose their families. By February 1865, the Confederacy had 400,000 men registered as soldiers. Of these, 198,494 were absent from duty, with over 100,000 listed as deserters. Lee reported that at least a hundred men were leaving his army each day; on one occasion, an entire brigade deserted. "Most of the desertions, lately," he added, "have been caused by letters from home."[12] The Yankees did

Scene at the latrines of Andersonville prison in Georgia. Thousands of Union prisoners lived, and died, amid the filth and heat of this horrible place.

their part, too, offering to pay each deserter for his musket and give him free passage to the North. Captured deserters might be branded with the letter D or shot by firing squad. The vast majority, however, reached home safely. There they were protected by their families, even by the local authorities.

Blacks were the Confederacy's last source of manpower. In the past Southerners had recruited soldiers from among their slaves. In 1703, for example, the South Carolina assembly ruled that masters could "arme and equipe any slave or slaves," and if a slave killed or captured an invader "he shall have and enjoy his freedom."[13] Blacks later served in the American Revolution and the War of 1812. In 1861 free blacks in New Orleans organized a regiment, but were judged unfit for Confederate service.

By 1865 Southerners took another look at arming their slaves. Many, as might be expected, opposed such a drastic move. The main justification for slavery had always been the "inferiority" of black people. Arming them during a crisis would be an admission that racism was wrong. How could a black person be inferior one moment, and then be called upon to take up one of the basic duties of a free citizen? Besides, hadn't Southerners condemned "demon Lincoln" for recruiting blacks?

Marse Robert wanted black soldiers. His argument was not based on principle, but on logic and necessity. He did not say, although he believed, that slavery was wrong. Slavery, he insisted, was doomed; it was only a question of who ended it and how. If the Confederacy lost the war, there would be no more slavery anyhow; Mr. Lincoln had seen to that. And if the Confederacy did not have more men, it would lose both its slaves and its independence. There was no choice but to arm the slaves in return for a promise of emancipation after the war.

Lee won his point, or at least part of it. On March 13 Davis signed the Negro Soldier Law. Although it allowed the enlistment of slaves, it made no mention of emancipation. Clearly, the law was merely a favor to the South's favorite general. Several companies of slave-soldiers were formed in Richmond, but when they paraded toward the end of the month, onlookers splattered them with mud. By then, however, the Confederacy had only two weeks to live.

Time was running out at Petersburg. The Union army numbered 150,000 men, with reinforcements arriving daily, while Lee's force of 35,000 men was steadily shrinking. Grant kept up the pressure, pushing and probing to find a weak spot. Slowly but surely, he extended his lines to the left, threatening Lee's right. Lee had to follow suit, or wind up with the enemy in his rear. But extending his line was like stretching a rubber band: the more he stretched, the thinner it became; eventually it would snap.

Lee decided to risk everything on a bold plan. He would abandon Petersburg and link up with the forces facing Sherman in North Carolina, led by Joe Johnston. True, Richmond would be left unprotected, but that no longer mattered. All that counted was the Confederacy's survival. A victory in North Carolina might—just *might*—allow him to return to Virginia with Johnston's force and defeat Grant. It was a long shot, but at least it was a chance.

Leaving Petersburg, however, was easier said than done. If Grant learned of the move, he would spring forward with every man and gun under his command. And if he caught Lee in the open, as he had been trying to do ever since the Wilderness, it would be all over. The only thing to do was create a diversion to open an escape corridor.

Lee turned to John B. Gordon, hero of the Bloody Lane at Sharpsburg, who had become a general. As one of the army's most aggressive field officers, Gordon was to launch a surprise attack on the center of the Union line. The effect would be like a boxer's hitting an opponent in the stomach to make him lower his hands and uncover his face. Similarly, Grant would pull troops from his left flank to protect his center, allowing Lee to dash through the opening.

Gordon moved out at 4:30 A.M. on March 25. His objective was Fort Stedman near the south bank of the Appomattox River. However, noise made by his waiting troops alerted the Yankee pickets.

"What are you doing over there, Johnny?" a picket shouted. "What is that noise? Answer quick or I'll shoot."

"Never mind, Yank," said a quick-thinking Rebel. "Lie down and go to sleep. We are just gathering a little corn. You know rations are mighty short over here." Despite the heavy fighting, a small patch of corn still stood between the lines.

"All right, Johnny," the Yankee replied. "Go ahead and get your corn. I'll not shoot at you while you are drawing your rations."

Gordon's men came closer, invisible in the darkness. Coming within range, he ordered a sergeant to fire his rifle as a signal to start the assault. The sergeant hesitated, unable to trick men who had trusted him. Gordon repeated the order—sharply. The sergeant obeyed, but in his own way. "Hello, Yank!" he yelled. "Look out; we are coming!" Having satisfied his conscience, he fired and the attack went forward.[14]

Fort Stedman was easily overrun. But Grant did not scare easily. Rather than weaken his left, as expected, he turned his artillery on the fort. Gordon retreated with a loss of forty-eight hundred men to the Yankees' two thousand. Not only had the attack failed, it alerted the Union commander to the Confederates' true situation. Had Lee been strong enough, Grant thought, he would have pressed the attack, even tried to break through to City Point. Clearly, he was grasping at straws.

It was Grant's turn to attack. On March 29 he sent Phil Sheridan on one of those smash-'em-up expeditions for which he was famous. Setting out with ten thousand cavalry and seventeen thousand infantry, Little Phil headed southeast, toward the Southside Railway, Lee's last link to the outside world. Ten thousand men under George Pickett and Fitzhugh Lee waited at Five Forks, a vital crossroads and the key to the Confederate right flank. Lee's orders were to defend Five Forks to the death.

The defenders held their ground, halting Sheridan in front of a log barrier. Little Phil got angry; he was not used to being stopped. That night, March 31, he held a war council. Pounding his fist into the palm of his hand, he gave his staff a stern talking-to. There would be no stopping tomorrow! Period. It was April Fools' Day, and he intended to make fools of the Rebels. "I tell you, I'm ready to strike tomorrow and go to smashing things!"[15]

Next morning, as the Yankees swept forward, they met disorganized resistance. Pickett and his officers were a mile to the rear, eating shad caught in a nearby stream. Sheridan easily found a weak spot and led his cavalry through in person. They came with a cheer, jumping the barrier and firing six-shooters at anyone in butternut. Five thousand Confederates were captured and hundreds killed.

Sheridan sent the good news to his chief, along with six captured battle flags. Grant was pleased. Lincoln, who was visiting City Point, was elated. The president grabbed the flags in his big hands. Gently unfurling them, he cried: "Here is something material—something I can see, feel, and understand. This means victory. This *is* victory."[16] Grant thought so, too.

Sunday, April 2, 1865. The Army of the Potomac pushed against Lee's sagging line with all its might. The assault began with an artillery barrage like the third day at Gettysburg. Only this time there was no contest; not only did Grant have more guns, he had heavier ones. Among them was "Dictator," a mortar mounted on a railroad flatcar. Mortars sent shells in high arcs over enemy walls and forts, even over the heads of friendly troops as they

advanced. Dictator, the largest, threw a two-hundred-pound shell two and a half miles. Each time it fired, the kickback sent it rolling hundreds of yards to the rear. A donkey engine then hauled it back into firing position.

"Dictator," one of the giant railroad mortars used by the Union army during the siege of Petersburg.

Union guns lit up the predawn sky with flashes of man-made lightning, and these were followed by the howl and shriek of shells. The vibrations shook the ground. Shock waves struck like hard fists, so that waiting troops felt as if invisible demons were banging on their skulls. Billy Yank's ears rang; the gunfire was so loud that men standing near the artillery had to put their fingers in their ears to avoid going deaf. After two hours, the guns fell silent to allow the infantry to pass. The Confederate line split wide open.

Lee, for a change, was sleeping in a house behind the lines. Awakened by the artillery, he came to the door in his nightshirt. Staff officers were racing about, shouting something about "Yankees" and "breakthrough." Just then, strange troops appeared to the east. A. P. Hill and a sergeant rode out to investigate. The sergeant returned a few minutes later, alone. Hill, he said, was gone, shot through the heart. "He is at rest now," Lee murmured, "and we who are left are the ones to suffer."[17]

There was no time for mourning. Lee sent for seven heavy guns to hold off the Yankees, while he dictated a telegram to the War Department in Richmond. It confirmed that his lines were broken and asked that the capital be evacuated by evening. He dictated calmly, yet was furious with that cold anger his staff dreaded. Furious at Grant, that stubborn, indomitable man. Furious at him-

The ruins of Richmond, April 1865. This scene is reminiscent of the bombed-out cities of Europe during the Second World War nearly a century later.

self for having to retreat. Furious, above all, at those government idiots in Richmond. "Well, Colonel," he told an aide, "it has happened just as I told them it would in Richmond. The line has been stretched until it has broken."[18]

All eyes were on Jefferson Davis when a telegram was handed to him in church later that morning. Reading it quickly, he hurried out of the building, his face pale as chalk. Citizens did not need a formal announcement; they knew Richmond was lost.

Panic spread through the city. Those who could, left by train, horse, wagon, and on foot. Slave dealers, unable to move their "stock," abandoned scores of chained blacks in the streets. Soldiers set fire to ironclads anchored on the James and ammunition dumps in the city. Richmond's main arsenal, containing 750,000 artillery shells, exploded like the crack of doom. Hot shell fragments set other buildings afire, turning much of Richmond into an inferno. The poor went on a rampage, breaking into private homes, shops, and government warehouses. Barrels of whiskey were rolled into the streets, their tops bashed in, and passersby invited to drink. The raw liquor was truly "fire water"; it filled empty stomachs, making people crazy drunk. Some fell in the gutter and were trampled; others lost their bearings and staggered into blazing buildings.

By the morning of April 3 it seemed that nothing could save the Confederate capital. Passing troops were too busy escaping to attend to the fires. All the bridges had been destroyed except Mayo's Bridge at the foot of Fourteenth Street. Barrels of gunpowder and tar were placed there, to be ignited when the time came. It came quickly enough. As the last troops crossed, an officer gave the order: "All over! Good-bye! Blow her to hell!"[19]

Already Yankee cavalry were galloping down Main Street, led by black troopers shouting "Richmond at last!" Then they and their white comrades went to work. Soldiers became firefighters. Military police guarded stores and dealt with looters; more than one thief was whacked across the shoulders with the flat of a sword.

Richmond's whites saw the conquerors in different ways. There were those who turned aside in disgust and despair; "the horrible Stars and Stripes" flying over the capital sent them home in tears.[20] Others were grateful to those who were saving their homes. "The Yankees have come! The Yankees have come!" a girl shouted, clapping her hands, "and now we'll get something to eat. I'm going to have pickles and molasses and oranges and cheese and nuts and candy until I have a fit and die."[21]

Lincoln wanted to see his prize. Next day, April 4, he arrived by boat accompanied by his twelve-year-old son, Tad, and an escort of a dozen sailors assembled at the last minute. He was unconcerned about his personal safety; assassination, everyone knew, was not an American custom. He often drove through Washington without a bodyguard.

The moment he landed, he was met by black people, who had been slaves only hours before. Shouting and singing, weeping and laughing, they crowded around their hero. "I know I am free," a woman cried, "for I have seen Father Abraham and felt him." "May de Lord bless you, President Linkum!" said a black man, removing his hat and bowing deeply. Lincoln removed his own hat and returned the bow. That bow was eloquent, one free man showing respect for another.[22]

Lincoln saw the sights, sat at Jefferson Davis's desk in the Confederate White House, and paid a social call. Sally Pickett was at home with her infant son when a knock came at the door. Opening it, she saw a tall, lean man in a black suit and a stovepipe hat. "Is this George Pickett's place?" he asked. It was, she answered, explaining that he wasn't home. "I know that, ma'am," he replied, "but I just wanted to see the place. I am Abraham Lincoln." The infant in her arms began to squirm and reach toward the stranger. The president took him in his arms and got a big, wet kiss. Returning him to his mother, he shook his finger and said, "Tell your father, the rascal, that I forgive him for the sake of that kiss and those bright eyes."[23]

Lincoln did not visit Mary Lee. When his soldiers arrived, they rushed to her house at 707 East Franklin Street. After putting out the fire next door, they posted guards to keep her safe and sent food every day. A strong supporter of the Confederacy, she was also an army wife and a mother. She knew that boys in blue were as homesick as boys in gray. Each morning she sent a breakfast tray to the guard who had watched over her and her daughters while they slept. Neighbors said this was "uncalled for," but Mary had a mind of her own.

Meanwhile, her husband led the retreat from Petersburg. His first destination was Amelia Court House, thirty miles to the west, where a supply train was supposed to be waiting with food. Due to a mix-up, however, it proved to be an ammunition train. A full day, April 5, was lost in gathering supplies from the surrounding area; there wasn't much, since farm families had scarcely enough for themselves.

On April 6 Sheridan caught three Confederate divisions in the open. They were crossing Sayler's Creek, a branch of the Appomattox River, when he struck. The action (it cannot be called a battle) cost the Rebels eight thousand men captured. Seven generals were among the prisoners, including Bald Dick Ewell and Custis Lee. Marse Robert saw the fleeing survivors from a hilltop. "My God!" he exclaimed. "Has the army been dissolved?"[24] Not yet, but the end was near.

The Rebels moved westward along the north bank of the Appomattox River. Grant meant to trap them by dividing his army into two unequal parts. The larger part, under Meade, followed close behind the enemy, slowing him down by making him fight constant rearguard actions. Sheridan moved parallel to the Confederates along the river's south bank. Grant wanted him to cut their line of retreat, allowing the main force to close in for the kill.

The Army of Northern Virginia was on its last legs. It was the return from Sharpsburg, the winter at Fredericksburg, and the retreat from Gettysburg rolled into one. Numb with fatigue, men marched asleep, awakening when they walked into one another or stepped into a rut. Their minds wandered, and they babbled nonsense or imagined themselves elsewhere; some swore they heard their wives' voices. Wagon horses collapsed, making it necessary to burn the wagons' contents to keep them out of the pursuers' hands. Sometimes the Yankees saved a wagon's contents. One wagon held millions of dollars in brand-new Confederate bills. The troopers played poker for million-dollar pots of useless paper.

"Freedom forever!" they shouted, laughing. "Rally round the flag, boys!" "We are coming, Father Abraham!"

Francis Lawley of the *London Times* accompanied the retreat. It was an unforgettable experience. He saw "every mud-hole and every rise in the road choked with blazing wagons, the air filled with the deafening reports of ammunition exploding and shells bursting when touched by the flames, dense columns of smoke ascending to heaven from the burning and exploding vehicles—exhausted men, worn-out mules and horses lying down side by side—gaunt famine glaring hopelessly from sunken lacklustre eyes—dead horses, dead mules, dead men everywhere—death many times welcomed as God's blessing in disguise."[25]

On April 7 Lee received a message from Grant urging him to surrender. "Not yet," said Longstreet, who had rejoined the army after recovering from his wound. Lee agreed. Honor demanded that he do everything possible before admitting defeat. He also knew Grant's nickname, and that worried him; he would fight to the last bullet, rather than surrender unconditionally. His reply was masterly. In the same sentence as he said things were not as bad as Grant thought, he asked about surrender terms.

Lee's destination was Appomattox Station, a railroad depot a mile from the village of Appomattox Court House. The supply trains waiting at the depot were his last hope. If he reached them in time, he might elude Grant and reach North Carolina.

Sheridan beat him to the punch. During the afternoon of April 8, his cavalry captured the trains. Then they dug in to await the infantry. That evening, while cooking supper, they saw the glow of campfires to the east. Confederate campfires! Little Phil had slipped ahead of Lee, cutting his escape route.

Lee met his commanders in the woods near Appomattox Court House. Pete Longstreet was there, along with Fitzhugh Lee, John B. Gordon, and William N. Pendleton, the army's chief of artillery. The headquarters wagons had been lost, so there were no chairs or camp stools. They sat around a small fire on blankets or saddles, discussing the situation. All agreed there was just one hope, and a mighty poor one at that. If the Yankees up ahead were cavalry, they might easily brush them aside. But if infantry were also present, it would be the end.

April 9, 1865. Palm Sunday, the Sunday before Easter. Lee awoke at 3:00 A.M. and put on his best uniform, which he had been saving for a special occasion. He then tied a red silk sash around his waist and buckled on a beautiful dress sword. On his legs he wore shiny boots that reached up to the knees, probably the only polished boots in the army. Asked later in the morning why he did this, he explained: "I have probably to be General Grant's prisoner, and I thought I must make my best appearance."[26]

At daybreak, after a short bombardment, the Army of Northern Virginia charged for the last time. Exhausted as they were, the chance to hit back renewed the soldiers' energy. All went well, at first. Giving the Rebel yell, they took the Yankee positions, little more than shallow rifle pits, and pushed ahead, driving the dismounted cavalrymen before them. But it could not last.

The cavalrymen suddenly parted and moved away from the center of the field. Behind them was a solid wall of blue. Sheridan's infantry, in a line of battle two miles wide, came forward. Off to their right, stood Sheridan with his mounted cavalry, ten thousand strong, backed by scores of big guns. They were silent and unmoving, their flags snapping in the breeze. With Sheridan in front and Meade pressing from behind, the Army of Northern Virginia was trapped. Its twenty-three thousand men faced eighty thousand enemy troops, with more arriving by the minute.

Lee was waiting a mile to the rear when a message came from Gordon, the assault leader. His men had been "fought to a frazzle," and he could make no headway.

So that was it. The dreaded moment had arrived. Marse Robert listened in silence, shook his head sadly, and declared: "Then there is nothing left me but to go and see General Grant, and I would rather die a thousand deaths."[27]

Officers who knew him feared he might do something rash. Gazing across the field toward Sheridan's troops, he said to himself, "How easily I could be rid of all this and be at rest! I have only to ride along the line and all will be over!" By that he meant it would be easy to commit suicide by riding in front of his lines and drawing Yankee fire. It was an emotional outburst from a proud man who had followed his conscience to the bitter end. "But it is our duty to live," he said with a sigh. "What will become of the women and children of the South if we are not here to protect them?"[28]

Lee waited under an apple tree while one officer rode out with a flag of truce and another carried a request to meet Grant. Around noon, word came that the Union commander would meet him in the village. The meeting place was a two-story brick house belonging to Wilmer McLean. By an odd quirk of fate, Mr. McLean, a farmer, had owned a house at Bull Run, where the Confederates won their first victory in 1861. A shell had smashed through a window, convincing him to move his family to this quiet village. But the war had caught up to the McLeans. *History* had caught up to them.

Lee arrived first and waited in the parlor. Grant came half an hour later. What a contrast they made! The Confederate chief stood straight as a ramrod in his splendid uniform. Grant, slightly stoop-shouldered, a cigar stub clenched between his teeth, had hurried there straight from the field. He wore no sword, and his mud-spattered pants were tucked inside muddy boots. Only the three stars on his shoulder straps indicated his rank. But he radiated self-confidence, and was clearly the boss.

They shook hands and sat down at a small table. Grant was nervous, and started to reminisce about Mexico. Lee brought him to the point: He wanted to hear the surrender terms. President Lincoln had set out the basic principle a few days earlier: "Let 'em up easy." The Confederates, he felt, were misguided people, not criminals. They were still Americans, and must be treated with respect. Under no circumstances should they be humiliated, further deepening their hurt and poisoning the peace.

Grant's terms were in line with the president's wishes. Lee and his men would be paroled on their promise not to fight again. Confederate officers could keep their pistols, swords, and horses; everything else must be surrendered at a formal ceremony. Lee

The McLean house at Appomattox Court House, Virginia, where General Lee surrendered on April 9, 1865

accepted the terms, relieved that his men would not be marched off to prison camps. The only problem, he said, was that ordinary cavalrymen and gunners owned their own horses. Grant did not wait to be asked for a favor; he said they could take their animals home "to put in a crop." He also promised to see that the starving army was fed. Lee signed the surrender document and the meeting ended.

George Gordon Meade brought the first news of the surrender to the Union troops. As Lee left the house, he leaped on his horse and galloped toward the nearest regiment. Solid, steady Meade was beside himself with joy. Waving his hat over his head, he made his horse dance in circles while yelling, "It's all over, boys! Lee's surrendered! It's all over!"[29]

The news spread like wildfire. The Yankees went wild. Victory! Victory! They had won the greatest war in American history. Gunners fired blank cartridges. Cavalrymen shot pistols into the air. "I cried and laughed by turns," recalled Colonel Elisha Hunt Rhodes, Second Rhode Island regiment. "I was never so happy in my life." Another compared it to all the Fourths of July, past and future, rolled into one. "The air is black with hats and boots, coats, knapsacks, shirts and cartridge boxes. They fall on each others' necks and laugh and cry by turns. Huge, lumbering, bearded men embrace and kiss like school-girls, then dance and sing and shout, stand on their heads and play leapfrog with each other."[30]

The racket annoyed Grant. There was no need to gloat over their victory, he thought. Staff officers were sent to stop the firing. The war was over, and the Rebels were their countrymen again. No one could (or should) ask for more.

Lee was heartbroken. Returning to his lines, he sat stiffly in the saddle, staring straight ahead. Cheering Rebels lined both sides of the road. But when they saw the expression on his face, the cheers froze in their throats. "General, are we surrendered?" they called, already knowing the answer.[31]

Marse Robert looked down, tears glistening in his eyes. "Men," he said haltingly, "we have fought through the war together. I have done my best for you. My heart is too full to say more." His lips moved as if to say "good-bye," but the words would not come.

Rank disappeared in the wave of grief that swept over the Army of Northern Virginia. Officers sat on their horses, sobbing unashamedly. Johnny Rebs threw their rifles away. "No Yankee will ever shoot at us with you," said a soldier as he smashed his weapon against a tree. "Blow, Gabriel! Blow! My God, let him blow, I am ready to die!" cried another, flailing his arms.[32] Many were too upset for words; they flung themselves to the ground and wept like children.

Their leader, however, was uppermost in their thoughts. It is one thing to cheer a victorious general, another to love a loser. Lee was unique among generals; his men loved him for himself, not only for his deeds. No matter what happened, he would always be their Marse Robert. "I love you just as well as ever, General Lee!" a soldier cried. "Goodbye, General, God bless you," men called over and over again.[33] Slowly, gently, he guided Traveller through the dense crowds. At every step, weeping men kissed the horse and caressed its master's boots. After resting under the apple tree, he went to his tent.

Next day, April 10, both commanders met briefly between the lines. Grant suggested that Lee ask all Confederate forces to surrender. Lee replied that he could not do so without consulting President Davis, who was at that moment fleeing southward. Grant dropped the subject. (Johnston surrendered to Sherman two weeks later.) As they parted, some of Grant's aides asked Lee's permission to visit old friends in the Confederate camp. He agreed.

On the way back, Lee met Meade.

"Good morning, General!" Meade called.

Lee did not recognize him. But when he came closer, Lee smiled and asked: "But General, what are you doing with all that gray hair in your beard?"

"You have to answer for most of it," Meade answered cheerfully.[34]

Grant's aides brought Longstreet, Gordon, and several other

Lee returns to the Army of Northern Virginia after leaving U. S. Grant at Appomattox Court House. Upon learning of the surrender, thousands of his men broke down and wept.

Confederates back to the McLean house to meet their chief. Grant made a beeline for Longstreet. Offering his hand and a cigar, he said, "Pete, let's have another game of brag to recall the old days." Longstreet never forgot their meeting. When he told about it afterward, he could only say: "Why do men fight who were born to be brothers!"[35]

Paroles were distributed on April 11. These were printed on slips of paper like bank checks, with a space for the date and the parolee's name, unit, and signature.

The formal surrender took place the following day in a field near Appomattox Court House. John Gordon led the Confederates. Maine's Joshua Lawrence Chamberlain, now a major general, commanded the Union force. Lee and Grant did not attend.

The ceremony promised to be unpleasant for Rebels. They would have to march between the blue ranks, stack their weapons, and hand over their battle flags. Those precious flags, torn and faded as they were, had become part of them. Parting with them would be like parting with dear comrades, living and dead. Some refused to give them up. Before setting out, they cut them into small pieces, which they took home as sacred relics.

Chamberlain respected these men, and wanted to make things as easy for them as possible. As Gordon, on horseback, led his troops forward, Chamberlain ordered his troops to hold their rifles in the salute position. Gordon had his men do the same. Honor was answering honor.

The ceremony lasted six hours. Now and then, Johnny Reb and Billy Yank exchanged words. "Well, old fellows, we have met again," a Rebel told members of the Twentieth Maine regiment. There was no anger in his voice, only pride mixed with sadness. Robert Bingham, a North Carolinian, remembered how once the Yankees had cheered when they overran his outfit. If they cheered today, he didn't know what he would do. He wept as he marched. Then his unit halted between the blue ranks. Turning his head, he looked at the Yankees. Tears were rolling down their cheeks, too.[36]

X ✦ WARRIOR AT PEACE

Go home and take up any work that offers. Accept conditions as you find them. Consider only the present and future. Do not cherish bitterness.

—Robert E. Lee,

April 14, 1865

Marse Robert was going home. After the surrender ceremony, he gave a familiar order: "Strike the tent!" Down floated the tent he had lived in since taking over the Army of Northern Virginia. It, together with the little personal gear he still had, was put on a wagon. Then, accompanied by members of his staff, he set out for Richmond on Traveller. Grant's aides had offered a cavalry escort, but Lee would not hear of it. He was among his own people, he said; surely there was nothing to fear from Virginians.

On April 15 the little caravan reached the James River opposite Richmond. It was raining, and a Union pontoon bridge offered the only way to cross. Since traffic was heavy, they had to wait their turn. They used the time to study the city they had fought so hard to protect. It was not the city they remembered. The waterfront lay in ruins. Beyond, they saw acre upon acre of burned-out buildings and chimneys standing amid the rubble.

News of Lee's arrival spread quickly. Crowds lined the way, along with Union troops watching for trouble. It was an emotional experience for everyone. The people of Richmond cheered and wept at the same time. "Here comes General Lee," a fellow shouted. "I am going to take off my hat to him!" A Union soldier standing nearby yelled, "Damned if I don't, too!"[1] Wherever Lee passed, Union men, common soldiers and officers alike, raised their hats.

These bluecoats were saluting a gallant foe, but also one they wished had fought with them instead of against them. There was no bitterness (at least none that was recorded) on their part.

The crowd was thickest in front of the red brick house on East Franklin Street. In a replay of Appomattox, people pressed in around Traveller, offering kind words and trying to touch their hero. Shaking as many hands as he could reach, Lee entered the house and closed the door. It was probably then that he learned that Abraham Lincoln had been shot the night before. His immediate reaction is unknown; he later called the assassination "a crime that no good man could approve."[2]

It seemed that Lee's life, too, was over. He was a defeated general. He was bankrupt. His property was gone. His links to George Washington had been cut when the Yankees took the Founding Father's relics away from Arlington for "safekeeping." He might even become a man without a country.

On May 29 Lincoln's successor, President Andrew Johnson, offered amnesty, or pardon, for Rebels who took a loyalty oath to the United States. The only exceptions were Confederate leaders, like Lee, who could ask the president for an individual pardon. Lee decided to apply immediately.

Being pardoned, however, was not easy. Northerners, particularly civilians who had never seen a battlefield, did not share Billy Yank's willingness to live and let live. Politicians and journalists thundered against the Confederate leadership. Those "butchers," they insisted, had given the nation four years of hell. And none more so than Robert E. Lee. According to the *New York Independent,* Lee was "the bloodiest and guiltiest traitor in all the South." He must be tried as a traitor. A New York politician led a crowd in chanting the expected verdict: "Hang Lee! Hang Lee! Hang Lee!"[3]

On June 3 a Federal grand jury indicted him for treason. News of the indictment rocked the South. Lee was the Southerners' hero, a good man who had done his duty. If Yankee fanatics could persecute him, then nobody was safe.

Offers of protection poured into the house on East Franklin Street. One day, for example, a man dressed in butternut asked to see the general. "General Lee," he said, "I followed you four years and done the best I knowed how. Me and my wife live on a little farm way up on the Blue Ridge. We heard the Yankees wasn't treating you right, and I come down to see 'bout it. If you will come up thar, we will take care of you the best we know as long as we live."

Touched by this simple man's generosity, Lee reached for a box of clothing, a gift from an admirer. "My friend," he said, "I don't need a thing. . . . I want to thank you for coming, and I want you to take this suit."

The man drew back, crossing his hands over his chest. "I can't take nothin' offen you!" he said firmly. But after a moment, he relaxed and touched the clothes. "Yes, I will, General. I will carry them back home, put them away, and when I die the boys can put them on me."[4]

Lee was in a delicate situation. The South was a powder keg, and a word from him could have set off an explosion. That must not be allowed to happen. So, instead of defending himself in public, he turned to U. S. Grant. He wrote to ask how the indictment squared with the surrender terms he had signed at Appomattox. It did not. Grant had promised the Rebels would be left alone if they lived up to the terms of their paroles. He, too, was an honorable man. If politicians disagreed, they must find someone else to do their dirty work; he would resign from the army and take the issue to the country. Nothing more was heard about the indictment.

Lee applied for amnesty on June 13. No reply came, nor would come in his lifetime. The application was put aside and not found until the 1970s. Only then, in 1975, was the pardon granted and his citizenship restored. Lee, therefore, spent his remaining years in the land of his birth, but was not legally a citizen or entitled to vote or hold an official position. Had he been allowed to run for public office, he would certainly have been elected. Worse men have sat in the United States Senate and House of Representatives.

Southerners needed someone like him in high office. The war had left the South in ruins. Confederate money was worthless. Handsome cities like Richmond and Charleston lay in ruins. Banks and businesses had closed their doors. The transportation system had broken down. The planters' investment of over two billion dollars in slaves, their chief form of wealth, had vanished. Farm animals were gone, taken by both Union and Confederate armies. Planting a crop, never easy, became backbreaking drudgery. In certain places, farmers hitched themselves to plows, while wives and children held the handles.

There were still plenty of defiant Southerners. They cursed the "damnyankees" and praised Lincoln's murderer, John Wilkes Booth. There were those who lived only for revenge. The Yankees, said a South Carolinian, have "left me one inestimable privilege— to hate 'em. I git up at half-past four in the morning, and sit up till twelve at night, to hate 'em."[5]

Hatred turned Confederate officers into refugees. Hundreds

settled in Cuba, Mexico, Canada, and England. A few enlisted in the armies of Romania, Egypt, and Korea. Still others had suffered deep inner wounds, wounds that destroyed their characters. It is no accident that outlaws like Jesse James and Cole Younger had served in the Confederate army, while gunfighters like "Wild Bill" Hickok were Union soldiers. Veterans were graduates of a great school of killing, the Civil War. It had shaped them as youngsters, teaching them that life is cheap and that problems can be solved by guns. There was even talk of setting up a Confederate colony in the jungles of Brazil, a country where slavery was still legal.

Robert E. Lee was no hater. His basic sanity and decency served his people well during these hard times. He knew the importance of not dwelling on the past, of not letting the past spoil the future. He never tired of telling Southerners that the Civil War *was* over. They had lost, and nothing could undo the past. Now they must get on with their lives.

In peace, as in war, Lee led by example. He refused to attend political meetings or discuss the war in public. He was forever urging former Confederates to become loyal Americans. To a woman who was preserving as a reminder of the war a tree trunk shattered by Union gunfire, he said: "Cut it down, my dear Madam, and forget it!" A Yankee-hating minister was reminded that the Bible says, "Love your enemies." Even during the war, Lee continued, "I have never seen the day when I did not pray for them."[6] Coming from Marse Robert, words like these commanded attention.

If Lee was no longer a soldier, what was he? It was a difficult question to answer. All he knew was that he, too, must get on with his life.

He could have enjoyed a comfortable life, had he been willing to cash in on his fame. Every week brought job offers promising easy money for little or no work. A New York trading company wanted to make him president at fifty thousand dollars a year, a *very* large sum in those days. An insurance firm offered ten thousand dollars just for the use of his name. Lee refused, saying his name was not for sale at any price. By doing otherwise, "I should be trading on the blood of my men."[7]

Finally, there came an offer he could not refuse. Early in August 1865 he was notified of his election as president of Washington College. The college is located at Lexington, Virginia, in the southern Shenandoah Valley, a vast upland with the Blue Ridge to the east and the Alleghenies to the west. Originally called Liberty Hall Academy, it was renamed for George Washington after he gave it a large donation. During the Civil War, the college was nearly destroyed by Union raiders; its neighbor, the Virginia Military Institute (VMI), was burned to the ground. Lee's election, the trustees hoped, would bring their school back to life.

Lee's interest in education dated at least from his years as superintendent of the U.S. Military Academy at West Point. The Civil War deepened that interest. At the height of the Battle of Chancellorsville, for example, he struck up a conversation with a German military observer. Instead of commenting on the battle, he spoke of how young Southerners might be educated after the war. Win or lose, he knew the South would need educated men to help it rebuild. The trustees' offer, therefore, fit in with his own needs and ideas. After thinking it over for a few days, he accepted. His salary would be $1,500 a year plus 20 percent of the tuition fees (students paid $75 a year) and the use of a house on campus.[8]

Lee was a hands-on president. He had come to Lexington to do a job, and he was determined to succeed. Rather than force students to take a set program, he shifted to an "elective" system, one of the first of its kind in the country. He introduced a wide range of practical subjects: engineering, mining, chemistry, accounting, business law. He started a school of journalism, the first anywhere in the world, and offered courses in photography. Enrollment grew from 87 full-time students in his first year to 348 four years later. Thanks to Lee, Washington College became one of the finest schools in the South.

Nothing escaped Lee's attention. He studied every account, supervised every repair, and read every report. Not only did he know each student by name, he knew everything about them. He knew what courses they were taking, their study habits, and their class standing. On the basis of classwork and written tests, every student received a weekly grade in every class. Lee went over these in detail, then discussed any weaknesses with the student and his

Robert E. Lee as president of Washington College about the year 1870. This is one of the last, if not the very last, pictures taken of the former chief of the Army of Northern Virginia.

professors. His aim was to help, not scold or punish. If a student needed a place to study, the president let him use a little office near his own. If he had personal problems, he knew where to find a sympathetic listener. A freshman from Tennessee had expected to find a ferocious warrior at the head of the school. Lee, however, was "almost motherly."[9]

Washington College had no written rules; all Lee demanded was that students be gentlemen, that is, live cleanly, respect others, and act honorably. Those who crossed the line found their "almost motherly" president to be a tiger. In 1865, for example, students demanded a week's vacation for Christmas. Lee allowed one day. Students circulated a paper saying they would cut classes during Christmas week. When Lee saw it on the bulletin board, he said loud enough for passersby to hear that anyone who signed would be expelled. If everyone signed, he would lock up the school and put the keys in his pocket. Word traveled fast. By evening, the petition was gone. The president, they knew, never made idle threats. If he promised to do something, that was that; you could count on it like tomorrow's sunrise.

The years at Washington College were among Lee's happiest and more rewarding. Content with himself, satisfied in his work, he came to regret his thirty-six years as a soldier. The greatest mistake of his life, he confessed, was having taken a military education. Whenever his students and faculty marched in procession with those of VMI, not even the beating on the big bass drum could make him keep in step. It was his way of showing that he had finished with soldiering.

Still, he could not close the door on his warrior life. The past intruded constantly, and where least expected. He might tell a student, a former soldier, that his service in the Army of Northern Virginia had made him a better man. Or he might warn a professor never to speak harshly of U. S. Grant, Grant of Appomattox, who had sent his defeated troops home with their self-respect. Traveller, of course, was a living reminder of bygone days. "Traveller," he wrote, "is my only companion; I may also say my pleasure. He and I, wherever practicable, wander out in the mountains and enjoy sweet confidence."[10]

After a day's work, Lee went for a long ride in the mountains around Lexington. That was the high point of his day, a chance to clear his mind and relax. Dressed in a gray uniform without insignia, high boots, and a broad-brimmed hat, he set out. He talked to Traveller, patted him, and let him stop to munch the grass whenever he pleased. Seldom did he pass a rider or a house without being recognized. Veterans snapped to attention and saluted. One fellow kept shouting "Hurrah for General Lee! Hurrah for General Lee!" until he was out of sight.[11] Another time, he met some children with dirty faces. He spoke to them about the importance of cleanliness. A little later, he rode past a log cabin, out of which came the same children with clean faces, combed hair, and fresh clothes. "We know you are General Lee!" said a little girl. "We have your picture."[12]

Sometimes he was caught in bad weather and had to spend the night with local people. Innkeepers refused to take his money. Mothers asked him to bless their children. One veteran asked Lee to take the bed, while he slept on the floor and his wife slept with the children. Nothing doing, Lee said; they must share the bed. Next morning, after his guest was gone, the soldier told neighbors that Marse Robert had been his guest.

"And where did he sleep?" they asked.

"Why, he slept with *me,*" he said, sticking out his chest.

"How did it *feel?*"

"I'll tell you, I never closed an eye. I didn't sleep a wink. I might have slept with God!"[13]

But Lee's riding days were coming to an end. The heart condition, which first appeared in 1863, grew worse. By the winter of 1869–1870, he was complaining about pressure in his chest and shooting pains in his arms; he could not walk more than a few yards without shortness of breath. To make matters worse, he had difficulty shaking off a cold, which left him very weak. His doctors ordered him south to escape the cold and damp of Lexington.

He set out early in March 1870, accompanied by his daughter Agnes. Stopping in Richmond, he was visited by John Singleton Mosby, a famous Confederate raider, and George Pickett. "Colonel, I hope we shall have no more wars," he told Mosby as they parted. Pickett was bitter, speaking of Lee as "that old man," adding, "He had my division massacred at Gettysburg."[14]

What began as a private trip quickly became a public event. As the Lees moved south by train, telegraph lines began to hum. Marse Robert was coming! At tiny depots and big cities, veterans turned out to give the Rebel yell and roar "Lee! Lee! Lee!" Parents held up their children to see him; often the first part of a little boy's name was Robert E. Lee. He was puzzled. "Why should they care for me?" he asked modestly. "I am only a poor old Confederate."[15]

Lee returned to Lexington feeling a little better. Only it did not last. On September 28, 1870, he came home after a long day at the

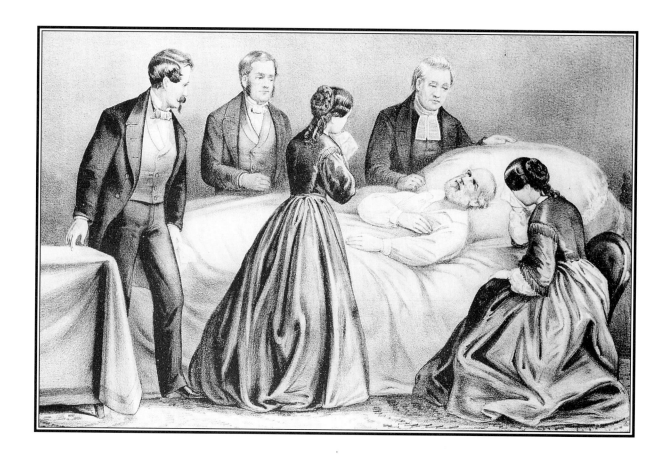

Robert E. Lee died at home, in bed, surrounded by his loved ones, after a brief illness. His passing was mourned throughout the South, which he had served with such devotion. Even former enemies praised his decency and humanity, which, they said, was worthier of a better cause than secession.

office and a meeting in the Episcopal church nearby. Taking his place at the head of the table, he started to say grace, but the words refused to come. He had suffered a stroke. Doctors were called, but they could do nothing. He was in God's hands, they told the family.

In the days that followed, he rallied a few times, and even regained some speech. But he always slipped back a little further each time. His mind wandered. Again it was wartime. Again he led the Army of Northern Virginia. Again he was on a battlefield. Again he heard the roar of the guns. And again, like Stonewall Jackson on his deathbed, he called for A. P. Hill. "Tell Hill he *must* come up!"

At 9:30 A.M. on October 12, Marse Robert gave the order for the last march: "Strike the tent." Then he quietly slipped away.

NOTES

Prologue

1. Margaret Sanborn, Robert E. Lee: A Portrait, 2 volumes (Philadelphia: Lippincott, 1967), 1:310.
2. Robert Stiles, *Four Years under Marse Robert* (New York: Neale Publishing, 1903), 21.
3. William Manchester, *American Caesar: Douglas MacArthur, 1880–1964* (Boston: Little, Brown, 1978), 41.

Chapter 1

1. Quoted in Earl Schenck Miers, *Robert E. Lee: A Great Life in Brief* (New York: Knopf, 1967), 14.
2. Sanborn, *Lee*, 1:3.
3. *Ibid.*, 1:48.
4. Stanley F. Horn, ed., *The Robert E. Lee Reader* (Indianapolis: Bobbs-Merrill, 1949), 33.
5. Gamaliel Bradford, *Lee the American* (Boston: Houghton Mifflin, 1929), 209.
6. Sanborn, *Lee*, 1:73.
7. A. L. Long, *Memoirs of Robert E. Lee: His Military and Personal History* (New York: J. M. Stoddart, 1886), 71.

8. Carl Sandburg, *Abraham Lincoln: The War Years*, 4 volumes (New York: Harcourt, Brace, 1939) 1:518.

9. Sanborn, *Lee*, 1:199.

10. *Ibid.*

11. Gene Smith, *Lee and Grant: A Dual Biography* (New York: McGraw-Hill, 1984), 50.

12. Nancy Scott Anderson and Dwight Anderson, *The Generals: Ulysses S. Grant and Robert E. Lee* (New York: Knopf, 1988), 113.

13. Ulysses S. Grant, *Personal Memoirs of Ulysses S. Grant and Selected Letters, 1839–1865* (New York: Library of America, 1990), 41.

14. Sanborn, *Lee*, 1:158.

15. Philip Van Doren Stern, *Robert E. Lee: The Man and the Soldier* (New York: McGraw-Hill, 1963), 77.

16. Sanborn, *Lee*, 1:170.

17. *Ibid.*, 1:171.

18. Douglas Southall Freeman, *Robert E. Lee*, 4 volumes (New York: Scribner's, 1934–1935), 1:245, 246.

19. Sanborn, *Lee*, 1:183.

20. *Ibid.*, 1:232.

21. Freeman, *Lee*, 1:301.

22. Sanborn, *Lee*, 1:224.

23. James C. Young, *Marse Robert: Knight of the Confederacy* (New York: Rae D. Henkle, 1929), 61.

24. Freeman, *Lee*, 1:376.

25. Anderson, *The Generals*, 137.

26. Philip Burnham, "Selling Poor Seven: The Struggles and Torments of a Forgotten Class in Antebellum America: Black Slaveowners," *American Heritage* (February–March 1993), 92.

27. Richard Wheeler, ed., *Lee's Terrible Swift Sword: From Antietam to Chancellorsville, An Eyewitness History* (New York: Harper & Row, 1982), 327.

28. Frederick Douglass, *My Bondage and My Freedom* (New York: Miller, Orton, and Mulligan, 1855), 253–254. Some spelling has been changed for the sake of clarity.

29. C. Vann Woodward, ed., *Mary Chesnut's Civil War* (New Haven: Yale University Press, 1981), 29. A mulatto is a person of mixed race.

30. Sandburg, *Lincoln*, 1:522.

31. Roy P. Basler, ed., *The Collected Works of Abraham Lincoln*, 8 volumes (New Brunswick, N.J.: Rutgers University Press, 1953), 7:281.

32. Freeman, *Lee*, 1:372–373.

33. Basler, *Lincoln Collected Works*, 3:145.

34. *Ibid.*, 2:130.

35. Anderson, *The Generals*, 156.

Chapter 2

1. Hazel C. Wolf, *On Freedom's Altar: The Martyr Complex in the Abolitionist Movement* (Madison: University of Wisconsin Press, 1952), 123.
2. Allan Nevins, *The Emergence of Lincoln*, 2 volumes (New York: Scribner's, 1950), 2:89–101; James Ford Rhodes, *History of the United States from the Compromise of 1850*, 7 volumes (New York: Macmillan, 1913–1916), 2:409.
3. Jules Abels, *Man on Fire: John Brown and the Cause of Liberty* (New York: Macmillan, 1971), 383.
4. Merton E. Coulter, *The Confederate States of America* (Baton Rouge: Louisiana State University Press, 1959), 14–15.
5. *Ibid.*, 12.
6. Horn, *The Robert E. Lee Reader*, 89–90.
7. Freeman, *Lee*, 1:442.
8. Smith, *Lee and Grant*, 103.
9. Vann, ed., *Mary Chesnut's Civil War*, 70, 71.
10. Belle Irvin Wiley, *The Life of Johnny Reb: The Common Soldier of the Confederacy* (Baton Rouge: Louisiana State University Press, 1978), 15.
11. Gerald F. Linderman, *Embattled Courage: The Experience of Combat in the American Civil War* (New York: Free Press, 1987), 81.
12. Belle Irvin Wiley, *Confederate Women* (Westport, Conn.: Greenwood Press, 1975), 142.
13. James I. Robertson, Jr., *Soldiers Blue and Gray* (Columbia: University of South Carolina Press, 1988), 13.
14. *Ibid.*, 14.
15. Belle Irvin Wiley, *Southern Negroes, 1861–1865* (Baton Rouge: Louisiana State University Press, 1965), 144.
16. *Ibid.*, 139. As food became scarcer, Rebels sent their servants home. By 1862 only officers had body servants.
17. Robertson, *Soldiers Blue and Gray*, 124.
18. Wiley, *Johnny Reb*, 90.
19. Robertson, *Soldiers Blue and Gray*, 67.
20. Carlton McCarthy, *Detailed Minutiae of Soldier Life in the Army of Northern Virginia, 1861–1865* (Richmond: Carlton McCarthy, 1882), 17.
21. Robertson, *Soldiers Blue and Gray*, 50.
22. Wiley, *Johnny Reb*, 214.
23. *Ibid.*, 211.
24. *Ibid.*, 36, 58.
25. Freeman, *Lee*, 1:538–539; Miers, *Lee*, 377–378.

26. Sanborn, *Lee*, 2:28.

27. Burke Davis, *Gray Fox: Robert E. Lee and the Civil War* (New York: Fairfax Press, 1981), 44–45.

28. Davis, *Gray Fox*, 60.

Chapter 3

1. Sandburg, *Lincoln*, 1:303.

2. Stephen W. Sears, *George B. McClellan: The Young Napoleon* (New York: Ticknor & Fields, 1988), 132.

3. *Ibid.*, 21.

4. Richard Wheeler, ed., *Sword over Richmond: An Eyewitness History of McClellan's Peninsula Campaign* (New York: Harper & Row, 1986), 190.

5. *Ibid.*, 164.

6. *Ibid.*, 118.

7. Coulter, *Confederate States of America*, 421.

8. James V. Murfin, *The Gleam of Bayonets: The Battle of Antietam and the Maryland Campaign of 1862* (New York: Thomas Youseloff, 1965), 50.

9. Bruce Catton, *Mr. Lincoln's Army* (Garden City, N.Y.: Doubleday, 1962), 19.

10. *Ibid.*, 169.

11. Wheeler, *Sword over Richmond*, 244; Clifford Dowdy, *The Seven Days: The Emergence of Lee* (Boston: Little, Brown, 1964), 126–127.

12. Peter Earle, *Robert E. Lee* (New York: Saturday Review Press, 1973), 76.

13. Wheeler, *Sword over Richmond*, 109.

14. John Bowers, *Stonewall Jackson: Portrait of a Soldier* (New York: Morrow, 1989), 27.

15. Lenoir Chambers, *Stonewall Jackson*, 2 volumes (New York: Morrow, 1959), 2:331.

16. Wheeler, *Sword over Richmond*, 249.

17. Bradford, *Lee*, 130.

18. Glenn Tucker, *High Tide at Gettysburg: The Campaign in Pennsylvania* (New York: Morningside Bookshop, 1973), 5.

19. Glenn Tucker, *Lee and Longstreet at Gettysburg* (Indianapolis: Bobbs-Merrill, 1968), 203.

20. Clifford Dowdy, *Death of a Nation: The Story of Lee and His Men at Gettysburg* (New York: Knopf, 1963), 65.

21. Wheeler, *Lee's Terrible Swift Sword*, 7.

22. Wiley, *Johnny Reb*, 30.

23. Bruce Catton, *Glory Road* (Garden City, N.Y.: Doubleday, 1952), 46.

24. Robert E. Lee, Jr., *Recollections and Letters of General Robert E. Lee*

(Garden City, N.Y.: Doubleday, Page, 1924), 74.

25. Coulter, *Confederate States of America*, 201.
26. Sandburg, *Lincoln*, 1:494.
27. Richard Wheeler, ed., *Voices of the Civil War* (New York: Meridian, 1990), 152.
28. Wheeler, *Lee's Terrible Swift Sword*, 9.
29. Wiley, *Johnny Reb*, 308.
30. Wheeler, *Sword over Richmond*, 326.
31. *Ibid.*, 325.
32. Wiley, *Johnny Reb*, 267.
33. Davis, *Gray Fox*, 105.

Chapter 4

1. Davis, *Gray Fox*, 110.
2. *Ibid.*, 120.
3. Bowers, *Stonewall Jackson*, 281.
4. Anderson, *The Generals*, 260.
5. Otto Eisenschiml and Ralph Newman, *The Civil War: The American Iliad as Told by Those Who Lived It* (New York: Grosset & Dunlop, 1956), 243.
6. Sandburg, *Lincoln*, 1:534.
7. Wheeler, *Lee's Terrible Swift Sword*, 45.
8. Robertson, *Soldiers Blue and Gray*, 62–63.
9. *Ibid.*, 43.
10. Murfin, *The Gleam of Bayonets*, 109.
11. Sears, *George B. McClellan*, 282.
12. Wheeler, *Lee's Terrible Swift Sword*, 85; Richard Wheeler, ed., *We Knew Stonewall Jackson* (New York: Crowell, 1977), 107.
13. Stephen W. Sears, *Landscape Turned Red: The Battle of Antietam* (New York: Ticknor & Fields, 1983), 162.
14. *Ibid.*, 201.
15. Murfin, *The Gleam of Bayonets*, 231.
16. Sears, *Landscape Turned Red*, 208; John M. Priest, *Antietam: A Soldier's Battle* (Shippensburg, Pa.: White Mane Publishing, 1989), 101, 208.
17. *Ibid.*, 127.
18. Sears, *Landscape Turned Red*, 202.
19. Stiles, *Four Years under Marse Robert*, 212.
20. Wheeler, *Lee's Terrible Swift Sword*, 122.
21. Murfin, *The Gleam of Bayonets*, 265.
22. Joseph T. Durkin, ed., *John Dooley: Confederate Soldier* (Washington,

D.C.: Georgetown University Press, 1945), 46–47.

23. Murfin, *The Gleam of Bayonets*, 293.

24. Priest, *Antietam*, 129–130.

25. Wheeler, *Lee's Terrible Swift Sword*, 124.

26. Priest, *Antietam*, 175, 210.

27. Catton, *Mr. Lincoln's Army*, 321.

28. Murfin, *The Gleam of Bayonets*, 298.

29. Sears, *Landscape Turned Red*, 318.

30. Slavery was abolished throughout the nation by the Thirteenth Amendment to the Constitution, ratified on December 18, 1865.

31. James M. McPherson, *Ordeal by Fire: The Civil War and Reconstruction* (New York: Knopf, 1982), 349.

32. Coulter, *Confederate States of America*, 265.

Chapter 5

1. Lee, Jr., *Recollections and Letters*, 80.

2. Davis, *Gray Fox*, 161.

3. Catton, *Glory Road*, 331.

4. Bowers, *Stonewall Jackson*, 310; Catton, *Glory Road*, 33.

5. Wheeler, *Lee's Terrible Swift Sword*, 250.

6. Stiles, *Four Years under Marse Robert*, 130–131.

7. Wheeler, *Lee's Terrible Swift Sword*, 253.

8. *Ibid.*, 268.

9. *Ibid.*, 288–289.

10. *Ibid.*, 285; Paul M. Angle and Earl Schenck Miers, eds., *The Tragic Years, 1860–1865: A Documentary History of the American Civil War* (New York: Simon & Schuster, 1960), 440.

11. Ernest B. Furgurson, *Chancellorsville 1863: The Souls of the Brave* (New York: Knopf, 1992), 38–39.

12. Stiles, *Four Years under Marse Robert*, 131.

13. Burke Davis, *They Called Him Stonewall: A Life of Lt. General T. J. Jackson, C.S.A.* (New York: Fairfax Press, 1988), 364.

14. McPherson, *Ordeal by Fire*, 306.

15. Stern, *Lee*, 166.

16. Anderson, *The Generals*, 288.

17. Furgurson, *Chancellorsville*, 37.

18. Wheeler, *Lee's Terrible Swift Sword*, 344.

19. Robertson, *Soldiers Blue and Gray*, 90.

20. *Ibid.*, 193.

21. Coulter, *Confederate States of America*, 462.

22. Wheeler, *Lee's Terrible Swift Sword*, 156–157.
23. Robertson, *Soldiers Blue and Gray*, 92.
24. Wiley, *Johnny Reb*, 63–66; Sanborn, *Lee*, 2:102; Robertson, *Soldiers Blue and Gray*, 89.
25. *Ibid.*, 85–86.
26. Bradford, *Lee*, 120.
27. Stern, *Lee*, 168.
28. Sanborn, *Lee*, 2:101.
29. Bradford, *Lee*, 158.
30. Sanborn, *Lee*, 2:101.
31. Bradford, *Lee*, 158.
32. *Ibid.*, 93.
33. Sanborn, *Lee*, 2:82.
34. *Ibid.*, 2:101.
35. Wheeler, *Lee's Terrible Swift Sword*, 163.
36. James M. McPherson, *Battle Cry of Freedom: The Civil War Era* (New York: Oxford University Press, 1988), 449.
37. Richard Wheeler, ed., *Witness to Appomattox* (New York: Harper & Row, 1989), 15.
38. Wiley, *Confederate Women*, 147.
39. Coulter, *Confederate States of America*, 422–423.
40. Wiley, *Confederate Women*, 170–171.
41. Belle Irvin Wiley, *The Plain People of the Confederacy* (Baton Rouge: Louisiana State University Press, 1943), 58.

Chapter 6

1. Basler, *Lincoln Collected Works*, 6:78–79.
2. Wheeler, *Lee's Terrible Swift Sword*, 341.
3. Catton, *Glory Road*, 161.
4. Furgurson, *Chancellorsville*, 60–61.
5. Wheeler, *Lee's Terrible Swift Sword*, 351.
6. *Ibid.*
7. *Ibid.*, 357.
8. *Ibid.*
9. Angle and Miers, *Tragic Years*, 502.
10. Catton, *Glory Road*, 211.
11. Wheeler, *Lee's Terrible Swift Sword*, 361.
12. Davis, *Gray Fox*, 187.
13. Chambers, *Stonewall Jackson*, 2:386.
14. Furgurson, *Chancellorsville*, 155.

15. *Ibid.*, 156.
16. Catton, *Glory Road*, 180.
17. Furgurson, *Chancellorsville*, 165.
18. Horn, *The Robert E. Lee Reader*, 285.
19. Furgurson, *Chancellorsville*, 173, 186.
20. *Ibid.*, 181–182. Howard was not ruined, and went on to become one of the army's outstanding Indian fighters on the Great Plains.
21. Davis, *They Called Him Stonewall*, 427.
22. Chambers, *Stonewall Jackson*, 2:426.
23. Horn, *The Robert E. Lee Reader*, 287.
24. Furgurson, *Chancellorsville*, 230.
25. *Ibid.*, 232–233.
26. Wheeler, *Voices of the Civil War*, 272–273.
27. Sanborn, *Lee*, 2:113.
28. Horn, *The Robert E. Lee Reader*, 290.
29. Sandburg, *Abraham Lincoln*, 2:96.
30. Wheeler, *Lee's Terrible Swift Sword*, 402.
31. Sanborn, *Lee*, 2:115.

Chapter 7

1. Davis, *Gray Fox*, 208.
2. George R. Stewart, *Pickett's Charge: A Microhistory of the Final Attack at Gettysburg, July 3, 1863* (Boston: Houghton Mifflin, 1987), 9.
3. Anderson, *The Generals*, 322.
4. Sandburg, *Lincoln*, 2:339.
5. *Ibid.*
6. Henry Steele Commager, ed., *The Blue and the Gray: The Story of the Civil War as Told by Participants* (Indianapolis: Bobbs-Merrill, 1950), 595.
7. Tucker, *High Tide at Gettysburg*, 88–89.
8. Catton, *Mr. Lincoln's Army*, 14.
9. Sanborn, *Lee*, 2:125.
10. Tucker, *High Tide at Gettysburg*, 119.
11. Richard Wheeler, ed., *Witness to Gettysburg* (New York: Harper & Row, 1987), 123.
12. Tucker, *High Tide at Gettysburg*, 177.
13. Wheeler, *Voices of the Civil War*, 300.
14. Earl Schenck Miers and Richard A. Brown, eds., *Gettysburg* (New Brunswick, N.J.: Rutgers University Press, 1948), 103; H. J. Eckenrode, *James Longstreet: Lee's War Horse* (Chapel Hill:

University of North Carolina Press, 1986), 186.

15. Tucker, *High Tide at Gettysburg*, 210.
16. Miers and Brown, *Gettysburg*, 118.
17. Wheeler, *Witness to Gettysburg*, 195.
18. *Ibid.*, 196.
19. William C. Oates and Frank A. Haskell, *Gettysburg* (New York: Bantam Books, 1992), 97, 99.
20. Wheeler, *Witness to Gettysburg*, 133.
21. Tucker, *High Tide at Gettysburg*, 316–317.
22. Stern, *Lee*, 180.
23. Angle and Miers, *Tragic Years*, 657.
24. Durkin, ed., *John Dooley: Confederate Soldier*, 104–105.
25. Stewart, *Pickett's Charge*, 96.
26. Tucker, *High Tide at Gettysburg*, 352.
27. Stewart, *Pickett's Charge*, 143.
28. Gregory A. Coco, *On the Bloodstained Field: 130 Human Interest Stories of the Campaign and Battle of Gettysburg* (N.P.: Wheatfield Press, 1987), 28.
29. Tucker, *High Tide at Gettysburg*, 352.
30. Oates and Haskell, *Gettysburg*, 208.
31. Stewart, *Pickett's Charge*, 150.
32. McCarthy, *Detailed Minutiae of Soldier Life*, 107.
33. Wheeler, *Witness to Gettysburg*, 237.
34. *Ibid.*
35. Stewart, *Pickett's Charge*, 170.
36. Anderson, *The Generals*, 343.
37. *Ibid.*
38. Wheeler, *Witness to Gettysburg*, 283.
39. Stewart, *Pickett's Charge*, 183.
40. Oates and Haskell, *Gettysburg*, 213–214.
41. Anderson, *The Generals*, 345.
42. Wheeler, *Witness to Gettysburg*, 241.
43. Stewart, *Pickett's Charge*, 198.
44. *Ibid.*, 247.
45. Catton, *Glory Road*, 323–324; Wheeler, *Witness to Gettysburg*, 245; Oates and Haskell, *Gettysburg*, 230.
46. Coco, *On the Bloodstained Field*, 14.
47. Horn, *The Robert E. Lee Reader*, 324.
48. Stewart, *Pickett's Charge*, 256–257.
49. Horn, *The Robert E. Lee Reader*, 340.
50. *New York Times*, May 13, 1957.
51. Horn, *The Robert E. Lee Reader*, 328.

Chapter 8

1. Wheeler, *Witness to Gettysburg*, 256.
2. Sandburg, *Lincoln*, 1:632.
3. Wheeler, *Witness to Gettysburg*, 5.
4. Grant, *Memoirs*, 208.
5. W. E. Woodward, *Meet General Grant* (New York: Horace Liveright, 1928), 256.
6. Belle Irvin Wiley, *The Life of Billy Yank: The Common Soldier of the Union* (Baton Rouge: Louisiana State University Press, 1978), 294.
7. Smith, *Lee and Grant*, 182.
8. T. Harry Williams, *Lincoln and His Generals* (New York: Knopf, 1952), 333. The president made Sheridan an inch shorter than his true height.
9. McPherson, *Ordeal by Fire*, 411.
10. Stiles, *Four Years under Marse Robert*, 239.
11. Smith, *Lee and Grant*, 187.
12. General Horace Porter, *Campaigning with Grant* (New York: Century, 1897), 47.
13. Wheeler, *Voices of the Civil War*, 381.
14. Anderson, *The Generals*, 375–376.
15. Wheeler, *Voices of the Civil War*, 385–386.
16. Smith, *Lee and Grant*, 194–195; Anderson, *The Generals*, 374.
17. Porter, *Campaigning with Grant*, 98.
18. Smith, *Lee and Grant*, 198.
19. McPherson, *Ordeal by Fire*, 416.
20. Smith, *Lee and Grant*, 202.
21. Wheeler, *On Fields of Fury*, 201–202.
22. *Ibid.*, 209.
23. Sanborn, *Lee*, 2:181.
24. Eisenschiml and Newman, *The Civil War*, 578–579. A parapet is an earthen mound in front of a trench; an abatis is a barricade of felled trees with their branches sharpened and facing toward the enemy.
25. Davis, *Gray Fox*, 324.
26. Wheeler, *On Fields of Fury*, 266.
27. Smith, *Lee and Grant*, 216, 226.
28. Stephen B. Oates, *With Malice Toward None: The Life of Abraham Lincoln* (New York: Harper & Row, 1977), 390.
29. Grady McWhiney and Perry D. Jamieson, *Attack and Die: Civil War Military Tactics and the Southern Heritage* (University, Ala.: University of Alabama Press, 1982), 12–19.

Chapter 9

1. Stern, *Lee*, 188.
2. Wiley, *Plain People of the Confederacy*, 10.
3. Robertson, *Soldiers Blue and Gray*, 78.
4. Linderman, *Embattled Courage*, 154.
5. Bruce Catton, *A Stillness at Appomattox* (Garden City, N.Y.: Doubleday, 1953), 203.
6. A. C. Inman, ed., *Soldier of the South: General Pickett's Letters to His Wife* (Boston: Houghton Mifflin, 1928), 140–141.
7. Horn, *The Robert E. Lee Reader*, 404.
8. Sanborn, *Lee*, 2:188–189.
9. Davis, *Gray Fox*, 355.
10. Coulter, *Confederate States of America*, 478. Prisoner exchanges were resumed in February 1865, with nearly a thousand men a day, mostly sick and wounded, returned to their own side.
11. McPherson, *Ordeal by Fire*, 468.
12. Belle Irvin Wiley, *The Road to Appomattox* (Memphis, Tenn.: Memphis State University Press, 1956), 72.
13. Wiley, *Southern Negroes*, 146.
14. Wheeler, *Witness to Appomattox*, 44–45.
15. Smith, *Lee and Grant*, 445.
16. Burke Davis, *To Appomattox: Nine April Days*, 1865 (New York: Rinehart, 1959), 60.
17. Davis, *Gray Fox*, 371.
18. Anderson, *The Generals*, 428.
19. Angle and Miers, *Tragic Years*, 1017.
20. A. A. Hoehling and Mary Hoehling, *The Last Days of the Confederacy* (New York: Fairfax Press, 1981), 199.
21. Mary Mayer Culpepper, *Trials and Triumphs: The Women of the American Civil War* (East Lansing: Michigan State University Press, 1991), 219.
22. McPherson, *Ordeal by Fire*, 480; Wheeler, *Voices of the Civil War*, 456.
23. Wheeler, *Witness to Appomattox*, 136–137.
24. Davis, *Gray Fox*, 380.
25. Angle and Miers, *Tragic Years*, 1027.
26. Sanborn, *Lee*, 2:222.
27. *Ibid.*, 2:221.
28. *Ibid.*, 2:222.
29. Bruce Catton, *Grant Takes Command* (Boston: Little, Brown, 1969), 469.
30. Robert Hunt Rhodes, ed., *All for the Union: The Civil War Diary of*

Elisha Hunt Rhodes (New York: Orion Books, 1991), 230; Catton, *Grant Takes Command*, 469.

31. Anderson, *The Generals*, 454.
32. Wiley, *Johnny Reb*, 148–149.
33. Davis, *Gray Fox*, 276.
34. Sanborn, *Lee*, 2:237–238.
35. Catton, *Grant Takes Command*, 472.
36. Joshua Lawrence Chamberlain, *The Passing of the Armies* (New York: G. P. Putnam's Sons, 1915), 261–265; Smith, *Lee and Grant*, 281–282.

Chapter 10

1. Sanborn, *Lee*, 2:242.
2. Charles Bracelen Flood, *Lee: The Last Years* (Boston: Houghton Mifflin, 1981), 44.
3. *Ibid.*, 58, 88.
4. Sanborn, *Lee*, 2:257–258.
5. Merton E. Coulter, *The South During Reconstruction* (Baton Rouge: Louisiana State University Press, 1947), 26.
6. Sanborn, *Lee*, 2:308.
7. Cleveland Amory, *Who Killed Society?* (New York: Harper & Brothers, 1960), 93.
8. Late in October 1870, only days after the general's death, the school was renamed Washington and Lee University. Lee's son, Custis, became president, an office he held for a quarter of a century.
9. Horn, *The Robert E. Lee Reader*, 478.
10. Lee, Jr., *Recollections and Letters*, 193. Traveller's skeleton is on display in the basement of the Memorial Chapel at Washington and Lee University.
11. Sanborn, *Lee*, 2:315.
12. Stern, *Lee*, 230.
13. Sanborn, *Lee*, 2:292.
14. Horn, *The Robert E. Lee Reader*, 493.
15. Smith, *Lee and Grant*, 330.

SOME MORE BOOKS

There are many thousands of books on the Civil War, and more appear each month. Here are a few of the ones I found most valuable, particularly as they relate to Robert E. Lee.

Abels, Jules. *Man on Fire: John Brown and the Cause of Liberty*. New York: Macmillan, 1971.

Anderson, Nancy Scott, and Dwight Anderson. *The Generals: Ulysses S. Grant and Robert E. Lee*. New York: Knopf, 1988.

Angle, Paul M. and Earl Schenck Miers, eds. *Tragic Years, 1860–1865: A Documentary History of the American Civil War*. New York: Simon & Schuster, 1960.

Basler, Roy P., ed. *The Collected Works of Abraham Lincoln*. 8 volumes. New Brunswick, N.J.: Rutgers University Press, 1953.

Bowers, John. *Stonewall Jackson: Portrait of a Soldier*. New York: Morrow, 1989.

Bradford, Gamaliel. *Lee the American*. Boston: Houghton Mifflin, 1929.

Brooks, Steward. *Civil War Medicine*. Springfield, Ill.: Thomas, 1966.

Burnham, Philip. "Selling Poor Seven: The Struggles and Torments of a Forgotten Class in Antebellum America: Black Slaveowners." *American Heritage* (February–March, 1993), 91–97.

Catton, Bruce. *Glory Road*. Garden City, N.Y.: Doubleday, 1952.

———. *Grant Takes Command*. Boston: Little, Brown, 1969.

———. *Mr. Lincoln's Army*. Garden City, N.Y.: Doubleday, 1962.

———. *A Stillness at Appomattox*. Garden City, N.Y.: Doubleday, 1953.

Chambers, Lenoir. *Stonewall Jackson*. 2 volumes. New York: Morrow, 1959.

Cleaves, Freeman. *Meade of Gettysburg*. Norman: University of Oklahoma Press, 1960.

Coco, Gregory A. *On the Bloodstained Field: 130 Human Interest Stories of the Campaign and Battle of Gettysburg*. N.P.: Wheatfield Press, 1987.

Commager, Henry Steele, ed. *The Blue and the Gray: The Story of the Civil War as Told by Participants*. Indianapolis: Bobbs-Merrill, 1950.

Coulter, Merton E. *The Confederate States of America*. Baton Rouge: Louisiana State University Press, 1959.

———. *The South During Reconstruction, 1865–1877*. Baton Rouge: Louisiana State University Press, 1947.

Culpepper, Marilyn Mayer. *Trials and Triumphs: The Women of the American Civil War*. East Lansing: Michigan State University Press, 1991.

Cunningham, H. H. *Doctors in Gray: The Confederate Medical Service*. Baton Rouge: Louisiana State University Press, 1958.

Davis, Burke. *Gray Fox: Robert E. Lee and the Civil War*. New York: Fairfax Press, 1981.

———. *They Called Him Stonewall: A Life of Lt. General T. J. Jackson, C.S.A.* New York: Fairfax Press, 1988.

———. *To Appomattox: Nine April Days, 1865*. New York: Rinehart, 1959.

Davis, William C. *Jefferson Davis: The Man and His Hour*. New York: Harper Collins, 1991.

Donald, David. "The Confederate as a Fighting Man." *Journal of Southern History* 25 (1959): 178–193.

Dowdy, Clifford. *Death of a Nation: The Story of Lee and His Men at Gettysburg*. New York: Knopf, 1963.

———. *The Seven Days: The Emergence of Lee*. Boston: Little, Brown, 1964.

Durkin, Joseph T., ed. *John Dooley: Confederate Soldier*. Washington, D.C.: Georgetown University Press, 1945.

Earle, Peter. *Robert E. Lee*. New York: Saturday Review Press, 1973.

Eckenrode, H. J. *James Longstreet: Lee's War Horse*. Chapel Hill: University of North Carolina Press, 1986.

Eisenschiml, Otto, and Ralph Newman. *The Civil War: The American Iliad as Told by Those Who Lived It*. New York: Grosset & Dunlap, 1956.

Flood, Charles Bracelen. *Lee: The Last Years*. Boston: Houghton Mifflin, 1981.

Freeman, Douglas Southall. *Lee's Lieutenants*. 3 volumes. New York: Scribner, 1972.

———. *Robert E. Lee*. 4 volumes. New York: Scribner, 1934–1935. This is the classic work on Lee, the starting point from which all other biographers begin. Richard Harwell edited an abridged version, published by Scribner in 1991.

Fuller, J. F. C. *Grant and Lee: A Study in Personality and Generalship*. 1932. Reprint. Bloomington: University of Indiana Press, 1982.

Furgurson, Ernest B. *Chancellorsville 1863: The Souls of the Brave*. New York: Knopf, 1992.

Genovese, Eugene D. *Roll, Jordan, Roll: The World the Slaves Made*. New York: Pantheon Books, 1974.

Grant, Ulysses, S. *Personal Memoirs of Ulysses S. Grant and Selected Letters. 1839–1865*. New York: Library of America, 1990.

Horn, Stanley F., ed. *The Robert E. Lee Reader*. Indianapolis: Bobbs-Merrill, 1949.

Lee, Robert E., Jr. *Recollections and Letters of General Robert E. Lee*. Garden City, N.Y.: Doubleday, 1924.

Linderman, Gerald F. *Embattled Courage: The Experience of Combat in the American Civil War*. New York: Free Press, 1987.

Long, A. L. *Memoirs of Robert E. Lee: His Military and Personal History*. New York: J. M. Stoddart, 1886. This valuable book, by Lee's military secretary, was reprinted by the Blue and Grey Press in 1983.

Maurice, Sir Frederick. *Robert E. Lee: The Soldier*. Boston: Houghton Mifflin, 1925.

McCarthy, Carlton. *Detailed Minutiae of Soldier Life in the Army of Northern Virginia, 1861–1865*. Richmond: Carlton McCarthy, 1882. Reprinted 1982 by Time-Life Books.

McPherson, James M. *Battle Cry of Freedom: The Civil War Era*. New York: Oxford University Press, 1988.

———. *Ordeal by Fire: The Civil War and Reconstruction*. New York: Knopf, 1982.

McWhiney, Grady, and Perry D. Jamieson. *Attack and Die: Civil War Military Tactics and the Southern Heritage*. University, Ala.: University of Alabama Press, 1982.

Miers, Earl Schenck. *The Last Campaign: Grant Saves the Union*. Philadelphia: Lippincott, 1972.

———. *Robert E. Lee: A Great Life in Brief*. New York: Knopf, 1967.

———, and Richard A. Brown, eds. *Gettysburg*. New Brunswick, N.J.: Rutgers University Press, 1948.

Mitchell, Reid. *Civil War Soldiers*. New York: Viking Press, 1988.

Murfin, James V. *The Gleam of Bayonets: The Battle of Antietam and the*

Maryland Campaign of 1862. New York: Thomas Youseloff, 1965.

Nevins, Allan. *The Emergence of Lincoln*. 2 volumes. New York: Scribner, 1950.

Oates, Stephen B. *With Malice Toward None: The Life of Abraham Lincoln*. New York: Harper & Row, 1977.

Oates, Colonel William C., and Lieutenant Frank A. Haskell. *Gettysburg*. New York: Bantam Books, 1992. A valuable account by a Confederate and Union participant.

Patrick, Rembert W. *The Fall of Richmond*. Baton Rouge: Louisiana State University Press, 1960.

Porter, General Horace. *Campaigning with Grant*. New York: Century, 1897. Reprinted by Time-Life Books, 1981.

Priest, John M. *Antietam: A Soldier's Battle*. Shippensburg, Penn.: White Mane Publishing, 1989.

Rhodes, James Ford. *History of the United States from the Compromise of 1850*. 7 volumes. New York: Macmillan, 1913–1916. Still a classic study.

Robertson, James I., Jr. *Soldiers Blue and Gray*. Columbia, S.C.: University of South Carolina Press, 1988.

Royster, Charles. *The Destructive War: William Tecumseh Sherman, Stonewall Jackson, and the Americans*. New York: Knopf, 1991.

Sanborn, Margaret. *Robert E. Lee: A Portrait*. 2 volumes. Philadelphia: Lippincott, 1966, 1967.

Sandburg, Carl. *Abraham Lincoln: The War Years*. 4 volumes. New York: Harcourt, Brace, 1939.

Sears, Stephen W. *George B. McClellan: The Young Napoleon*. New York: Ticknor & Fields, 1988.

———. *Landscape Turned Red: The Battle of Antietam*. New York: Ticknor & Fields, 1983.

———. *To the Gates of Richmond: The Peninsula Campaign*. New York: Ticknor & Fields, 1992.

Smith, Gene. *Lee and Grant: A Dual Biography*. New York: McGraw-Hill, 1984.

Stamp, Kenneth M. *The Peculiar Institution: Slavery in the Ante-Bellum South*. New York: Knopf, 1956.

Stern, Philip Van Doren. *An End to Valor: The Last Days of the Civil War*. Boston: Houghton Mifflin, 1958.

———. *Robert E. Lee: The Man and the Soldier*. New York: McGraw-Hill, 1963.

Stewart, George R. *Pickett's Charge: A Microhistory of the Final Attack at Gettysburg, July 3, 1863*. Boston: Houghton Mifflin, 1987.

Stiles, Robert. *Four Years under Marse Robert*. New York: Neale Publishing, 1903.

Tucker, Glenn. *High Tide at Gettysburg: The Campaign in Pennsylvania.* New York: Morningside Bookshop, 1973.

———. *Lee and Longstreet at Gettysburg.* Indianapolis: Bobbs-Merrill, 1968.

Wheeler, Richard, ed. *Lee's Terrible Swift Sword: From Antietam to Chancellorsville, An Eyewitness History.* New York: Harper & Row, 1982. This and the following books edited by Wheeler are invaluable collections of eyewitness accounts of the Civil War.

———. *On Fields of Fury. From the Wilderness to the Crater: An Eyewitness History.* New York: Harper Collins, 1991.

———. *Sword over Richmond: An Eyewitness History of McClellan's Peninsula Campaign.* New York: Harper & Row, 1986.

———. *Voices of the Civil War.* New York: Meridian, 1990.

———. *We Knew Stonewall Jackson.* New York: Crowell, 1977.

———. *We Knew William Tecumseh Sherman.* New York: Crowell, 1977.

———. *Witness to Appomattox.* New York: Harper & Row, 1989.

———. *Witness to Gettysburg.* New York: Harper & Row, 1987.

Wiley, Belle Irvin. *Confederate Women.* Westport, Conn.: Greenwood Press, 1975.

———. *The Life of Billy Yank: The Common Soldier of the Union.* Baton Rouge: Louisiana State University Press, 1978.

———. *The Life of Johnny Reb: The Common Soldier of the Confederacy.* Baton Rouge: Louisiana State University Press, 1978.

———. *Lincoln and Lee.* New York: Oxford University Press, 1966.

———. *The Plain People of the Confederacy.* Baton Rouge: Louisiana State University Press, 1943.

———. *The Road to Appomattox.* Memphis, Tenn.: Memphis State University Press, 1956.

———. *Southern Negroes, 1861–1865.* Baton Rouge: Louisiana State University Press, 1965.

Williams, T. Harry. *Lincoln and His Generals.* New York: Knopf, 1952.

———. *McClellan, Sherman and Grant.* New Brunswick, N.J.: Rutgers University Press, 1962.

Woodward, C. Vann, ed. *Mary Chesnut's Civil War.* New Haven: Yale University Press, 1981.

Young, James C. *Marse Robert: Knight of the Confederacy.* New York: Rae D. Henkle, 1929.

INDEX